AMERICAN WHISKEY

Richard Thomas

Foreword by Robin Robinson

CIDER MILL
PRESS

BOOK
PUBLISHERS
KENNEBUNKPORT, MAINE

13-Digit ISBN: 978-1-64643-305-6
10-Digit ISBN: 1-64643-305-X

This book may be ordered by mail from the publisher. Please include $5.99 for postage and handling. Please support your local bookseller first!

Books published by Cider Mill Press Book Publishers are available at special discounts for bulk purchases in the United States by corporations, institutions, and other organizations. For more information, please contact the publisher.

Cider Mill Press Book Publishers
"Where good books are ready for press"
PO Box 454
12 Spring Street
Kennebunkport, Maine 04046
Visit us online!
cidermillpress.com

Typography: Clarendon, Historycal, Warnock Pro, WhiskeyLabel
Image Credits: see page 543

Printed in China
1 2 3 4 5 6 7 8 9 0
First Edition

CONTENTS

FOREWORD

The new whiskey revival caught the drinking public off guard in the early 2000s. Once relegated to the nether zones of bottom shelves or back corners of dark bars, a new generation unafraid of flavors brought whiskey back to the front and center of drinking culture. Old drink recipes from the pre-Prohibition days were revitalized, featuring aged grain spirits mixed with real ingredients, not premade powder mixes. Cocktail ice became an obsession as we tasted our first real Manhattans, Old Fashioneds, Sazeracs, and Whiskey Sours, presented in the way they were meant to taste in their original incarnations. And, most importantly, we began to relearn the names and rediscover the tastes of whiskey brands that had either faded into the dust or carried the stigma of "old man's booze."

In the same way that the wine awakening of the 1980s taught us that Americans make quality wine to rival France and Germany, this new whiskey revival reminded us that we are a land of global-quality whiskey makers as well. The American wine boom brought us from the rigidness of brand-centric names like Paul Masson, Gallo, and Riunite to varietal grapes from specific regions. We had to learn new words like merlot, pinot noir, and chardonnay, while at the same time we discovered Napa Valley, Sonoma, the Russian River, and Willamette Valley. It was a new vocabulary, a new geography, and Americans sought out new guides to help them navigate: Frank Schoonmaker, Hugh Johnson, and Kevin Zraly were among those trained in the grape who gave us the backgrounds, regional influences, our first tasting notes, and even pronunciations that added to our enjoyment of wine.

Here in the 21st century, whiskey, and primarily American whiskey, has now ascended to the mantle once held by wine. It spurred a new generation of craft distillers to where no other country on the planet has more licensed distilleries than the US—over 2,100 at last count. Whiskey is now arguably in its "third wave" where it has crossed over from the hardcore first adopters and later through the influencers and advocates who spurred its popularity. Whiskey is now part of the American lifestyle, part of every drinker's vocabulary, and the iterations that continue to appear on the nation's shelves are testament to its longevity. And with that, a new guide was needed. Richard Thomas's *American Whiskey* arrived at the right time.

For over ten years, Richard's well-known online magazine, *The Whiskey Reviewer*, kept pace with the consistent drumbeat of new brands, new innovations in the whiskey world, and the personalities that keep the industry moving forward. Reviews of brands, insightful opinions, features on the makers, and a solid connection with the education of whiskey production is what makes his site a browser bookmark. Richard brought the best of that in the first edition of *American Whiskey*, a rich compendium of brands, bottles, and backgrounds. But this is not a "listicle" bound in a hard cover. Richard continues to offer insights on how and why a whiskey is unique or different from the next one around the corner. His tasting notes offer more than just a haiku of descriptive terms, they're full thoughts on flavor. He's painted mini-biographies of some of the luminaries of the industry and why their influence is worth noting as you sip their creations. And while the first pages give the reader the background, history, categories, and vocabulary of whiskey making, he adds to that vast knowledge throughout the book, slipping in key information in different reviews and features on personalities.

It's a fun exploration from cover to cover.

This is a dynamic industry where change is constant, where new innovations, new brands, and new people continue to drive it to new heights. And with that, this revised edition of *American Whiskey* is keeping pace with those changes. Tuck it under your arm as you peruse the aisles of your favorite whiskey shop; keep it handy as you're pinged on your phone about a friend's new favorite brand. Or casually read it while sipping a whiskey at a favorite bar and see how many new friends you make, and how impressed they'll be with your whiskey knowledge. For that, you can thank this book and its author.

Robin Robinson

Author, *The Complete Whiskey Course: A Comprehensive Tasting School in Ten Classes*

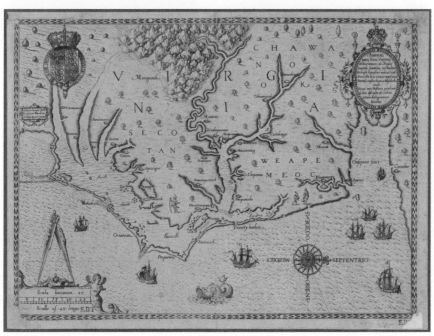

More than other spirits, even other aged spirits, whiskey is intertwined with history. Ten years old is a mature age for an American whiskey. Stop and think about where you were 10 years ago today, what you were doing and what a different person you were. That was when the youngest spirit from a freshly bottled example of a 10-year-old bourbon or rye, for age statements denote a minimum, was entered into the barrel. Excepting single-barrel offerings, some of the content will be older still. Think about everything that happened while that spirit sat quietly in the barrel, part of it steadily evaporating as it matured.

Although it cannot be said that whiskey matches the human lifetime (70-year-old whiskeys are extremely rare, even in Scotland, and are absolutely unheard of in America), the age of a mature bottle of whiskey exceeds the time frame of two presidential terms. Your whiskey could easily have an age statement greater than most pets. A high school graduate requires less time to become an MD than what is required to age mature whiskey.

How American whiskey came to be what it is today is a story filled with as much myth as fact. Its roots are not rebellious farmers in western Pennsylvania or the Reverend Elijah Craig in Kentucky, but in the Virginia of colonial America, where in 1620 Sir George Thorpe produced the first documented spirits distilled from fermented corn.

It was a very early beginning, even relative to the old country. Whiskey

ILLICIT DISTILLATION OF LIQUORS—SOUTHERN MODE OF MAKING WHISKY.—[SKETCHED BY A. W. THOMPSON.]

was produced in Thorpe's native Britain, but it was such a minor concern that the notoriously rapacious state didn't bother taxing alcohol production until 1644.

By the time the British Parliament loosened the licensing for distilleries in 1823, thereby creating the environment that gave rise to Scottish malts as we now know them, a Scotsman named Dr. James Crow had just moved to Kentucky. A decade later, Crow would begin drawing the various strands of Kentucky whiskey production together, studying them in a laboratory, and establishing the practices to make a spirituous liquor that today is recognizable as bourbon whiskey.

But if you're after the story of how bourbon whiskey or rye whiskey came into being, there are plenty of books and documentary films out there. In this book, I'm concerned with American whiskey as it exists today: an industry that is firmly centered in two states in the American Mid-South, Kentucky and Tennessee, but can truly be said to have spread from coast-to-coast for the first time in the country's history. The best place to start telling that story is with America's great failed experiment in social engineering, Prohibition.

Prior to the 1920 ratification of the 18th Amendment, which outlawed making and selling alcohol nationally, the growing power of the temperance movement had already shuttered whiskey distilling in several states. Tennessee saw the manufacture of liquor prohibited in 1909, and

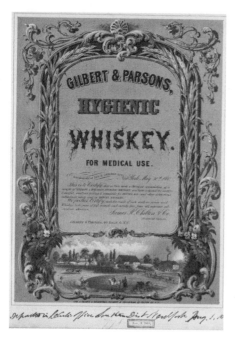

the ownership and transportation of it in the state was banned by the 1917 "Bone Dry Bill." It was nationwide Prohibition, however, that wiped what had been an almost national industry off broad swathes of the map.

Folks in the whiskey business responded to Prohibition in different ways. A few managed to stay in operation. The sale of whiskey by prescription, ostensibly for medicinal purposes, was allowed, with licenses to do so issued to six companies. By 1928, stocks of aged whiskey were already running low, thanks to strong "medicinal" demand and the bootlegging activities of fellows like George Remus and Lewis Rosenstiel. This allowed some distillers to stay in operation and survive.

Others from the business got by as

best they could, bided their time, and hoped to go back to work in the future. James B. Beam was one such whiskey man, and began rebuilding his distillery in 1933, shortly after Prohibition was repealed. Abraham Bowman dived back into making whiskey on his vast property in Fairfax County, Virginia, in 1934. Lem Motlow, owner of Jack Daniel's, had to wait until 1938 and the repeal of Tennessee's state-level Prohibition to do the same.

Some people just gave up and moved on, however, reckoning that an amendment to the U.S. Constitution had never been repealed and never would be. Others might have wanted to get back into the business, but couldn't, at least not where they had originally operated. Most urban distilleries saw their valuable buildings converted to other uses during the 13 years of Prohibition. Many states also retained Prohibition-era laws hindering or blocking the production of spirits, even after drinking became legal again (laws that stayed on the books until the modern craft distilling movement!).

After all was said and done, what had been an industry found across the Mid-South, Midwest, and Northeast now existed only in a handful of states. Although Kentucky had previously enjoyed a reputation for making particularly good bourbon, Virginia had a fine reputation for it as well, while Pennsylvania and Maryland had their own distinctive styles of rye whiskey. New York was a major whiskey producer, Ohio made lots of bourbon, and Peoria, Illinois, was once the single largest producer of whiskey in

America. After Prohibition, the center of gravity shifted more and more to Kentucky.

As bad of a body blow as Prohibition was to the American whiskey industry, more was to come. Anticipating the coming of the Second World War, the government raised taxes on spirits from $2.25 to $3.00 per proof gallon as part of the Defense Tax Act of 1940 (taxes would rise to $9.00 per proof gallon in 1944), this at a time when the median income was less than $1,000 a year. When the war effort was in full swing, controls on whiskey industry necessities like grain, wood, copper, and fuel came with it. Whiskey distillers were also ordered to produce industrial alcohol for the war effort, which gave them

steady work, albeit while disrupting their actual business.

Even after Prohibition and wartime restrictions became a memory and rising prosperity meant high liquor taxes bit consumers a little less fiercely, larger economic forces continued to eat away at the national whiskey industry. Industrial consolidation was a broader trend that saw small and medium-size producers in many industries either bought out, often to be shuttered, or else driven out of business. Although some distilleries and the brands associated with them, such as Jim Beam and Jack Daniel's, rose to prominence in this era, generally speaking the 1950s and 1960s were a time that saw round after round of consolidation, closures,

and the trading of brands like so many baseball cards.

The final act in the contraction of America's whiskey industry was the whiskey crash of the 1970s. Majestic Distilling Company in Maryland, maker of Pikesville Rye (now made by Heaven Hill), ceased production in 1972. Hiram Walker closed its huge plant in Peoria, Illinois, in 1979. Philadelphia's Continental Distilling (which made Rittenhouse Rye, also now made by Heaven Hill) went bust in the early 1980s. In 1988, the Canadian drinks goliath Seagram shut down its plant in Dundalk, Maryland where Calvert Whisky was made. By 1989, the American whiskey industry had returned to its post-Prohibition low-water mark. Bomberger's in Pennsylvania shut down production that year, taking Pennsylvania rye whiskey with it, once a proud tradition in American whiskey that stood as a peer to Kentucky bourbon. The industry had shrunk down to a presence in just four states, and in one of those it scarcely had a toehold.

Both Kentucky and Tennessee remained bastions of the industry, of course. Heaven Hill's original distillery in Bardstown, Kentucky, would burn down in a 1996 fire that would go down as one of the worst disasters in whiskey history, but that same year would see Brown-Forman open the renovated Labrot & Graham Distillery and introduce Woodford Reserve. By that point in time, something of an equilibrium had been reached, and the nadir of the industry had left these two sister states in possession of the overwhelming majority of America's whiskey industry.

The other two remaining outposts were Indiana and Virginia. In Indiana, Seagram operated a venerable production plant that would, after the

fall and breakup of that conglomerate, become known at first as LDI and now as MGP. In Virginia, the A. Smith Bowman distillery left the increasingly crowded northern Virginia suburbs in 1988 for its current home in Fredericksburg. However, in doing so it left behind its cookers and fermenters, and for decades would be reliant upon finishing distillate from what is now Buffalo Trace Distillery to continue making whiskeys like Virginia Gentleman Bourbon.

From that late 1980s low point, whiskey making would rebound to become a coast-to-coast industry by the early 2010s. According to Bill Owens, founder and president of the American Distilling Institute, 1,527 craft distillers were operating in the United States by late 2018, and of them, some 570 were making whiskey. Kentucky and Tennessee still dominate the industry, and by a wide

margin at that—Kentucky alone produces 95% of all the bourbon made in the United States, after one discounts Tennessee Whiskey as bourbon, that is—but American whiskey making has returned to something resembling its pre-Prohibition form, minus the disreputable rectifiers (whose products were often the equivalent of Everclear colored with tobacco spit). The difference between the time before Prohibition and today is that instead of being bounded by the Atlantic Ocean and the Mississippi and Tennessee Rivers, whiskey production now has a firm foothold in the Rocky Mountains and on the West Coast, too.

WHAT IS AMERICAN WHISKEY?

Part of understanding American whiskey is having an awareness for what makes it American, and for that one needs at least a basic grasp of whiskeys as they exist around the world. In its broadest strokes, whiskey is made by milling grain; cooking it so the starch can be converted to sugar; fermenting that sugar into alcohol; distilling that alcohol into a much higher concentration, but not so high that the spirit loses the character of the source grains and yeast (i.e., becomes vodka); and is entered into a barrel for a period of maturation.

The spirit is found in the details, though. There are five major whiskey regions around the world: Canada, Ireland, Japan, Scotland, and the United States. Three of them—Ireland, Japan, and Scotland—have much in common with each other and make for a useful point of comparison. Briefly, all three countries produce malt whisky (or whiskey in Ireland), which is made from 100% malted barley in a pot still,

and grain whisky, which is made from a mix of grains in a column still. Both types are usually, but not exclusively, aged in casks that have already been used to mature some other form of liquor. If the grain or malt whiskey produced by a single distillery is bottled, it is called a single-malt or single-grain whiskey. If the two are mixed together or whiskeys from other distilleries are brought into the mix, they become blends.

All three regions have their own unique characteristics that make them distinctive from each other. Ireland also produces pot still whiskey, made from a mix of malted and unmalted barley; Japanese whisky doesn't even have a legal or regulatory regime defining and governing what it is, but it largely mirrors the Scottish industry on which it was modeled. Even so, this cursory look at Ireland, Scotland, and Japan provides a backdrop for defining American whiskey as a category all its own.

MILLING, MASHING, FERMENTING, DISTILLING, FILLING, MATURING

The distinctions between American whiskey and the rest of the world's starts with the basics of production, because even where the steps are the same, Americans sometimes have their own names for different articles of equipment.

Making whiskey starts with a mill, where grain is ground into a meal.

To this meal, water is added to make a porridge-like substance. Much is made of Kentucky and Tennessee's limestone geology, because that limestone removes iron and adds calcium to the water, features that were essential to distilling whiskey before modern times. Limestone-filtered spring and well water is still helpful,

but today one can manually remove unwanted minerals from the water.

The porridge is poured into a cooker, where it is heated to help with the process of converting starches in the grain into sugar. Different grains have different optimum temperatures in this process, so they are usually cooked in sequence, with the grain requiring the most heat going first. For example, most bourbon is made with a mash bill (grain recipe) of corn, rye, and malted barley, with corn requiring the longest cooking time and highest heat, around 220°F. Rye requires less time and lower heat, around 170°F, so it is added after the corn mash has cooled. Malted barley requires only 150°F, so it goes in last. Unless a whiskey is made from just one type of grain, some version of this sequence is used in cooking the mash.

In bourbon, malted barley provides most of the enzymes necessary to convert the cooked starches into sugar, and usually it is present in the mash bill solely for this purpose and not to add to the flavor. In some whiskeys, other malted grains carry out this task. Whenever a mash bill doesn't have a malted grain of some kind in it, processed enzymes are added to the mash instead.

Once the cooking process is complete, the mash is piped over to a fermenter (outside of the United States the mash is often called "wort" and the fermenter a "wash back"). Added to this is yeast, which converts the sugar to alcohol and carbon dioxide, the latter bubbling up and escaping into the air. Fermentation produces a lot of heat, and too much heat (95 to 104°F) kills yeast, so fermenters have coils of pipes in them to circulate cool water, maintain a stable temperature, and keep the process going.

After a few days, the alcohol content of the mash is 7 to 10%. Some distilleries extend the fermentation beyond this, which produces some additional alcohol and, more importantly, more of the chemical compounds that contribute to the flavor. Different strains of yeast reflect their individual identities during the latter point, and most distilleries place a strong emphasis on the quality of their yeast. Four Roses has five separate yeast strains in use, while the legendary distiller Booker Noe used to tell stories of his grandfather, Jim Beam, making yeast on his back porch and taking home samples from the distillery for safekeeping.

Following fermentation, the mash is sent to the still(s) for distillation. Here one sees a small, but key, difference in the way Americans make whiskey compared to the rest of the world. Outside the United States, distillers tend to separate the grainy solids out of the mash to create the wort. Americans usually send the mash over whole, solids and all.

Most American whiskey, including all the major categories, must be distilled to no higher than 80% alcohol (160 proof). Distilling higher than this strips out much of the flavor; distilling to 90% or higher would make the liquid an odorless and flavorless neutral grain spirit or vodka.

In America, the column still used to be king. In 1990, all of the whiskey-making distilleries in the country were using a column still design, with the single exception of A. Smith Bowman in Virginia. All of the big and medium-size distilleries continue to do so, but in the mid-1990s, the column still's stranglehold began to weaken. Prichard's, Old Potrero, and Woodford Reserve all opened in this span, and all three used pot stills. The mid-2000s saw the emergence of modern craft whiskey, and that first batch of small distillers were reliant either on pot stills or a hybrid design that combined the pot and column systems. Almost all the whiskey made in America today comes from the giant column stills, but those columns are dwarfed in number (albeit not in volume) by the plethora of small pots and hybrids operated by craft distillers around the country.

The traditional and most iconic whiskey still, the pot still, is also the simplest to explain. Basically, it's a copper pot that is partly filled with alcohol-bearing liquid (in America, this is the grainy mash, still bearing solids). Heat is applied, sufficient to vaporize the alcohol, but not the water in the mash. Usually this is done with steam coils, but sometimes the flame of a natural gas burner is used instead.

What is Proof?

If you pick up a bottle of Scotch in Scotland and a bottle of bourbon in Kentucky, two hard differences are found right there on the bottle. First, the European bottle is slightly smaller, holding 700 milliliters instead of 750 milliliters. Also, Scotch refers to alcohol by volume (ABV) as a measure of how much alcohol is in the bottle; the bourbon has both that and proof on the label.

Nowadays, one usually sees proof only on bottles of American spirits or spirits destined for import into the United States. ABV is used everywhere else, and as a measure, proof is simply double the ABV, so it may seem superfluous. The term has more antique origins, however, and began with an early method used to demonstrate the strength of spirituous liquors.

Proof dates back to 16th-century Europe. Back in those days, a pellet of gunpowder was soaked in the spirit and set on fire. If the gunpowder burned steadily, without either sputtering or exploding in a flash, it was said to be "100 proof," or completely proven. Sputtering or flashing meant less or more alcohol was in the spirit.

This crude gunpowder system was relied upon generally before the instruments necessary to take more accurate measurements were invented, but continued to be used in 19th-century America wherever such instruments were unavailable. In the Wild West, one might not have been able to measure specific gravity, but gunpowder was readily available. In 1848, the United States officially based alcohol proof on ABV and established 100 proof as 50% alcohol, creating a system separate from those used in Europe. That system continues to this day as an American affectation.

The alcohol-bearing vapor rises from the rounded belly up the swan neck of the pot still, and an interesting point of design is that the taller and thinner the neck, the purer the spirit will be. The heavier compounds in the vapor, such as oils and congeners, will tend to condense and drop back down into the still as reflux rather than rise to the top of the neck. Once at the top, a pipe called a lyne arm carries the vapor on to be condensed and to enter the next stage of distillation.

Pot stills can feature many tweaks, especially for the swan neck, such as the onion or boil ball, pinched waists, flat tops, and vapor columns. These are usually much more important to, and characteristic of, Scottish pot stills than the pot stills seen in America, so the most important takeaway is that if you see a pot still and the neck looks odd, that is probably a design feature meant to increase or minimize reflux. With traditional pot stills, at least two runs through a still is necessary to reach the desired strength of alcohol for making whiskey. In America, those two runs are usually referred to as the stripping run and the spirit run. In Scotland, they use double sets of stills, while Irish producers use a triple set for triple distillation.

If you are on the Kentucky Bourbon Trail, you can see examples of these two sets just 25 miles apart: Woodford Reserve has an Irish-style triple set, while Town Branch has a Scottish-style double set of pot stills. Mike Sherman, vice president of Vendome Copper & Brass Works (the premier still builder in the United States) says, "[Pot stills] do tend to be a little more labor intensive to run and they do not have the production capacity of a continuous column, but they are very versatile and have more of a 'hands-on' approach to distilling."

The column still is also known as the patent, continuous, and/or Coffey still. The latter name refers to Irishman Aeneas Coffey, who perfected some precursors of the column still and patented his design in 1831. The simplest way to think of it is that the column stacks several pots on top of each other, because within the column is a series of perforated copper plates. The mash is poured in near the top and steam rises up from the bottom. As the mash makes its way down, alcohol vapor is extracted from the mash and rises up the column, where it is collected and condensed.

Column stills in Ireland and the UK (and in much of world, for that matter) are quite different from column stills in America. Outside of the United States, a column still usually comes in two columns, which are referred to as an analyzer and a rectifier. This two-column design is meant to work with a mash that the grainy solids have been removed from; the resulting spirit is pretty close to vodka and similar to American light whiskey.

An American column still (sometimes it is called a beer still) is a single column, attached to a pot-like device called a doubler or thumper, where the vapor receives a second round of distillation. Often a doubler or thumper will even resemble a pot still in its outward

appearance, although a doubler will contain a condenser as well as a pot-shaped distillation unit. Unlike Irish and Scottish column stills, American stills are designed to work with mash (i.e., the grain solids remain). Those solids are gone by the time the doubler or thumper comes into play, enabling them to continuously run a second distillation. Thumpers are usually used with smaller column stills, and the doubler (with its condenser) is attached to larger column stills.

The big and medium-size whiskey makers use a column still because it is a highly efficient piece of equipment for large-scale production. On the virtues of column stills and economies of scale, Sherman says, "Continuous columns tend to be much easier to run and produce a more consistent product. As long as you have fermented mash available to feed the continuous column, it will keep running for days. Some distilleries will run for a week or two straight before shutting it down."

The hybrid stills that are common at many small distilleries are exactly what they look like: a pot still with a short column still in the place of the traditional swan neck. In terms of operation, hybrids reverse the American column design. The pot still makes the stripping run, while the short column still makes the spirit run.

For a smaller distiller, this design is more cost-effective. I've never seen a column still in any operation that I wouldn't describe as at least medium size, and pot stills require at least a pairing to be commercially viable. Hybrid stills allow a small distiller to make a full distillation run from a single piece of equipment, and using the small column for the second half of the run allows for some fine-tuning of the end product.

Distillation produces new-make whiskey (also called "white dog") and a by-product, the spent mash, which still carries plenty of nutritious stuff. Almost without exception, this stuff is pumped or scooped out of the still, dried, and passed on to farmers as animal feed.

The new whiskey, including even whiskeys destined for bottling as "unaged" or "white," is then entered into a barrel. It may seem paradoxical that a spirit designated as not aged would go through this step, but time in a barrel is required by law if a spirit is to be called whiskey, even if that time amounts to just a minute.

This bizarre stipulation, which will be explored in depth later on, is another one of those little differences that make American whiskey distinctive. In Ireland and Scotland, a whiskey must be aged for at least three years to earn its name; the United States mandates aging, but has no statutory minimum except for categories such as "straight" and "bottled in bond."

For whiskeys that will be matured, however, water is added to the whiskey to reduce the alcohol content to 125 proof or less. Putting higher-proof alcohol in the barrel is cheaper and more efficient because it requires fewer barrels to deliver the same amount of whiskey at bottling. Lowering the entry proof means more water in the barrel, and water is useful for breaking down certain chemical compounds so they can oxidize. This process reduces the dry, bitter, and astringent aspects of a whiskey's flavor, which collectively are known as its "woodiness."

Once in the barrel, the whiskey goes into storage for months, years, or (rarely) decades. At the big distillers, this could take place in a multi-story warehouse sporting specially designed racks, known as a "rick-house"; for a small "nano-distillery" in a city, the barrel could just be going down to the cellar. The racks in rickhouses are designed not just for ease of storage, but also to ensure consistent ventilation for all barrels stored in the building. However, depending on the distiller's location, the top floor of a towering rickhouse becomes an oven in the summer (much like an attic), while the bottom floor is usually cooler than the ground beneath a shady tree.

Depending on the distillery and its method, maturing whiskey in charred, new white oak barrels accounts for all of the whiskey's color and 40 to 80% of its flavor. Yet maturation is about more than just time in the barrel; aging whiskey is like a square dance, in which climate and method of storage join hands with time and wood.

Almost all the whiskey made in America comes from big distillers, and these distillers share many characteristics when it comes to barrel aging. The barrels they use are made from white oak harvested in an area

running from Missouri and Arkansas over to West Virginia and east Tennessee, and as far south as northern Alabama. Most of those barrels receive a #3 or #4 char, which breaks down a lot of hemicellulose into wood sugars, producing those sweet caramel, brown sugar, and toffee flavors American whiskey is known for. Deeper charring also mellows tannins and puts additional spice and vanilla into the whiskey, while cutting back on oak lactones.

The big distilleries are found in a region running right through the middle of the region where all that oak comes from: southern Indiana, central Kentucky, and central Tennessee. The climate in that region varies but slightly between its northernmost and southernmost points, and thus the entire area experiences sweltering summers (which expands the liquid and drives whiskey into the wood) and chilly winters (which contracts the liquid and pulls it back out).

Method of storage varies quite a bit among the big distillers. The most common type of rickhouse has always struck me (the son of a Kentucky horse farmer) as a sturdy tower of racks sheathed in a tobacco barn, but one several stories tall. The core of the building is its ricks, or tiers of barrel storage racks. These are designed for ease of storage and removal, as well as to allow for regular and uniform air circulation around the barrels and throughout the building. Usually there are three racks of barrels on each floor.

Around the ricks is a wood-planked building with some windows and a tin roof. The thermal properties of these buildings ensure that on a scorching August day, the ground floor will be a good bit cooler than a spot just outside the doorway, while the top floor will be dry and perhaps as hot as 130 or 140°F. Thus, barrels stored at the top are "cooked" and age faster, whereas barrels placed at the bottom of the building enjoy a slower, more mellow spell of maturation.

Even among the Kentucky majors, however, there are some serious variations. Maker's Mark rotates its barrels to ensure a more uniform aging process, while Four Roses uses single-story rickhouses to achieve a similar effect. Some rickhouses have both tin roofs and tin sheathing, effectively making them ovens in summertime. Others are built of brick, fieldstone, or cinder block, materials that offer better insulation and thus warm up and cool down more slowly than rickhouses sheathed in wood planks or tin sheets, shielding their contents from extreme turns of the weather.

Since the mid-2000s, maturation has gone coast-to-coast and consequently added many more variables. For starters, the white oak used by many small cooperages around the country is often harvested in their local areas, and the growing seasons for trees in places like Minnesota, Washington state, and Maine are quite different from that of the Ozarks. The results can be a tighter or looser grain structure in the wood, thus allowing more or less whiskey into the wood's fibers. American white oak is not the only type of wood in use nowadays either, with exotic local oak species (such as Westland's Garryana oak),

imported European oak, and even maple in use as either stave inserts, barrelheads, or whole barrels.

In terms of climate, the whiskeys of Pennsylvania, Maryland, and Virginia might not have been aged in conditions so different from that of the Ohio Valley, but those matured in Colorado, Texas, New Mexico, and Washington mature under very different conditions indeed. As for storage, although some craft distillers use ricks or racks, they never have warehouses several stories tall. Many palletize their barrels (barrels are set standing on their heads on pallets, with pallets stacked atop each other) or else use the dunnage system (barrels stacked atop each other on their sides, three high). Finally, some craft distillers are using climate-controlled warehouses to store their whiskey, particularly in the Southwest, thus eliminating the factor of climate altogether.

No story illustrates how changing any of these conditions can profoundly alter the maturation of whiskey better than the 2012 release of Colonel E.H. Taylor Warehouse C "Tornado Survivor" Bourbon. Warehouse C, a brick rickhouse built in 1881, had its roof torn off and some of the masonry damaged by a tornado in 2006. The barrels, however, were undamaged and left to rest where they were while the building was repaired. As a result, the building received much more light during the day than usual, with the barrels on the roof receiving the full brunt of the summer sun, and the building's ventilation characteristics changed radically.

These conditions were present for just a matter of months while the roof was repaired, a brief period in almost a decade's worth of aging behind the "Tornado Survivor" bourbon, yet they had an outsize impact. One result was the doubling of the expected Angel's Share, which refers to the whiskey that is lost to evaporation, to an average of 63.9%. Another was the creation of a bourbon that was ambrosia. That marvelous outcome was so unexpected that Buffalo Trace was inspired to build Warehouse X in 2013, a whiskey maturation laboratory controlling for light, ventilation, humidity, and temperature.

Once a distiller has decided maturation is over and dumps the barrel, the whiskey is filtered to at least remove solids (usually bits of charcoal from the charred insides of the barrel) and often more. Chill filtration is a common procedure, intended to remove certain oils that make a whiskey appear cloudy if it gets cold. However, some distillers use post-maturation filtration as a way to target and remove certain chemical compounds from the whiskey that they don't want to influence its flavor.

The final step before bottling is to add filtered water and "cut" the whiskey down to the desired alcohol content. The minimum in America, 40% alcohol by volume (ABV) or 80 proof, is a point in common with most other countries. As a rule, however, American whiskey tends to be stronger than its foreign counterparts. Scotch whisky is usually bottled at 40% or 43% ABV, and less frequently at 46% ABV. In America, the usual range is 40% to 50%, with greater emphasis placed on the range of 45% to 50% (90 to 100 proof), especially for premium expressions. Some expressions are bottled uncut, as barrel-proof or cask-strength releases. These are usually unfiltered too, except to remove solids, and are as close to straight-from-the-barrel whiskey as most drinkers can get.

TYPES OF AMERICAN WHISKEY

ALL BOURBON IS WHISKEY, BUT NOT ALL WHISKEY IS BOURBON

What makes one whiskey a bourbon and another an American malt is defined by federal law and refined by regulations from the agency principally responsible for enforcing standards, the Alcohol and Tobacco Tax and Trade Bureau (TTB), part of the U.S. Department of the Treasury. These rules name what I like to think of as the major American categories in the first clause of "Class 2; Whisky" in 27 CFR 5.22: bourbon, rye, wheat, malt, and rye malt whiskeys.

All five categories are governed by identical rules. They are made from fermented grain; distilled to not more than 80% ABV (160 proof); and entered into charred, new oak barrels at not more than 62.5% ABV (125 proof) for maturation. A sometimes overlooked rule is that this categorization "also includes mixtures of such whiskeys of the same type," so a distiller can mix bourbons from different distilleries and still call it bourbon.

What separates bourbon from rye, malt, and wheat whiskey is the mash bill. Each type is identified by its primary grain, which must be 51% or greater of the mash bill. As anyone who has been on more than one American distillery tour has had drummed into them, bourbon is made with 51% or greater corn; rye is 51% or greater rye; wheat is 51% or greater wheat, and so on. Nothing is said regarding what the remainder of the grain recipe needs to be.

So, although the traditional recipe for bourbon is a large helping of corn, some rye for extra flavor, and a little malted barley to convert starch to sugar for fermentation, nothing legally stipulates this recipe. This is why there are wheated bourbons, substituting wheat for the rye, and (as we shall see) 100% corn, two-grain, four-grain, and even nine-grain bourbons. The same principle applies to all the other major categories.

In my mind, the mandate for charred, new oak barrel aging is one of the signatures of American whiskey. Other whiskey industries can use charred new oak, but are not required to and for the most part do not, preferring to rely upon casks that have been used in the maturation of other kinds of liquor instead. Most Scottish, Japanese, and Irish stocks are aged in former bourbon barrels or casks made from former bourbon barrel components, with a smattering of Sherry butts, Port pipes, and various other odds and ends. Aging in charred, new oak barrels is where American whiskey derives its vanilla and caramel flavors, its color, and some of its characteristic sweetness; it is said an American whiskey derives between 40 and 80% of its flavor from aging in new oak, depending on the methods of a particular distillery.

A further stipulation applies to just bourbon. An obscure bit of federal law, 27 CFR 5.23(a)(2), allows for additives only if they are customarily used. The TTB has an internal regulation that additives are not customary to bourbon and cannot be used, ever. So, a bottle of just plain bourbon (for the meaning of other designations, such as "straight," see page 30) is made with just water, grain, and yeast, but a bottle of just plain rye, wheat whiskey, and so on might contain a tiny amount of added coloring or flavoring.

CORN WHISKEY, TENNESSEE WHISKEY, LIGHT WHISKEY, AND BLENDS

The idea of 100% corn bourbon might seem somehow wrong. When I've met people who hold that misconception, it's usually due to a misunderstanding about either corn whiskey or bourbon's relation to Tennessee Whiskey. Corn whiskey is similar to the five major American categories: it too is distilled to not more than 160 proof and entered into barrels at not more than 125 proof. Corn whiskey is also mostly corn, and before it goes into the barrel, a corn whiskey and a bourbon might be the very same distillate.

The differences between corn whiskey and bourbon are found in the specifics of the mash bills and how they are aged: corn whiskey must be made from 80% or greater corn and aged in either used oak barrels or uncharred new oak barrels. If a corn whiskey distillate is aged in a charred, new oak barrel, it becomes bourbon. Most bourbon distillates do not have enough corn in them to become corn whiskey, however, no matter what kind of barrel they are aged in. The two categories overlap, but the most important distinction is in their maturation. It makes a world of difference in terms of flavor, and corn whiskey serves as a good comparison point for what aging in charred, new oak does for the major categories of American whiskey.

Tennessee is known for its whiskey because two of the major brands, including America's top-selling whiskey, are both labeled as such: Jack Daniel's and George Dickel. Once upon a time, and insofar as the law was concerned, Tennessee whiskey meant whiskey from Tennessee and that was it. It was about as stringent as saying Ohio or Missouri whiskey.

That changed with the passage of the Tennessee Whiskey Law of 2013. This state law defined Tennessee Whiskey as being made in the same way bourbon is, but with the added step of filtration in sugar maple charcoal prior to barrel aging, a step known as the Lincoln County Process (LCP). No further guidance is given on what the Lincoln County Process is, and every distiller of Tennessee Whiskey has its own particular version. Prichard's Distillery was given a "grandfather" exemption, because it has been in operation since the 1990s and calls its non-LCP products Tennessee whiskey as well.

My opinion is that by defining Tennessee Whiskey in this way, the law makes the category a major and distinctive variant of bourbon. Sometimes folks erroneously believe bourbon cannot have higher than 80% corn in it because George Dickel Nos. 8 and 12 have over 80% corn in their mash bills, whereas none of the popular Kentucky bourbons of the 1950s and 1960s did. But those details are a matter of choice, not law.

In 1968, as American palates were changing and vodka was becoming increasingly popular, light whiskey was introduced as a category. Accordingly, it is a whiskey distilled to a higher strength and purity, between 80% and 90% ABV. Like corn whiskey, it is matured in used or uncharred new oak barrels. One rarely sees light whiskey on the shelf as such these days; a major exception was the limited-edition 14-year-old light whiskey released by Utah-based bottler turned small distiller High West, and some other small distillers are making and marketing light

whiskeys. Usually they appear in blends of sourced whiskeys.

As far as American blended whiskeys are concerned, the rules and terminology are complex and make for awfully boring reading. Suffice it to say, if a bottle says blended on it, it contains more than one type of whiskey. Some of the contents might not even be whiskey.

Finally, what happens if someone makes a whiskey that doesn't match any of the types described here? Then one is free to call it pretty much anything that isn't described here. Remember the basics: it must be fermented from a grain mash; distilled to lower than 95% ABV; aged for at least a brief period in a wood barrel of some kind; and be bottled at least 40% ABV/80 proof. "American Whiskey," "Four Grain Whiskey," "[Enter State Here] Whiskey," "Sour Mash Whiskey," and other titles have all been used to describe creations that fall between the cracks. So long as the name doesn't violate truth in advertising laws, it works.

AMERICAN SINGLE MALT

When it comes to food and drink, regional appellations and meaningful, specialized categorization can only ever be good things. They add to richness and complexity, and so it was that American whiskey became all the poorer during the mid-20th century, as its distinctions shrank down to Kentucky bourbon, Kentucky rye, and Tennessee Whiskey. The modern whiskey boom turned that around,

reviving some old categories and adding new ones. None has gotten more attention than the American Single Malt movement.

In 2016, several producers (Balcones, Copperworks, FEW Spirits, Headframe Spirits, Santa Fe Spirits, Triple Eight, Virginia Distilling, Westland, and Westward) of American malt whiskey came together to form the American Single Malt Whiskey

Commission (ASMWC) and lobby for the introduction of a new single malt category into the federal regulations governing what whiskey is. Almost two dozen more distilleries have since joined the movement. According to them, the following characteristics define an American single malt:

- A mash bill of 100% malted barley
- All whiskey distilled entirely at one distillery
- Mashed, distilled, and matured entirely in the US
- Matured in oak casks not exceeding 700 liters
- Distilled to no more than 160 proof
- Bottled at 80 proof or higher

At the time of writing, members of the ASMWC told me they fully expected the Federal Alcohol and Tobacco Tax and Trade Bureau (TTB) to adopt this standard by Summer 2022. That said, the same thing was expected last year, and the gears driving federal regulators turn slowly. The main thing is that they have not said "no" yet, and so long as they do not say "no," they will eventually say "yes."

The interesting twist in all of this is the TTB already has a defined category for malt whiskey. One stipulation is that they be 51% or more malted barley, similar to the way that bourbon, rye, and wheat whiskeys are all 51% or more of their signature grain. Nothing about a 100% malted barley whiskey contradicts this requirement, although it does move away from the mixed mash bill formula that characterizes so many American whiskeys.

Of more importance is that the definition does not require the use of new barrels. That use of new wood is required by all four of the current major categories (bourbon, rye, wheat, and malt), and is accordingly regarded by most as a signature of American whiskey as we know it. Some American single malts use new oak barrels and some do not, and while discarding that requirement grants American whiskey makers more freedom, it also clearly has an eye on commonality with the malt whiskeys made according to the Scottish and Irish models. However, a difference between this standard and that of the Scottish and Irish model is that the latter are required to use copper pot stills; the American standard doesn't specify that either.

If the American single malt category comes into being as the ASMWC envisions it, what I see is a split developing between two different approaches to making American

malts. The new version, the American single malt, will more or less follow the guidelines above, more closely mirror other malt whiskeys made around the world, and be the purview of America's small and mid-size distillers. The older version is the one currently defined—at least 51% malted barley mash bill, aged in new barrels—and is made not only by craft distillers, but also by some of the big guys. Heaven Hill and Woodford Reserve both make malt whiskeys in this vein, with Heaven Hill's being 65% malt and Woodford's being 51%.

Although I am sure everyone concerned would wish for a less confusing set of terms than American malts and American single malts, the formalization of the latter can only be a good thing. These developments add value and help consumers more easily understand what is in the bottle. In particular, it will make those bottles more approachable to foreign drinkers, already familiar with Scottish and Irish malts but only just becoming acquainted with rye or wheat whiskey.

Singles, Smalls, Straights, and Bondeds

A handful of terms found on American whiskey labels refer to the qualitative points of most or all whiskeys, rather than their category. Some of these are enforced by law and some are a matter of custom or marketing.

"Straight Whiskey" is defined by federal law and regulations, and can be applied to bourbon, rye, wheat, malt, rye malt, corn, and other whiskeys, corresponding to the rules governing

them. As a practical matter, no light whiskey can be a straight whiskey, but most anything else can be. A whiskey is "straight" if it has been aged for two or more years. If a straight whiskey has been aged fewer than four years, an age statement is required on the label. Also, a straight whiskey contains no additives. Bourbon already cannot have any additives as per TTB regulations, but other major types of whiskeys can, so the straight designation is a doubly important indicator for them.

Under the Bottled in Bond Act of 1897 (one of the early progressive measures from the era that gave us Upton Sinclair's *The Jungle*), a whiskey can be labeled as "bottled in bond" if the whiskey comes from a single distillery and was distilled in a single distilling season; the whiskey was aged for a minimum of four years at a bonded warehouse (i.e., under the supervision of the taxman); it was bottled at 100 proof, no more and no less; and the label identifies where it was made and, if different, where it was bottled.

"Bottled in bond" status was an important marker for quality in the pre-Prohibition era, and became a sleepy holdover from a bygone era by

WHY RYE CAN GUM UP THE WORKS

Rye whiskey with a high percentage of rye grain in the mash bill is notoriously difficult to make. When I asked Larry Ebersold and Greg Metze, the former master distillers of what is now MGP, and thus the makers of most of the sourced rye whiskey on the shelves today, what their thorniest career challenges were, both pointed to the creation of MGP's widely used 95% rye, 5% malted barley whiskey.

Rye is stickier than other grains commonly used in making whiskey. Thus, a mash made largely out of rye tends to become a viscous goo. This is one of the reasons why the Kentucky style of rye whiskey uses the bare minimum of rye grain called for by law (Kentucky rye whiskeys often use 51 to 53%), because minimizing the rye avoids its troublesome, syrupy nature.

This stickiness and viscosity can cause fermenters to overflow and flood the room with foam, but a more common problem with making rye whiskey with lots of rye in it is clumps of grain sticking to the still and its steam coils, where they are scorched and burnt. Making these whiskeys with very high rye content requires either lots of patient experimentation (which was what Ebersold and Metze did) or specialized equipment, like an agitator in the still to keep the rye mash from sticking to the interior. Another option, but not one often used in the United States, is to separate out the solids and turn the mash into a wort, and send that all-liquid wort to the still.

the late 20th century, before becoming popular again in recent years. The influx of mass-market bourbons that were as good or better than the bonded standards (Wild Turkey 101, for example, which is older than the bonded minimum and a hair stronger) made the demarcation irrelevant for a time. However, the disappearance of so many age statements from premium whiskeys in the mid- to late 2010s and rising prices have caused many enthusiasts to return to bonded whiskeys as their go-to favorites.

Two marketing terms have found widespread usage in modern American whiskey: "small batch" and "single barrel." Small batch was in vogue in the 1990s, and although less popular today, the term remains in use. Part of the reason why it isn't as catchy a term as it used to be is that most craft whiskey is, by any definition, small batch. The number of craft distillers that produce enough whiskey for a batch to draw on more than a dozen or two dozen barrels at a time is small. Mass-market whiskeys are made in batches drawing on several hundred barrels at a time. Making them that way means barrels with outlier flavors can be used, because these traits tend to disappear in the huge batching, meaning the process is less fussy. A smaller batch has less wiggle room, so "small

batch" implies more care on the part of the distillery and, thus, higher quality. The problem with the term "small batch" is that no formal line determines what is or is not a small batch. Usually it is thought (and is often the case in practice) that a small-batch whiskey is made with fewer than two dozen barrels. However, there are some examples of small-batch whiskeys that were or are made with several dozen barrels, and in theory the term could be applied to whiskeys made with batches of hundreds of barrels (although making such a claim is so egregious that it might run afoul of truth in advertising laws if word got out).

"Single barrel" is another term that doesn't have the direct force of law behind it, but unlike small batch, the meaning is clear: all the whiskey in the bottle comes from just one barrel. "Single barrel" implies higher quality because a distillery is unlikely to choose an inferior or peculiar barrel for bottling in this way. Another aspect of single-barrel bottlings is that they lack the consistent flavor profile that most batched whiskeys have. Individual barrels sit within a spectrum of flavors, so two barrels of identical age that sat right next to each other in the warehouse could come out with noticeably different tastes.

High Grains and Extra Wood

A term you may see on a distillery's website, on the back label of a bottle of whiskey, or mentioned on a whiskey blog is "high-rye bourbon." This

refers to a bourbon with an unusually high proportion of rye in the mash bill. As the variety of whiskey mash bills in production has proliferated, the concept has grown to include many variations.

One of the problems with referring to high-rye bourbon or high-anything whiskey is that, like small batch, no hard definitions apply. Different distilleries and pundits have different definitions, and place the minimum for a high rye at 25% rye, 28% rye, or 30% rye. Some refer to wheated bourbons with a similar proportion of wheat in the mix as "high wheaters." High-corn bourbon is more consistently, although still not exclusively, defined as a bourbon made with 80% or more corn. I've taken to referring to a whiskey that isn't an American malt with 20% or more malted barley in the mash bill as high malt, because at that point the malt contributes to the flavor of the spirit and isn't just there for its starch-converting enzymes.

This concept extends beyond bourbon. The traditional Kentucky approach to making rye has been described as high corn, because the style is defined by having just enough rye grain in the mash bill to qualify as rye whiskey (51 to 53% in the known examples). This leaves plenty of room for corn, often above 30% of the content, making for a rye whiskey that is bourbonesque. The possibilities go on and on. The key is knowing that if a high grain is indicated, what it means is that a heavy helping of the secondary or tertiary grain was used in the mash bill, and the flavor should follow correspondingly.

In the 2010s, a practice that became widespread in American whiskey was secondary maturation or "finishing." In most instances, this

involves putting mature whiskey in a cask already used to mature wine, beer, or another spirit for a period of a few months to a few years, so as to add that drink's flavors to the whiskey. At this point, it's hard to think of a cask that hasn't been used to create a barrel finish: George Dickel even introduced a Tabasco barrel-finished whiskey, as Tabasco sauce is made using chilies that have been aged for three years in former bourbon barrels.

A subset of secondary maturation that is peculiarly American is double oaking. Reintroduced with Woodford Reserve Double Oaked in 2012, under this method a whiskey receives a finish in a charred, new oak barrel, doubling down on the quintessentially American style of aging in new oak. Sometimes the second round of barrels has received an extra-long preparatory toasting and only a light charring, a practice designed to boost the sweet flavors that can be extracted from the wood. The result is often a sweet vanilla bomb of a whiskey.

Although some Scotch and Irish whiskeys also use new oak for secondary maturation, this method is not really the same because most or all of the whiskey was aged in used oak during primary maturation. Recall that new oak is used sparingly in most other whiskey industries.

What Is Craft Whiskey?

In the early and middle 2010s, it was not uncommon to see journalists and bloggers scoff at the very notion of "craft distilling." One frequent criticism was that although craft brewing offered a very different and often superior product to big beer, the whiskeys made by the big distillers in Kentucky and Tennessee were already quite good, and frequently better than what was being made by the craft distillers. Also, naysayers have complained that "craft" is a poorly defined concept, because production at the big distillers and small distillers is often equally artisanal.

The facts support the croaking on some points, but not on others. By definition a craft distillery is a small one, and craft distilling is a sector with some hard definitions behind it. For starters, at the state level the licenses for small distillers, often called a craft distiller's license or a farm distilling license, usually have fixed upper limits for production. The California Craft Distillers Act of 2015 set an upper limit of 100,000 proof gallons per year for their craft licensing; in 2016, Illinois raised the upper limit for their craft licenses from 35,000 gallons to 100,000 gallons.

Craft distilling's two national industry groups apply their own definitions. The American Distilling Institute (ADI) sticks by the 100,000 proof gallon limit, while the American Craft Spirits Association (ACSA) applies a limit of "not removing fewer than 750,000 proof gallons from bond" per year (i.e., paying the taxman and shipping the liquor). Both groups take the

same interest in independent ownership, however, mandating a craft distillery retain at least a 75% stake in itself. A number of early craft distillers are no longer certified by ADI or members of ACSA because a big liquor company bought into them.

To put those numbers into perspective, the 2011 expansion of Wild Turkey boosted their production capacity to 11 million proof gallons per year. Although they are undoubtedly one of the "Kentucky majors"—one of the leading distilleries in America's biggest whiskey state—Wild Turkey is not thought to place in even the upper half of that class in terms of its production capacity. The biggest distilleries in the whiskey industry make a lot more. Bardstown Bourbon Company, a new distillery that operates as a contract producer for sourced brands, is thought of as just a medium-size distillery. It has grown by leaps and bounds since its opening, moving from a capacity of 1.5 million proof gallons to 6 million per year. At the lower end of the spectrum, the Old Forester Distillery on Louisville's Whiskey Row produces 100,000 proof gallons per year (filling about 14 barrels a day), which is slightly bigger than most craft distilleries, but utterly dwarfed by even medium-size plants.

As to whether the small distillers produce better products in the same way that craft ales and lagers were often better than big beer, the naysaying is on better footing. They are absolutely right that even mass-market staples like Jim Beam and Evan Williams are a damn sight more enjoyable relative to whatever you might compare them to than a can of Coors is when held up against the typical craft brew. The big distillers of Kentucky and Tennessee do what they do very well; there is no denying it, and taking them head-on is a Herculean task that only a handful of small distillers has proven to be up to.

That said, there are plenty of niches that aren't occupied by the big boys. Even with the plethora of sourced brands based on MGP's 95% rye whiskey, it is hard to imagine what rye whiskey (and with it mixology culture) would look like today if the craft scene hadn't exploded at the same time that the cocktail boom caught whiskey makers by surprise, spiking the demand for rye whiskey between 2010 and 2012. Likewise, although American malts are a small sector, it is one dominated by small distillers.

Also, craft distilleries are driving innovation in whiskey making. Their smaller scale of production allows them to experiment in a way that a big distillery, with its large-scale production equipment, cannot. Indeed, as the big distillers have started producing experimental whiskeys and releasing them as limited editions, such offerings have largely come from what are essentially micro-distilleries built on the existing distilling grounds.

Another critique of the craft movement is that it implies certain artisanal qualities that either aren't present at small distilleries or are actually omnipresent in the industry. There is some truth to the claim: a great deal of human intervention and handicraft goes into making whiskey even at the most automated distilleries, where many matters of production are controlled from a single console.

However, I think it specious to claim there isn't a difference between a distillery where people are still turning steam valves by hand and the automated processes in place at a medium or large distillery. The difference is largely a romantic one, found more in the heart and imagination than facts and figures, but it is there. Part of what makes the big distillers so good at what they do is that they have invested so much in understanding and controlling their production process. Still, when one considers that heritage is something every whiskey nerd prizes, it's hard to understand what drives the criticism of a movement made up mostly of distilleries that, in terms of scale, facilities, and style, have far more in common with the distilleries that were around during the pre-Prohibition era than anything going on with the majors of Kentucky and Tennessee.

AMERICAN WHISKEY TODAY, BY THE STATE

Profiling the hundreds of whiskeys described in the following pages was both the most enjoyable and the most onerous task in writing this book. I take as much interest in what small whiskey distillers in America are doing as anyone in the field, but the tasting notes I started with were insufficient for the picture I wanted to present, and I had to taste several dozen expressions for this work.

Because I wanted to present references to things that could be reasonably purchased and enjoyed, my first rule was to exclude all onetime, unique releases, because these automatically become unicorns (i.e., extremely expensive and extremely hard to acquire). In many ways they are harder to get than even the famed Pappy Van Winkle bourbons, which has a new batch released every year. Whiskeys like the excellent Heaven Hill 27-Year-Old Barrel Proof Bourbon, on the other hand, are scarce when they come out and become only more so thereafter.

My exclusion of one-shot releases did not extend to those that are part of a continuing series, such as Parker's Heritage or Four Kings. The reasoning there is simple: even if the individual releases aren't repeated, the series itself is something to look for every year, a point that is quite helpful in the practical business of acquiring a bottle of these serial whiskeys.

Another issue I confronted was the question of balancing a presentation of American whiskeys from coast-to-coast with the hard fact that nearly all of the whiskeys made in the United States come from Kentucky and Tennessee. This is visible not just on store and bar shelves everywhere, but also on bookstore shelves as well; there are a surfeit of books out there about Kentucky bourbon, but not even one book that gives a decent look at current whiskeys and producers from California, Texas, and Virginia.

Ultimately, about a third of the expressions covered here are from Kentucky and Tennessee. America's two leading whiskey states have the two largest sections, but the overall focus is on the country as a whole.

When I started *The Whiskey Reviewer* in 2011, it was possible for me to imagine covering every craft whiskey released in the United States. Within a couple of years, that had become a ludicrous ambition and has remained an impossibility ever since. There are far too many distillers making a vast number of expressions, many are extremely difficult to get at, and not all of them are worth the effort of doing so. It was not feasible to cover a whiskey for every one of the 50 states—not because of a lack, but due to the breadth of offerings out there—a point that underscores how far distilling in America has come.

THE THIRD WHISKEY STATE

Thanks to the craft distilling boom that started in the middle 2000s, the American whiskey industry has grown to become well and truly national for the first time. The pre-Prohibition whiskey industry looked a lot like Major League Baseball of the same era: the teams were started in the Midwest, Northeast, and the Upper South, and so were the distilleries. Nowadays, several Western states have a much bigger footprint in the whiskey business than states like Ohio, Maryland, and Illinois, all substantial players before Prohibition.

The pre-Prohibition, World War I era of American Whiskey was different from today in another way too. Back then, Kentucky and especially Tennessee were not the goliaths of the industry in terms of output and reputation that they became during the latter half of the 20th century. In those bygone times, Kentucky is best described as the first among equals. By the 1960s, Kentucky clearly led the industry, and the sister state of Tennessee was right behind her.

A decade into the 21st century, it was clear that craft whiskey was fast becoming a coast-to-coast phenomenon, with more than just singular outposts scattered about here and there. It was not long after that I began posing the bronze medal question: What would become America's third whiskey state? A handful of states boasted a whiskey-making sector that was numerous, vigorous, and well-established enough to place them in contention for that third-place slot, behind the leading pair of Kentucky and Tennessee, so my question was a fair and sincere one.

My view was the third-ranking state should have a rich and revived whiskey heritage or else host some of the forerunners of the craft whiskey movement (or both); it should also be home to a substantial small distilling sector that includes some of craft whiskey's best-known names; and, since craft whiskey is identified with innovation and being where the big distillers aren't, that sector should be producing some of the most interesting expressions in craft whiskey. These criteria are why I never thought of Indiana as being in contention for America's third whiskey state, as MGP gave them the heritage, but the Hoosier state was otherwise lacking.

For a decade players came and went, but three states were continuously in contention for the title: Colorado, Pennsylvania, and Texas. By 2020, I had finally drawn the conclusion that this particular bar debate had been settled—for me at any rate—and Texas had won the marathon. For heritage, Texas has two of craft whiskey's trailblazers in Balcones and Garrison Brothers, whereas Colorado has only the one (Stranahan's) and Pennsylvania relies on its legacy as the country's top pre-Prohibition rye whiskey state. Texas has been a leader in innovation, making early use of exotic grains like blue corn and its regionally derived mesquite smoking techniques; in adapting their production process to fit the extremes of local climate; and in carving out their own niche in American malt whiskey. It is also a state boasting as many well-known small and midsize whiskey names as anywhere. Finally, the state's industry keeps on growing, as each year seems to bring new start-ups to the state and distillers like Balcones grow from small to a midsize producers.

I am sure I will spend much of the 2020s engaged in friendly debates in bars and at conventions about this, but facts are stubborn things. No matter how you slice it, Texas either rivals or exceeds the rest of America in every conceivable whiskey industry category. Except Kentucky and Tennessee—the gulf between whiskey's sister states and the rest of the country is enormous, and I do not expect it will be closed in my lifetime.

ICON KEY

 PROOF

*V=VARIES

 COLORING

 NOSE

 FLAVOR PROFILE

 NORTHEAST

 REGION

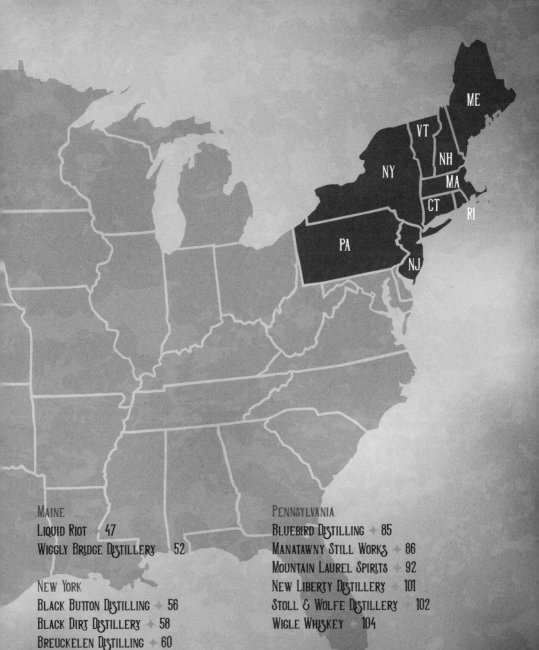

— LIQUID RIOT —

Most distilleries these days have a bar attached. Brewstilleries are a small but growing part of the American craft whiskey scene. Only a few have a restaurant attached. Portland's Liquid Riot makes spirits and beer, sells them over the bar, and serves food, all under one roof. I can count the number of folks doing that in the United States on one hand. Liquid Riot is run by two brothers, Eric and Ian Michaud, with Ian running the whiskey side of things. The labeling nods both to Portland ("Old Port") and to the city's distilled spirits history. Maine passed a prohibition law in 1851, and some years later

a rumor got around that Portland's mayor, Neal "The Napoleon of Temperance" Dow, was sitting atop a large stash of alcohol. Those discontented with prohibition turned another law Dow had sponsored against him, procuring a citizen's search warrant for the liquor in June 1855. There actually was a stockpile of "medicinal spirits" in City Hall, which is where a crowd gathered, reportedly growing to some 3,000 by that evening. The crowd became unruly, Dow called out the militia, and the militia fired on the crowd. Thus went the Portland Rum Riot of 1855.

90 Liquid Riot's bourbon is made from an unorthodox mash bill, using the traditional corn and rye, but relying on buckwheat in place of malted barley.

It has a light copper coloring in the glass, and a swish and coat released a scattered sheet of tears.

The nose is sweet with red fruits and molasses, with a note of hot cinnamon to spice it up.

The flavor leans toward the spicy side, however, with cinnamon and ginger in the main. A note of toasty wood imprints a dry character to it as well, but not in the tannic or overtly oaky way. The sweetness fades down to a glazing of nondescript sugar. The finish runs light, short, and dry.

Liquid Riot Rye Whiskey

Liquid Riot doesn't specify their exact mash bill for their whiskeys, describing them only in the most general terms. So, they state their rye is made with rye grain and malted barley, but not in what proportions. My guess is that the malted barley proportion must be relatively high, because the end product didn't turn out like very high rye, no-corn whiskeys from traditionally inspired distilleries.

In the glass it is quite amber, surprisingly so given that many ryes come out as copper in color. This is darker and redder. Coating the glass yields a sweeping display of chunky legs.

A sniff at the glass gives me the pumpernickel scent I usually associate with the presence of malted rye (I don't know if it is actually there, but that is what I got), but quite dry in this instance. I pick out a hint of lemon zest as well.

The flavor follows in that vein: pumpernickel spices with sweeter citrus notes, coupled to a seasoning of vanilla. It's a moderate, smooth whiskey, going down with a short, but spicy finish.

Whatever it is they are doing for their rye, I'm much fonder of it that I am of their bourbon. The latter was merely okay, whereas the rye is quite good.

— WIGGLY BRIDGE DISTILLERY —

Wiggly Bridge Distillery is one of a handful of small businesses run by David Woods Sr. and David Woods Jr. in York. Endowed with a can-do, DIY entrepreneurial style, the pair set out to make their own spirits, with David Jr. going so far as to teach himself copper fabrication through watching YouTube videos and trial and error to build their tiny, 60-gallon still. The distillery is named for a local landmark, which happens to be the smallest suspension footbridge in the world, a quaint feature nestled into a beautiful landscape.

WIGGLY BRIDGE BOTTLED IN BOND BOURBON WHISKY

100 Their bourbon is made from a mash bill of 57% corn, 38% rye, and 5% malted barley, so it's a high-rye whiskey. It's aged for the bonded minimum four years in small barrels.

In the glass, the bourbon has a light amber look. Coating the glass leaves a few thick legs behind.

The nose carries graham crackers that have been frosted with cinnamon, honey, and vanilla drizzle.

The flavor is classic bourbon territory, and not as spicy as the high-rye recipe might suggest: brown sugar, vanilla, a little cinnamon, and a tannic, oaky note. The finish runs off the latter, spicy, a bit woody, and with a hint of char.

This bourbon is simple and straightforward, but nice.

WIGGLY BRIDGE NEW ENGLAND SINGLE MALT WHISKY

80 This American malt whisky is so new that (at the time of writing) Wiggly Bridge hadn't even updated their website to reflect its existence! As a single malt, we can guess that it is made from 100% malted barley. What makes this American malt so noteworthy is how amazingly Scotch-like it is, being quite reminiscent of a youthful malt matured somewhere by the sea; no surprise, York is a coastal town.

That similarity to Scotch begins with the look, which resembles white wine once it is in the glass. A swish and coat stream skinny little legs.

The nose smacks of cereals and seaweed, and it's not altogether pleasant.

Thankfully, the flavor springs explosively out of that foundation. Leaving the seaweed behind altogether, it is honey sweet with a dash of cinnamon and a touch of ash. The finish winds down a little ashy and a little oaky.

NEW YORK

New New York's repute in American whiskey presents an interesting juxtaposition. The Empire State rates quite highly among certain drinks writers and independent experts, many of whom still consider it the country's number three whiskey state (although I wonder if said judgement is influenced by those experts being based in New York City). Yet among enthusiasts, the notion of New York bourbon prompts a response straight from a Pace picante sauce commercial: "This bourbon says it comes from New York City?" followed by an indignant shout of "NEW YORK CITY!" There are some people, it seems, who just cannot accept Yankee whiskey. My mother is among them.

Although I believe the decade-long contest over who was taking American whiskey's third-place slot is now over (see page 42), New York's claim was strong when it was in the running. It had history, the breadth of distilleries, and owned a proud standing within the craft movement. The state's small distilleries are as vibrant as any to be found in the country, and New York boasts a member of the first proper wave of craft distillers in Tuthilltown, opened in 2004. That groundbreaking distillery was followed by other early entrants, such as Finger Lakes Distillery, which got into the scene before growth exploded and went into overdrive after 2010.

New York City hosts the largest urban micro-distillery scene in the country, one that includes Arcane, Breuckelen, Kings County, Moto, New York Distilling, Van Brunt Stillhouse, and Widow Jane. The statewide micro-distilling sector is also among the country's largest, and that sector overall contributes its share to the diversity of American whiskey with expressions like Kings County's Peated Bourbon.

In pre-Prohibition times, and especially during the 19th century, New York was a major distilling state. In 2017 it took a step toward reclaiming that heritage by starting the Empire Rye movement, founded by Black Button, Coppersea, Finger Lakes, Honeoye Falls, Kings County, New York Distilling, Tuthilltown, and Yankee Distillers. "The state has a long tradition of making rye," says Bourbon Empire author Reid Mitenbuler, "which went dormant for a good chunk of the twentieth century."

Although New York made a lot of rye whiskey back in the day, it has not been identified with a regional style in the same way as Pennsylvania, Kentucky, and Maryland, so Empire Rye is a modern creation. The Empire Rye press materials state that in place of mandating a style, distillers are "given ample space to express their creativity" while the regional classification focuses on origin and sourcing issues. Appropriately for a state that broke open craft distilling as an agricultural issue, Empire Rye whiskeys must comply with "New York Farm Distiller (Class D) requirement that 75% of the mash bill be New York grain; in this instance that 75% MUST be New York State-grown rye grain, which may be raw, malted or a combination." The other requirements that stand out are that all Empire Rye whiskeys must be at least two years old, and with a lower entry proof (115 instead of 125) than mandated by Federal law.

— BLACK BUTTON DISTILLING —

Black Button Apple Pie Moonshine

40 "Apple Pie" is a classic concoction, using apples and spices to make otherwise unpalatable, unaged spirits tasty. It's especially well known in the South as a spin on corn whiskey, and that is the form the Yankees at Black Button took with their own corn whiskey. The original Black Button Moonshine upon which this is based has since been discontinued, but the Apple Pie iteration is still going strong.

The root is a corn whiskey, to which the Rochester-based distillery has added New York–made apple cider, vanilla, and cinnamon. It's roughly as strong as fortified wine and therefore a very easy sipper, and a flavorful cocktail ingredient.

As befits the name, the drink has a golden, apple juice–like appearance in the glass.

The nose, however, is pretty husky, leaning hard into the grassy side of corn whiskey.

The spices and cider make almost no appearance, and that is pretty misleading given what comes next: a mellow, easy-drinking experience of what is essentially liquefied apple pie filling.

Black Button Four Grain Bourbon Whiskey

The recipe chosen for this four-grain bourbon was 60% corn, 20% wheat, 9% rye, and 11% malted barley, and with some pride the distillery boasts it was all sourced from the state of New York.

For a young bourbon, it's quite smooth, and that starts with the nose. It's got a clear scent of caramel and citrus zest.

A taste gives more caramel, now cut with grassiness and marshmallow, with a dash of black pepper and toasted cereals coming on at the end. That gives way to more pepper and a sliver of woodiness on the short and smooth finish.

Black Button Empire Rye

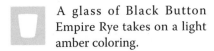

Black Button's contribution to the growing class of Empire Rye whiskeys is made with 94% rye and 6% malted barley. I suspect that mash bill was chosen to quash the knee-jerk reaction some enthusiasts must label any 95% rye mash bill as having been sourced from Indiana's MGP Distillery.

A glass of Black Button Empire Rye takes on a light amber coloring.

The nose from that pour carries the scent of the coarse-milled rye grain used to make pumpernickel coupled to vanilla.

The flavor follows in this vein: pumpernickel rye, vanilla, a grain of pepper, and a pinch of charcoal. The finish is a light one, starting out sweet and spicy, but fading fast onto that grain of pepper. This is a straightforward rye whiskey, but tasty and easy drinking.

— BLACK DIRT DISTILLERY —

Named for a band of "black dirt" that lies in an ancient glacial lake in upstate New York, the distillery is an outgrowth of the Warwick Valley Winery & Distillery, found in the Hudson Valley foothills. It's not widely known, but Warwick Valley is New York's first micro-distillery, having begun operations in 2002. They started out with brandy, but when the whiskey boom took off they hopped on the bandwagon and started making bourbon from corn grown in their rich, regional soil.

Black Dirt Bourbon Whiskey

Black Dirt's bourbon has evolved over time, mostly gaining age, but it has always been made with 80% corn, 8% rye, and 12% malted barley. That makes this a proper high-corn bourbon, and recent batches have all been at least three years and several months old. Black Dirt uses barrels charred to both level 3 and 4.

The nose has a toasted popcorn character, with a chip of oak and a spoonful of vanilla.

The texture is just a bit on the thin side, but nonetheless it delivers a flavor that is just as toasty and earthy as it is sweet, making this a fair choice for anyone shopping around for a bourbon that moves away from the usual brown sugar and vanilla-forward profile. It's got the vanilla for sure, but it also has a fire-roasted sweet corn current, and those two elements are rounded out by a note straddling a point somewhere between ultra-dark cocoa and coffee.

— BREUCKELEN DISTILLING —

Breuckelen Distilling, with its spin on the spelling of "Brooklyn," was started by Brad Estabrooke, a former securities trader at Deutsche Bank. Similar to the origin stories of many craft distilleries, Estabrooke left a white-collar career that had nothing to do with the booze business to get into spirits making. In 2010, he found an old boiler room to use as a space at 77 19th Street in Sunset Park, which is why his whiskeys are titled "77."

Breuckelen 77 Local Rye & Corn Whiskey

90 77 Local Rye is made from a mash of 90% rye and 10% corn, using added enzymes and no malted barley. According to Estabrooke, the reason they use enzymes directly rather than relying on the malted barley to provide them is that when they got started there were no area malt houses that could provide them with the New York–grown grain he wanted. If using enzyme additives sounds odd, remember that anytime you see a whiskey using 100% anything with no malted grains, enzymes were added. It was aged for just over two years in full-size barrels.

In the glass, it has the expected orange-copper rye color, and drops a few skinny tears.

The nose is predominately pumpernickel, with a whiff of mustiness, perhaps even moldiness, and a tinge of juniper.

A sip shows it to be a young whiskey, because it's a bit medicinal around the edges, but it's not harsh. A straightforward profile blends caramel and rye spice for a sweet start, before the whiskey turns dry at the end. The finish continues as dry and a bit spicy.

Breuckelen 77 Bonded Rye Whiskey

100

Bonded whiskeys coming from small distilleries are prime examples of the maturity of the craft movement, and this expression is a particularly strong example. It garnered praise even among bloggers who are known to be generally skeptical, if not downright reflexively critical, of craft whiskeys.

Technically, this is a rye whiskey, but this is a different animal, being made with a 100% rye mash bill. It was aged in standard 53-gallon barrels for the statutory minimum of four years.

The nose here is light and airy, akin to a pile of Jewish rye bread, sliced fresh from the oven and served on an oak platter, but with caramel drizzled atop. That might not sound very appetizing, but it is certainly pleasant enough to smell.

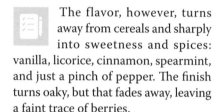

The flavor, however, turns away from cereals and sharply into sweetness and spices: vanilla, licorice, cinnamon, spearmint, and just a pinch of pepper. The finish turns oaky, but that fades away, leaving a faint trace of berries.

This is another one of those whiskeys that isn't deep or truly complex at any given point in the tasting of it. Instead, it shows sophistication in how it evolves over time.

Breuckelen 77 Local Rye & Corn Bottled in Bond Whiskey

100

Breuckelen is one of a handful of distilleries that can claim more than one bottled in bond expression (and keep in mind that hundreds of micro-distilleries out there cannot even claim one). This is the bonded version of their Local Rye & Corn Whiskey, described above and quite distinct from the bonded rye, making it both older and stronger.

Compared to its younger sibling, this bonded whiskey has a nose oozing with caramel, cinnamon, and oak, with just a touch of corn syrup.

That sweetness expands, if anything, on the palate, leaving the spiciness as a moderate, supplemental note. This is surprising given the 90% rye mash bill, as usually a whiskey so stacked up with rye would have a bold, spicy body. That finally appears in the finish, which carries cinnamon and pepper in equal measures.

Brownstone 6-Year-Old
Malt Whiskey

100

I first became acquainted with the Brownstone Malt when I visited Brad Estabrooke at his distillery in 2019; he wanted to show me something he was working on, and that sampling gave me something to look forward to. Made from 100% malted barley, Brownstone is aged in charred, new 53-gallon barrels for six years, before bottling at 100 proof. Given that many American-made single malts mimic the Scotch and Irish model of using predominately used barrels for aging their whiskey, the use of new barrels (ala other American whiskeys like bourbon and rye) is an authentic, grounding touch.

A pour of Brownstone lives up to the name, presenting a solid, middle amber look. I enjoyed looking at this particular pour more than usual, as the liquid was so viscous it sustained a bubble in the middle of the glass, one that lurked under the surface for almost a minute after swishing.

The nose had a dark, moody character. Golden raisins, molasses, cinnamon, and musty wood came into the nostril and squatted there, taking its leave only grudgingly.

Sipping gave me a mix of anise, fennel, cinnamon, and nutmeg for spices, brown sugar, and dried burley tobacco, and this rounded out with a sliver of toasted oak. The finish unfolded with lingering spiciness and a faint trace of wood. This is a flavorful whiskey, one that is sweeter than most American Malts, but in a way that manages to avoid leaning into bourbon territory. It is dark and hefty, sweet and spicy, and a must-have for anyone who is cultivating enthusiasm for the burgeoning American Malt sector.

— KINGS COUNTY DISTILLERY —

Because Colin Spoelman and David Haskell were "home distilling" long before they decided to turn pro, they got their license on April 14, 2010, and began mashing their first commercial batch the next day. Thus began the first legal distillery to operate in New York City since Prohibition.

Kings County, now the largest distillery in the city, takes its name from the place it can be found, because Kings County is Brooklyn, and Brooklyn is Kings County. The two have exactly the same boundaries. When Spoelman and Haskell got started in East Williamsburg, they were the smallest commercial distillery in America, and this when the craft spirits movement was still in its infancy and there was little need to make distinctions between micro- and nano-distilleries. In those days, they were operating with a set of stainless steel stills made by Hillbilly Stills in western Kentucky. Although their first release was a legal moonshine, they were making bourbon almost from the beginning, and the oldest barrel of aging whiskey they have in inventory was 7½ years old at the time of writing.

By 2012, Kings County was ready for its first expansion, and moved to the Paymaster Building in the Brooklyn Navy Yard. New equipment has followed the new facility; now Kings County relies on a pair of Forsyths pot stills, imported from Scotland, and a recently added 5,000-liter stripping still made by Louisville's Vendome. Their cookers come from Vendome, and their wood fermenters are built by Isseks Brothers (one of the family companies that builds those rooftop wooden water tanks New York is famous for).

Expansion doesn't always mean moving to a new building or adding a second facility, even for a small distillery, and Kings County is a case in point. The new stripping still, which was fired up in early 2019, greatly expands Kings County's production capacity. On their Forsyths pot stills, they were producing the equivalent of one standard 53-gallon barrel of spirits per day, but that has now increased fivefold.

Reflecting the experimental nature of their hobbyist roots, Kings County is a sweet-mash distillery, but hasn't always been that way. In its early days, it had production runs that were both sour mash and sweet mash, and eventually chose to settle on the latter. Some of the whiskey it has aging comes from sour-mash production runs, so future sour-mash releases remain a possibility. Another holdover from Spoelman and Haskell being hobbyists is that they use yeast from Brewhaus, a popular vendor of supplies for home brewing and distilling.

Another point reflecting that experimental spirit are the barrel stocks Kings County uses. In the several years they've been building their inventory of aged whiskey, Spoelman and Haskell have used almost every size of new oak barrel made in America. Nowadays, they have settled on 15-gallon barrels from Minnesota's The Barrel Mill and 53-gallon American Standard Barrels (ASBs)

from Independent Stave in Kentucky. Spoelman says that his "15s [are] good for four, and 53s we assume will age seven to 12 years like in Kentucky, but we have not pulled any 53s yet, and our oldest is just shy of six years now." About a quarter of the inventory is set aside for long-term aging.

Kings County Bourbon Whiskey

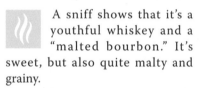 Whereas the larger trend in craft whiskey has been to reach for unorthodox grains and four-plus grain mash bills, Kings County chose to simplify when it came to its bourbon: going with 70% corn, 30% malted rye, and no third grain. The corn is from its home state and, peculiarly, the malted barley is from the UK. The whiskey was aged a minimum of two years. It's often seen in "pocket-size" bottles, with Kings County's minimalist, its label of typewriter print wrapped around the bottom.

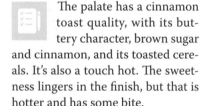 A sniff shows that it's a youthful whiskey and a "malted bourbon." It's sweet, but also quite malty and grainy.

The palate has a cinnamon toast quality, with its buttery character, brown sugar and cinnamon, and its toasted cereals. It's also a touch hot. The sweetness lingers in the finish, but that is hotter and has some bite.

KINGS COUNTY DISTILLERY
straight bourbon whiskey
45% alcohol by volume, 200ml

KINGS COUNTY PEATED BOURBON WHISKEY

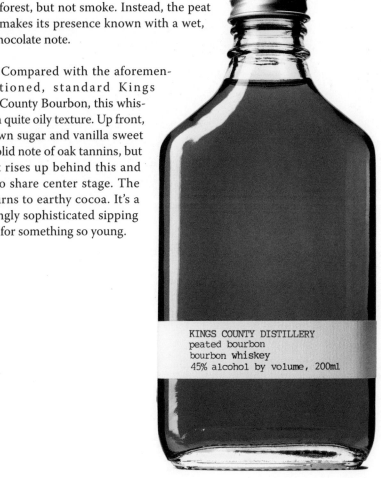

90 Arguably the most eyebrow-raising expression to come out of this distillery is their peated bourbon, which has become famous for its smoky, pseudo-Scotch character. That tack had never been tried before, despite the wide interest in craft distilling for using various smoked grains. Kings County took its basic bourbon mash bill, which was already using malted barley imported from the UK, and put a twist on it by splitting the malt content between 15% peated and 15% unpeated malted barley. It has been aged in charred new oak for 18 months.

The nose smacks of brown sugar and pine forest, but not smoke. Instead, the peat makes its presence known with a wet, earthy chocolate note.

Compared with the aforementioned, standard Kings County Bourbon, this whiskey has a quite oily texture. Up front, it is brown sugar and vanilla sweet with a solid note of oak tannins, but the peat rises up behind this and comes to share center stage. The finish turns to earthy cocoa. It's a surprisingly sophisticated sipping whiskey for something so young.

KINGS COUNTY DISTILLERY
peated bourbon
bourbon whiskey
45% alcohol by volume, 200ml

KINGS COUNTY DISTILLERY
chocolate "flavored" whiskey
40% alcohol by volume, 200ml

KINGS COUNTY DISTILLERY
chocolate "flavored" whiskey
40% alcohol by volume, 200ml

COLIN SPOELMAN

Depending on how you look at it, Colin Spoelman making whiskey in Brooklyn is either the most unlikely or the most natural outcome you could imagine for him. He grew up in Kentucky and, as detailed in the book *The Kings County Distillery Guide to Urban Moonshining*, brushed elbows with local moonshiners frequently. Yet it wasn't what he set out to do when he left Kentucky, and that journey took him to what, at the time, was the most improbable place in America to found a distillery: New York City.

Spoelman met David Haskell while both were at Yale studying architecture and urban planning; "Not an obvious background for whiskey," Spoelman admits. But they teamed up and started distilling as hobbyists after moving to New York. They feel this has given them a different grounding than those coming from the liquor industry or a training program, one full of trial and error.

In a story familiar to the craft whiskey scene, they also drew on experience from their non-distilling careers. Haskell was, and is, an editor at *New York* magazine, which helped with marketing, as well as writing the aforementioned book. One of Spoelman's early jobs in New York was working for the fragrance department of Estée Lauder, which gave him some formal sensory training.

Eventually the pair moved from making whiskey as a shady hobby to making it commercially, founding their distillery in a 325-square-foot room in East Williamsburg. However, starting at the nano-distillery scale in the midst of America's largest city was not their biggest difficulty. Nor were the inevitable growing pains. Instead, Spoelman points to America's three-tier liquor sales system (separating producer and retailer with a middleman, the distributor) as their biggest hurdle.

"You can create a great product that people all over the country want to buy," says Spoelman, "but you still have to convince a middleman in each state, often one that makes decisions on a whim and guesswork, to try your product. Then and only then do you get to convince a retailer, who is also working mostly on a whim and guesswork, to buy the product so as to make it available to those fans. It's very much a business that works on hustle."

Spoelman is proudest of his aged whiskeys, like his bottled in bond bourbon. "Bottled in bond incorporates three things very important to whiskey: a place, in a single distillery; a person, in a single distiller; and a time, of at least four years and from a single season. We were always holding barrels for a bonded whiskey, knowing that it would show best what a distiller can do within the law, and communicates the integrity and authenticity that people often associate with American whiskey. You can't source bonded whiskey, and so it really represents a distillery as opposed to a brand."

KINGS COUNTY EMPIRE RYE

102 For its own contribution to the Empire Rye category, Kings County chose a mash bill of 80% Danko Rye (noted in bread for its cocoa and baking spice flavors) and 20% English barley. They age it for at least two years, but not for as long as three.

This one takes up a bronze look in the glass.

The nose comes forward with rich chocolate and caramel coupled to tangerine cream, followed by a second, and almost larger, wave of oak and cinnamon.

The flavor follows in much the same vein, albeit with these two aspects arriving together rather than single file. The finish is dry, woody, and spicy. This particularly Brooklyn take on Empire Rye is big bodied, well-rounded, and I would love to see a bonded version

KINGS COUNTY 7–YEAR–OLD SINGLE BARREL BOURBON

107 In 2013, Kings County pot distilled a batch of bourbon, filled a barrel with some of it, and that barrel sat aging in the stifling attic of their Brooklyn Navy Yard building for seven years. That single barrel gave about a third of its contents up to the angels, pointing back to just how stuffy that aging room can get in summertime. This became the first entry in the Brooklyn distillery's new single barrel bourbon series, as well as an addition to the swelling ranks of craft bourbons that would be classed as mature, even by the standards prevalent in the Upper South. It's wonderfully balanced, displaying some sophistication and a good character.

Roasted in the barrel, this one came out with a deep red, amber appearance. .

The nose turned out to be quite fruity, hand in glove with a traditional bourbon scent, so much so it was like having a plate of freshly made crackerjacks and caramel apples placed in front of you: the caramel is very much present, along with toasty sweet corn and fresh red apple. It is the toasty corn aspect that serves as something like a boundary, allowing one to pull the two distinct threads apart.

A sip morphs into an apple pie, served with a caramel drizzle. The toasty corn returns later on, rising on the back end. That corn aspect fades, leaving a sliver of oak to linger in the finish.

— TACONIC DISTILLERY —

The provenance on Taconic whiskeys is a bit convoluted. The company got started in 2013 and had to change its name a couple of years later. Some of their whiskeys are sourced and some are not, but for a time even the in-house stuff wasn't made at the actual Taconic facility, but at a sister outfit before being matured on the Taconic property.

Taconic Founder's Rye Whiskey

 The nose of this 90-proof rye smacks of tropical banana and sweet peppers.

 On the palate, it's more banana, supplemented by notes of spices and green oak. The finish runs clear and smooth, with a tinge of tart melon on it.

— TUTHILLTOWN DISTILLERY —

Ralph Erenzo did not move to a rural property in Gardiner, New York, with the intent of starting a distillery. Erenzo, a longtime fixture in New York City's rock climbing scene instead wanted to establish a rock climbing camp there. His neighbors opposed the idea, and while casting about for alternate projects he discovered that the state had recently lowered the cost of a distilling license from $65,000 to $1,500. In 2003, Erenzo partnered with technical designer Brian Lee to build a distillery in one of the old granaries of Tuthilltown Gristmill. In 2005, they produced their first batch of vodka. The first Hudson whiskeys followed not long after.

As part of the first wave of craft distilleries, Tuthilltown has seen its share of changes. They started out with a 100-liter pot/column hybrid still from the German firm CARL. That still remains, but today it is used mostly for making neutral spirits. Their whiskey is now made with two pairs of stills, a set of 850- and 600-gallon stills for stripping and a set of 500- and 250-gallon stills for rectification. Their original fermenters were 250-gallon open-air vats, but these have since been replaced by eight 3,000-gallon tanks made by Criveller.

William Grant & Sons bought Tuthilltown's Hudson Whiskey brand in 2010 but did not acquire the distillery until April 2017. Since then, production has been increased by approximately 30%, and in November 2018 they added a fourth rickhouse.

That steady growth has also led to changes in where Tuthilltown sources its materials. The commitment to buy grain from New York family farms remains firm, but initially the distillery met its needs working with a nearby farm. Now their demands are such they must buy from farms all over the Empire State.

Hudson whiskeys come off the still at 140 proof and go into the barrel at 114 proof. Those barrels are made by Kentucky's Kelvin Cooperage, using white oak sourced from the Ozarks; the barrels receive a medium toasting and a level 3 char, and these days Tuthilltown is buying three sizes of barrels for aging their whiskeys: 15, 26 and 53. In the past, their Hudson Baby Bourbon was aged in 3-gallon and 14-gallon barrels, and that upward shift in barrel stock is an example of the transition from Craft Whiskey 1.0 to 2.0. The whiskey in the midsize barrels, the 15- and 26-gallon casks, receive at least two years of aging, while the standard 53-gallon barrels are used for about four years.

Following through on the new ownership and production upgrades, the Hudson Whiskey brand received a comprehensive revamp in 2020, with all new names and bottle designs. The line also saw a brand extension, with expressions like Four Part Harmony 7-Year-Old Four-Grain Bourbon added. Just as Tuthilltown/Hudson Whiskey helped lead the way for craft distilling in New York, and across the country, they now serve as a solid example of such a distillery fifteen years on, in mid-career.

HUDSON
BRIGHT LIGHTS, BIG BOURBON

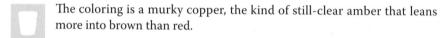

92

One of the early expressions from a distillery that started making whiskey in 2006, Hudson Baby Bourbon was an archetype of "Craft Whiskey 1.0." The "Baby" in the name refers to the maturation in combination of 3-gallon (for six months) and 14-gallon (for the following 18 to 24 months) barrels. Since the 2000s, the use of small barrels has shifted more toward 25- and 30-gallon sizes. Since the rebranding, Baby Bourbon received a mash bill tweak and became Bright Lights, Big Bourbon.

The coloring is a murky copper, the kind of still-clear amber that leans more into brown than red.

The nose is grainier than sweet, as well as woody; the latter aspect has just a hint of astringency to it.

The flavor is also grainy and woody, with the vanilla one expects as a standard element of a bourbon very muted indeed. It's there, but in the distant background. This is corn whiskey aged in different sizes of small barrels, and it shows. It has that green husk character of corn whiskey, which I like, but the plain fact is that barrel maturation should moderate that flavor profile, and here it does not. Instead, this bourbon has corn whiskey character with the overtly woody nature of a typical small-barrel bourbon thrown on top.

Hudson
Whiskey
NY

Bright Lights, Big Bourbon

New York   750 ml
Straight Bourbon Whiskey   46% alc/vol

NY MADE

Manhattan Rye was named not because of proximity to the borough, but because it's supposed to be a fine choice for making Manhattans. It's a 100% rye mash bill whiskey, almost all of it locally sourced, distilled in a copper pot. It was aged for less than four years, relying heavily on small barrels.

92

In the glass, it is the expected burnished copper. A swish and coat yield plenty of runny legs.

The nose packs a solid dose of pumpernickel and a strong current of green wood, with light notes of cherry and fig.

The liquid sits light and a bit watery on the tongue. It's not light on flavor, though. The rye spice is there, leaning increasingly into peppered territory as the taste unfolds. A touch of vanilla and raisins rounds things out. Not entirely simple, but still very straightforward. Most important is that the customary small-barrel whiskey astringency, such a common feature of early craft whiskey products, is a minor presence here. It's there, but it's very much in the background, perhaps partly covered by the pepper. Compared to the Hudson Baby Bourbon, it's a big improvement.

The finish leaves behind a little spice and raisin, and goes down a bit too hot to be branded merely warm.

This 100% rye whiskey is first aged in small, new white oak barrels and then given a finish. The finishing wood is Hudson's own old whiskey barrels, sent to a maple syrup producer in Vermont to create whiskey-aged maple syrup. Thus infused with the flavor of sweet maple, the barrels are sent back to give this rye its secondary maturation, for a total aging of "not more than four years."

92

It has a rich, deep red amber color in the glass, and the liquid is quite viscous. It carries itself with visible weight in the swish, and the coat drops only a few thin, lazy legs. This kind of appearance suggests two things: a good new make, but also a lot of wood influence. Both aspects are very much in force throughout the tasting.

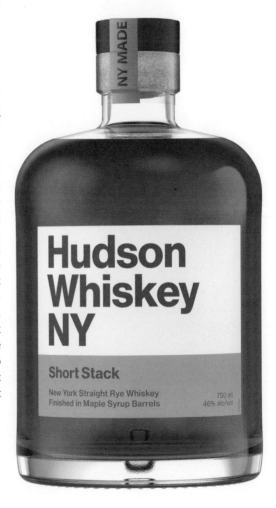

The nose is rye-driven anise plus the atmosphere of a musty old woodshed full of green, freshly split hardwoods.

The flavor is also a matter of rich, sweet rye spices and maple on the one hand, and oak-driven spiciness and astringent woodiness on the other. It is also just a touch hot. The wood finally comes to dominate in the finish, with the oaky and astringent aspect of the palate being what lingers on, although this fades quickly.

With its clear use of barrel stock that isn't just small, but tiny, this rye is over-woody in the way that so many early craft whiskeys were. Yet here, the fine qualities of the spirit are just as evident.

— WIDOW JANE DISTILLERY —

Located in the Red Hook part of Brooklyn, Widow Jane was founded by the same fellow behind Cacao Prieto, the maker of "beans-to-bar" fresh chocolates, and is now owned by Samson & Surrey. The name of the distillery is drawn from the water used to cut the bourbon (between dumping the barrel and bottling), which comes from the Widow Jane Mine. If that sounds strange, the mine was a limestone mine, principally used to furnish cement factories. Thus, the water has the same qualities as what is used by distillers in Kentucky. Some of their whiskeys are sourced and some are produced in-house, but all are cut with that water.

WIDOW JANE BABY JANE BOURBON WHISKEY

91

The version of this in-house whiskey that I tasted was one year old, but other batches may vary.

The nose was sweet, strongly vanilla-forward, and a touch nutty.

The liquid had a thin texture, and it led with a corn syrup flavor, plus notes of vanilla and nutmeg. The finish wound down fast, first with candy corn and then turning dry before fading out.

WIDOW JANE 10–YEAR–OLD SINGLE BARREL BOURBON WHISKEY

91

When Widow Jane is mentioned, it's usually because of this bourbon.

The nose has the expected candy corn and vanilla notes, but also a touch of milk chocolate and a twist of lemon peel.

It has a syrupy feel on the palate, and a sip yields a complex mélange of vanilla, oak, earthy chocolate, rye spice, herbs, and pepperiness. All of that runs on into the finish, the earthy chocolate excepted, and fades off bit by bit to leave an herbal trace at the end. It's a bourbon that brings a lot to the table.

LISA ROPER WICKER

In my mind, few personal stories illustrate the craft distilling boom more than that of Lisa Roper Wicker. Like so many people in the sector, she didn't start out intending to make booze (she studied journalism at Indiana University), but once she got her feet wet, she knew what she wanted to do. Also like so many in the field, that initial exposure didn't come from whiskey; in Wicker's case, it was making wine in Indiana, starting in 2002.

She spent several years in Indiana, all the while putting together her technical education in dribs and drabs at Purdue, the University of California-Davis, and on the job. In particular, she points to oenologist/microbiologist Ellie Butz as a mentor in winemaking, and retired Woodford Reserve distiller and current consultant Dave Scheurich for distilling. If she had to do it over again, she would probably have studied agriculture or food chemistry as an undergrad instead of journalism, but everything she has encountered has contributed in some way to her whiskey career, from technical writing to the basic mechanics she learned from her father, an engineer.

The first step to whiskey came when she was hired to build a winery in Kentucky, whereupon she met Steve Beam. She was thinking about making brandy at the time, and soon found herself working evenings in his distillery, Limestone Branch, collaborating on the production of brandy. When the winery's owners divorced and that project came unglued, Wicker went over to Limestone Branch. She was at Limestone Branch for almost three years, working on some of the moonshine Tim Smith toted around on the Discovery Channel program *Moonshiners* among other things. But when Luxco bought a controlling interest in the distillery, Wicker was fired.

On her last day at Limestone Branch, Palmetto Distillery in South Carolina offered her a job. Wanting to keep a foot in Kentucky, however, Wicker arranged to consult with them instead, thus beginning that stage of her distilling career. After a winter at Palmetto, she went to work at Starlight Distillery in Indiana. One of the owners of Starlight happened to be involved with the distilling program at Mount Vernon in Virginia, which is how she met the director of trades there and started volunteering in March 2016.

That led to Wicker becoming a consultant at Mount Vernon (she is now the main consultant). Then Drew Kulsveen at Willett suggested she work on the Preservation Distillery in Bardstown. Initially she was to stay on as distiller there, but formed her consultancy, Saints & Monsters, instead. Her first client was Samson & Surrey, who tasked her to work primarily with Widow Jane, presumably because it was the only brand in their portfolio that did not retain the services of the founder/previous owner. By spring 2018, she was vice president and head distiller for Samson & Surrey, before becoming president and distiller for Widow Jane.

Now she splits her time between Bardstown, Kentucky, and Brooklyn, transitioning a brand from relying on sourced whiskey to its in-house distilled spirits.

PENNSYLVANIA

— BLUEBIRD DISTILLING —

Bluebird Distilling is found in Phoenixville, due northwest of Valley Forge National Historical Park. Founder Jared Adkins has a story familiar to anyone who knows people who start craft breweries and distilleries: he ditched his white-collar job to start his own booze-making business.

BLUEBIRD FOUR GRAIN BOURBON WHISKEY

92 This bourbon is a conventional four-grain whiskey, made with corn, rye, wheat, and malted barley.

It has a very light amber coloring in the glass, just a step removed from copper. A swish and coat of the glass reveal ample and heavy tears.

The nose is quite toasty and malty, and a little musty as well, but a candied spiciness is at the fore, akin to the dried fruits in a very boozy fruitcake. This is accented by traces of oak and vanilla.

On the tongue, it is much more oaky, presenting a strong current of musty wood. The sweetness comes in the form of spiced apricots in the main, with a teaspoon of vanilla and a trace of toasty char. The finish is light on warmth and turns to a butterscotch flavor, while retaining a little spiciness and woodiness.

If what you are looking for in craft whiskeys is something outside the box, this bourbon is a good bet.

BLUEBIRD RYE WHISKEY

96 Bluebird chose to give the Pennsylvania style a twist for their rye whiskey; it is 100% rye, but with no malted rye in the mix.

In the glass it has a middling amber appearance, being coppery with brown highlights darkening things up slightly.

The nose is simple and straightforward: pumpernickel rye meets Fig Newton.

A sip reveals a silky texture that belies a very slight astringency on the back end of the palate. Leaving that astringent part aside, the whiskey doubles down on the rye and fig nose. The finish turns over to a light pinch of raw ginger, and fades on just a light sense of warmth. It's a simple, mid-bodied, yummy rye, perfect for easy drinking.

— MANATAWNY STILL WORKS — FOUR GRAIN AMERICAN WHISKEY

This distillery is located in the northern suburb of Pottstown, with a tasting room in Philadelphia.

MANATAWNY KEYSTONE WHISKEY

Keystone Whiskey is made from a four-grain mash bill, using the unusual mix of barley, wheat, rye, and oats. No single grain crosses the 51% threshold necessary to make it a rye, wheat, or malt whiskey, but it is known to emphasize the malted barley.

Despite being billed as heavy on the malted barley—and make no mistake, the malt is very much present in the nose—the oats jump out at you. A little soft sweetness also comes across, presumably from the wheat.

It's a thin liquid on the palate, but one that carries flavors of maple syrup, spices, and cereals. The finish is a tad peppery while retaining the cereals note from the palate.

A young whiskey to be sure, but the unorthodox mash bill gives it a character that is able to come across precisely because of that youth.

Pennsylvania Rye Revival

In the couple of decades before the mixology craze of the late 2000s, if you asked for a Manhattan, it was often made with bourbon, this despite the cocktail traditionally calling for rye whiskey, which had become a small category. Until the initial sourced brands based on MGP's 95% rye whiskey began appearing in the middle part of that decade and just a few years before ambitious bartenders began turning to vintage recipes for their crafty cocktails, asking for rye meant asking for Kentucky rye. With its minimal rye mash bill (51 to 53% rye content), Kentucky ryes were so close to their big sister bourbons that, in a cocktail, one could scarcely tell the difference.

That was a sad state for rye whiskey to fall into, because it once included a style of whiskey making that rivaled Kentucky bourbon in popularity: Pennsylvania rye. "Monongahela (Western Pennsylvania) rye whiskey's century of dominance began prior to the Western Insurrection of 1791 (the Whiskey Rebellion)," says Sam Komlenic, a Pennsylvania whiskey historian and the copy editor at *Whisky Advocate*, "and lasted until well after the Civil War, waning significantly for the first time around 1880."

Pennsylvania's Old Overholt was once one of the country's premier whiskey brands, enjoying a reputation to rival anything that came from the Bluegrass State, complete with devoted admirers that included presidents and celebrities.

Historic American Buildings Survey, Creator. A. & H.S. Overholt Company Distillery, Frick Avenue, West Overton, Westmoreland County, PA

By the late 1980s, the Overholt brand had been traded to the parent company of Jim Beam and consolidated into Beam's production, becoming a Kentucky rye. In 1989, the last operating distillery in the Keystone State was shuttered. Pennsylvania rye was dead.

Legend has it that Kentucky whiskey began with farmer-distillers fleeing westward to avoid those onerous whiskey taxes imposed under President George Washington. Certainly those migrants added to the sparse population of frontier Kentucky, but farmer-distillers were already at work in the territory before there was even a United States. Nevertheless, as Kentucky bourbon developed into something we can recognize today, during the mid- to late 19th century, rye whiskey evolved in parallel with it in Pennsylvania and Maryland. Kentucky made a lot more whiskey than the two eastern states put together during that time, but no one doubted eastern rye as a peer of Kentucky bourbon.

The two styles couldn't have become more different while remaining American whiskeys. Whereas Kentucky bourbon came to rely mostly on corn, with a little rye for seasoning and some malted barley to convert grain starch to sugar for fermentation, Pennsylvania rye leaned heavily on its signature grain, using a mix of rye, malted rye, and malted barley.

Pennsylvania distilleries eschewed both sour-mash whiskey making and the yin and yang of hot summers and (even colder) winters for barrel aging, preferring to use the sweet-mash method and to age in heated brick warehouses. Another Pennsylvania idiosyncrasy was the widespread adoption of the three-chambered charge still, which used principles similar to American column stills and was, curiously, sometimes made mostly from wood. This technology was reputed to leave more of just about everything that contributes to flavor, such as esters and fusel oils, in the spirit. The result was a whiskey noted for its boldly spicy flavor and big-bodied, chewy character.

Yet many of these characteristics proved double-edged and played a role in the decline of Pennsylvania rye vis-à-vis bourbon and other cheaper whiskeys. "Pennsylvania rye was more expensive to produce, using all fresh mash every time, with no sour mash backset," explains Komlenic. "The use of the slower three-chamber still in many larger Pennsylvania rye distilleries added substantially to the actual distilling time itself. Their masonry warehouses were steam-heated in colder months, never going lower than about 70 degrees. Whiskey that was more expensive to make eventually collided with the public's changing tastes, and the outcome of that equation proved disastrous to Pennsylvania's rye whiskey distillers."

After Prohibition, many Keystone State distillers found they couldn't reopen even if they had wished to, because during the intervening 13 years their old buildings had been repurposed. "Many of these distilleries were in areas where industry was expanding, especially steel and glass," says Wayne Curtis, drinks author and journalist. "With their riverfront or adjacent locations and access to rail, the distillery sites were in demand for other industries, and so were not only decommissioned, but taken apart and replaced. Meantime, Kentucky was enduring a sort of economic lethargy, and so the distilleries [there] were simply mothballed."

Following Prohibition's repeal, 34 distilleries would reopen in Kentucky versus just 12 in Pennsylvania. The economic disruptions of Prohibition and the Second World War coupled to changing tastes and industrial consolidation continued to erode the state's whiskey industry.

Pennsylvania rye was dead and buried in 1990, its corpse fleeced and its famous brand names carried off to Kentucky. Its cousin, the Maryland style of rye, had met a similar fate years earlier. Some two decades later, however, the rise in micro-distilling revitalized that bygone style.

The one caveat is that no distillery has brought all the known aspects of the Monongahela style into a single operation. Sweet-mash whiskey making is widespread in Pennsylvania (indeed, in craft whiskey generally), and some distillers are using very high-rye, no-corn mash bills, but no one has a whiskey on the shelves that was matured in warehouses heated to 70 degrees all winter. West Overton Village Distillery Museum has started making whiskey aged in heated warehouses, but has yet to release any of it. Also, the only distiller using a three-chamber still isn't anywhere near Pennsylvania.

Colorado's Leopold Bros. (see page 486), a distillery that was already making a Maryland-style rye whiskey, has had a three-chamber still built. "[They claim] the technology is what made for a more distinctive taste," says Curtis. However, although the Maryland style of rye has more rye in it than the almost-bourbon Kentucky-made ryes, it is not the potently rye-driven Pennsylvania style. Leopold Brothers has yet to release a full-on Monongahela rye whiskey made with their three-chamber still, so we have no way to compare how different the three-chamber still is from the hybrid stills most Pennsylvania craft distillers are using today.

Arguably the distiller closest to making an authentic Pennsylvania-style rye today is Mountain Laurel, with their Dad's Hat offering. "They seem to be the only distiller in the state to use only rye, malted barley, and a bit of malted rye to most accurately replicate the traditional Monongahela-style mash bill," says Komlenic.

A close second would be another eastern Pennsylvania outfit, Bluebird Distillery, which uses a 100% rye mash bill. Two other distilleries that actually are in the traditional heartland of Pennsylvania whiskey making, the western part of the state, are Liberty Pole and Wigle. Both take the no-corn approach, using wheat instead. My experience is that the results are a softer whiskey compared to the almost all-rye whiskeys I've tried (in much the same way that wheated bourbon is softer), more in tune with what I imagine the antique Maryland whiskeys were like. But as Komlenic says (and I concur), mash bill isn't everything.

Pennsylvania rye is now making a comeback, but the state's big distiller-produced brands are gone. It is possible that one of the craft distillers exploring Pennsylvania's lost style of whiskey making could be acquired by a major spirits company and grown into a medium-size approximation of what was lost, but that is the most I can realistically envision. Because of that, I don't think it appropriate to measure modern Pennsylvania rye against forebears like the classic Old Overholt, or to demand modern distillers mimic every single aspect that was commonly (but perhaps not universally) applied at the turn of the 20th century.

Instead, it is better to see the revival for what it is: adding richness to the character of American whiskey. "Monongahela rye was a shining star for decades," says Curtis, "and it would be great to see it come back. I haven't yet come to a determination of what 'it' is, but I'm pleased to see the experiments and debate going on to define Pennsylvania rye."

MOUNTAIN LAUREL SPIRITS

Pennsylvania is in the seventh busiest state in the Union for craft distilling, according to the American Craft Spirits Association. That is impressive, but it pales in comparison to the Keystone State's former status as one of the country's leading producers of whiskey, with a style all its own and rivaling that of Kentucky bourbon (see pages 88–91). That approach to making rye whiskey is starting to make a comeback in the modern craft whiskey movement, and at the forefront is Mountain Laurel Spirits, makers of Dad's Hat Rye Whiskey.

Dad's Hat was started by Herman Mihalich and John Cooper, a couple of friends who met in college and had a love of Pennsylvania rye whiskey and a deep pool of scientific and business skills to draw on. That allowed the pair to develop a production process at Michigan State University's Artisan Distilling Program in 2010 and lay a solid plan for financing and building a distillery. They got the distillery built on time and on budget, hit the ground running, and started production in September 2011.

In keeping with the Pennsylvania tradition, Mountain Laurel Spirits is a sweet-mash distillery, relying on a copper still and production tanks made by the German company CARL. They are presently mashing four times a week, which allows them to make, according to Mihalich's estimates, the equivalent of 10,000 bottles a month (this after aging and the Angel's Share). That mashing starts with their grain, of course, almost all of which comes from Meadow Brook Farms in Riegelsville, just an hour's drive from their Bristol, Pennsylvania, location. When their grain needs exceed what Meadow Brook can provide, the remainder comes from elsewhere in the state. Dad's Hat Rye Whiskey is made from a mash of 80% rye and 20% malted

barley, with no corn and no added enzymes.

The yeast is something Mihalich and Cooper brought with them from Michigan State, and after their second distillation they have a new make somewhere between 145 and 160 proof. This is cut down to 120 proof for barrel entry, but lately they have been experimenting with lower-entry proofs. Compared to Pennsylvania's pre-Prohibition whiskey industry, the only things missing from Dad's Hat are a three-chamber still and heated warehouses for climate-controlled aging.

Their 15- and 53-gallon barrels come from McGinnis Wood Products, a cooperage in Cuba, Missouri. Missouri is a major supplier of oak for barrel coopering, so there is nothing exotic about the wood, as there might be from a cooper in Minnesota or Washington; Dad's Hat just gets solid, new white oak barrels. Dad's Hat uses #4 char for their 15-gallon barrels and #3 for the standard, 53-gallon barrels. For their Port- and vermouth-finished expressions, Dad's Hat gets used barrels from California.

DAD'S HAT BOTTLED IN BOND RYE WHISKEY

100 This was one of the first bonded whiskeys to come from a small distillery, part of a landmark development heralding the growing maturity of the craft whiskey sector. Recall that the Bottled-in-Bond Act of 1897 requires a minimum of four years of aging and that all the whiskey in the batch comes from a single distilling season. For a new distillery, keeping back part of its inventory for those four years is a major commitment.

In the glass, this has that orange-highlighted amber almost standard to ryes, which reminds me so much of polished copper. It's a bright, clear liquid that drops big, thick, and runny legs.

The nose is spicy and herbal, with the latter a mixture of eucalyptus and mint. A drop of earthy, plumlike sweetness and a pinch of pine needles round things out. After the whiskey has breathed some, it adopts a minor toasted element.

The liquid sits lightly on the palate, and tastes sweet, spicy, and herbal in just about equal measures. The finish was also on the light side, fading swiftly. Overall, Dad's Hat Bottled in Bond is a balanced, light-bodied, easy-drinking whiskey.

HERMAN MIHALICH

As CEO and distiller of Mountain Laurel Spirits, aka Dad's Hat Rye, Herman Mihalich is at the forefront of the revival of a great American whiskey tradition. Yet like many small distillers, he started in a completely unrelated field. This isn't to say that Mihalich's personal story doesn't have rye-soaked roots, however.

Mihalich grew up in an apartment above the family-owned tavern in Monessen, Pennsylvania, a speakeasy gone straight started by his grandfather, Matt Mihalich. Monessen is a town on the Monongahela River, south of Pittsburgh, so the place naturally served robust, Monongahela-style rye whiskey. Memories of the heyday of the family's watering hole served as Mihalich's inspiration to both get into rye whiskey and for what he would call it, Dad's Hat.

That would need to wait for the 21st century, though. Mihalich graduated with a BS in chemical engineering from the University of Pennsylvania in 1980. After a couple of years working as a chemical engineer, he went back to school, shifted away from science, and got his MBA from the Wharton School in 1984. That turn to business eventually led to a quarter century working in the chemical, flavor, and fragrance industries. That is what Mihalich was doing in 2006, when he read an article by Eric Asimov in the *New York Times*, predicting that rye whiskey was poised for a comeback. Mihalich showed it to John Cooper, a friend from his Wharton School days, and the two started talking about bringing rye whiskey making back to its home state of Pennsylvania.

Mihalich's chemical engineering background gave him a start in distillation, which the pair built on by attending the Artisan Distilling Program at Michigan State University. They also researched Pennsylvania whiskey history extensively. The target Mihalich had in mind was Sam Thompson Pennsylvania Rye, the favorite brand of his father and grandfather. To this day, Mihalich has a couple of vintage bottles of Sam Thompson that he uses as a tasting point of reference.

Dad's Hat Pre-Prohibition Style Rye Whiskey

95 At a time when the big distillers are taking age statements off some fan favorite brands and making their whiskeys a little younger, Dad's Hat decided to make their staple expression older, raising the bar from three years to "at least four years" of age.

This has a sticky look in the glass, so sticky in fact that it is reluctant to drop any tears at all. The coloring is the light amber so typical of rye whiskey.

The scent is a mix of pumpernickel bread and dried red fruits, with a hint of spearmint.

The flavor is much more restrained than the generous nose, however. It's quite spicy, with a pinch of charred oak shavings. On the backside, a little sweet tobacco leaf rolls up and over the tongue. The finish runs spicy and a bit woody, lasting for a decent amount of time, but certainly nothing lengthy.

The extra aging has made this iteration of Dad's Hat mellower than the other younger, earlier expressions I've had from them. It's quite an easy-drinking sipper. Moreover, anyone who wants more rye out of their rye whiskey will appreciate the virtues of Dad's Hat Pre-Prohibition.

A pour of this 94-proof rye reveals an orange, mid-amber appearance, and giving the glass a swish leaves behind scattered, skinny legs with a thick, solid crown.

The nose certainly has a sweet wine quality, reminiscent of Ruby Port, and is balanced by holiday spices and a generous helping of dried mint flakes, with a hint of woodiness sitting just behind the crowd.

The flavor follows in that vein, albeit with a twist: it's Port-sweet, but just briefly, and then up comes a hot cinnamon-and-pepper spiciness, poured from a cup of green pine. The finish is short, clear, and offers just a tiny bit of wood and spice.

Compared to the vermouth-finished (see facing page), the finishing cask is much more evident here. Of course, the thing about that is if you're a fan of Dad's Hat, you like their very bold, very rye-forward style, so that isn't a characteristic you want pushed off center stage. As much as I like Port, and usually like a Port-finished whiskey, I don't think this one quite worked out.

DAD'S HAT RYE WHISKEY FINISHED IN VERMOUTH BARRELS

94

For this one, Dad's Hat takes their staple rye, ages it for nine or 10 months in 15-gallon new oak barrels and finishes it for three to six months in Quady Winery's Vya Sweet Vermouth casks.

A pour has a middling amber look in the glass, a bit darker than the usual color for a rye. Coating the glass leaves it awash with stubby tears.

The scent carries a mix of dried fruits, something like trail mix without the nuts, accented with spices and vanilla. Those spices run quite dry, providing some contrast against the fruitiness.

The flavor has a strong current of pepperiness and a chunk of barrel char sitting at the end of the road. The whiskey then winds down on that dry pepper and barrel char.

My take is that the sweet vermouth influence on the whiskey is limited principally to the nose, and makes little impact elsewhere. Otherwise, the whiskey is quite like the other expressions on the youthful end of Dad's Hat's line.

— NEW LIBERTY DISTILLERY —

This north Philadelphia distillery makes its whiskey with malted barley from Deer Creek Malthouse in nearby Chester County. Of course, the distillery named this offering for Pennsylvania's Dutch heritage, but whiskey making itself isn't actually part of the Dutch liquor tradition.

NEW LIBERTY DUTCH MALT WHISKEY

95
This is bottled after six to 18 months of aging.

The nose carries notes of toffee, dried fruits, and cut grass.

Those aspects carry over into the flavor, joined by a little spiciness. From there, the finish turns toward earthy coffee and chocolate.

— STOLL & WOLFE DISTILLERY —

The Stoll side of Stoll & Wolfe refers to Dick Stoll, the final master distiller of the famous Bomberger's Distillery in Schaefferstown, which was the last working distillery in Pennsylvania until modern times. Bomberger's went bankrupt in 1989, and if that name sounds familiar, it's because the distillery was the original home of Michter's and also made the famed A.H. Hirsch 16-Year-Old Bourbon.

Stoll subsequently left the whiskey business until he was brought out of retirement and formed a partnership with the Wolfes. The next step was to outsource production to another distiller, so they could contract distill to Stoll's specifications and not rely on sourced whiskey. Thus, they get to build their brand with Stoll's rye while working on their own distillery in central Pennsylvania.

Stoll & Wolfe Pennsylvania Rye Whiskey

90

This is a sweet-mash whiskey, as opposed to the more common sour mash. This means each batch starts over from scratch, rather than using leftovers from the previous batch to kick-start the process. The mash bill is 65% rye, 25% corn, and 10% malted barley, which is not in keeping with the no-corn style of either Pennsylvania or Monongahela rye, but still has more rye in it than the Kentucky style. It is aged for less than two years in 30-gallon barrels.

It has a spicy character in the main, with notes of butterscotch, vanilla, and green oak. The spice turns to peppermint in the finish, but is joined by some astringency, the latter pointing to the small-barrel aging.

WIGLE DISTILLERY

Pittsburgh's Wigle Distillery plucked its theme out of western Pennsylvania's Whiskey Rebellion, which rumbled from 1791 to 1794. A local farmer and distiller named Phillip Wigle punched out a tax collector, which was reputed to be the first violent act of the rebellion. Wigle was later convicted of treason and sentenced to meet a traitor's death at the gallows, but seeing as how Wigle was a tax evader and not a traitor, President Washington later pardoned him.

The distillery named for this pugnacious fellow began producing in December 2011 and has grown considerably in the decade since then. Wigle uses two pot stills made by the German company CARL. The main whiskey-making still is their 950-liter unit, but they have used a second 650-liter still for special projects or extra production. However, they mainly use the smaller still for other spirits, such as gin or rum.

Wigle buys its barrels from Kelvin Cooperage and has transitioned from smaller barrels to aging over 90% of their whiskeys in standard 53-gallon barrels. They buy barrels charred to levels 3 and 4, but prefer the deeper, heavier "alligator" char of level 4. Their locally sited warehouse is sided with corrugated metal sheeting and has 20-foot ceilings, and it is easy to imagine how the environment in that building varies wildly with the seasons and weather.

This is a craft distillery that is especially keen on its yeasts, drawing on a wide variety of sources, following much experimentation. Co-founder Alex Grelli says they use "Bretanomyces, Belgian yeast strains, yeast slurries from local breweries, malt whiskey yeasts, and spontaneous fermentation from endogenous yeast." They also put a premium on using organic grains grown within 250 miles of the distillery.

I visited Wigle in February 2020, on the eve of the pandemic lockdown. At that time, they were in the midst of adding a full kitchen and bar as part of a $3.4 million renovation, one that would also add a Whiskey Rebellion museum. Those projects have now all come to fruition, so visitors to the distillery have more to look forward to than the core attraction of tasting Pennsylvania rye, and seeing how it's made.

WIGLE SINGLE BARREL STRAIGHT BOURBON

100

Wigle definitely put an interesting twist on their bourbon, in that it is a wheated bourbon with slightly more malted barley than wheat in the mash bill: 69% corn, 15% wheat, and 16% malted barley. The proportion of malted barley in a whiskey mash is often half as much as that, since the grain is usually there only for the enzymes that convert grain starch to sugar. Here, it is as present and as much a flavoring element as the wheat, so should we call this a wheated bourbon, a malted bourbon, or both?

We live in a time when retail shenanigans have made Blanton's Single Barrel absent from store shelves and driven its market value (i.e., what you would pay for a bottle on demand) to an insane point north of $300. With that in mind, fans of single barrel bourbons should begin to turn to the releases coming out of the craft sector and try them. They are a damn sight cheaper and many of them, such as this one, are just as good.

Once in the glass, Wigle Single Barrel Bourbon is bronzed.

The nose is like a cross between cherry and pumpkin pie; cherry leads, coupled to a dollop of maple syrup, but beyond that is the ginger and nutmeg one gets from the pumpkin spice jar.

The flavor smears a layer of caramel to those same elements found in the scent, with a dose of Red Hots cinnamon coming up on the back end. The finish is light at first, but grows with time, coming over as a gentle, lapping wave of spiciness.

Wigle Deep Cut Bottled in Bond Rye Whiskey

When Pittsburgh's Wigle Distillery turned five years old in 2017, they marked the occasion by releasing a four-year-old bottled in bond version of their Deep Cut Rye Whiskey. Moreover, this release comes from whiskey aged in 53-gallon American Standard Barrels, not the 25- or 30-gallon barrels that are common in craft whiskey these days, to say nothing of the smaller barrels that were usual back when Wigle got started. The mash bill for Wigle's rye is similar to Stoll & Wolfe, being 65% rye and the rest corn and malted barley.

The look of this whiskey is that orange-style amber that a proper rye whiskey should have. The swish and coat of the glass leave me with a curtain of big, thick tears, and plenty of them.

The nose is well inside the expected rye whiskey profile: plenty of sweet, herbal spiciness, with spearmint and dill in particular coming forward, along with solid notes of vanilla and dry, toasty wood.

On the palate, the sweetness becomes a current of dried stone fruits, while the spiciness becomes hotter, yet also more moderate at the same time. That aspect moves away from herbs, becoming a mix of spearmint with hot, peppery cinnamon. Yet the sweet side and the vanilla balances it out splendidly, so it isn't too dry or peppery. The finish rolls out of the hot minty note that is present throughout, and as that fades away I am left with the vanilla.

Wigle Straight Wheat Whiskey

Wigle makes its wheat whiskey from a conventional, three-grain mash bill with a majority of wheat, plus rye and malted barley. It's a three-year-old whiskey aged in 30- and 53-gallon barrels.

The scent is full of apples and pears, plus a sliver of oak.

A sip of this rich, silky whiskey shows it to be very barrel-forward, with caramel and more of that oak coming out first. That gives way to a current of apples and citrus with a strong note of cloves, much like a dish of baked apples with a sweet orange squeezed over the top.

RHODE ISLAND

— SONS OF LIBERTY BEER — & SPIRITS COMPANY

Sons of Liberty is another brewstill-ery, a class of booze maker that does both beer and whiskey. That often corresponds to a focus on American malts, because beer isn't made from corn, and that is the case here. The company is all about taking their beer wort and making American single malts from them.

BATTLE CRY AMERICAN SINGLE MALT WHISKEY

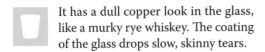 This is mostly malted barley, with a little bit of malted rye thrown in. Although it's not all malted barley, it's still all malted. The whiskey was aged in charred, new white oak with toasted French oak inserts.

It has a dull copper look in the glass, like a murky rye whiskey. The coating of the glass drops slow, skinny tears.

The nose gives me a rich scent full of gingerbread with a hint of red fruits.

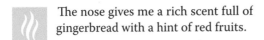 On the palate, that gingerbread flavor acquires a sprinkle of pepper. Balancing this is some anise and more of that murky, winey red fruitiness. The finish stays in that ginger and pepper vein, and lasts a decent amount of time.

The takeaway is that if you like your whiskey spicy, this is a simple, straightforward, but tasty whiskey, and one that holds up well on the rocks.

92

This whiskey was distilled from the wort used to make a stout, and having had that stout as well, I can tell you it's an excellent example of why whiskeys made from beer are so fascinating. If nothing else, the pairing makes for a killer boilermaker.

The mash is made from husked chocolate malt, crystal malt, pale malt, biscuit malt, and roasted barley, fermented with classic American Ale yeast. This is then double-distilled in a pot still, and the whiskey is aged in 10- and 30-gallon new American oak barrels with French oak inserts for 16 months or more.

In the glass it has a bronzed, mid-amber coloring, and the coat drops a storm of heavy tears.

The nose smacks of heavy, dark cake spice, soft chocolate, and cherries, like a blend of rum cake with black forest cake. Add to that a spoonful of vanilla extract.

On the palate the creamy texture clashes a bit with the flavor, which turns drier and spicier than the nose suggests. The cake spice goes gingered and peppery, rising above and over the sweeter chocolate, vanilla, and red fruitiness. The finish is a light, quick thing, but peppery and a little ashy while around.

This is a pretty straightforward dram, but a surprisingly flavorful and mature one for so young a spirit. It just goes to show you that with a good base and a good choice of barrel stock (using the French oak inserts, in this instance), you can bring a whiskey pretty far along in less than a few years.

VERMONT

— APPALACHIAN — GAP DISTILLERY

N amed for a path through the Green Mountains of Vermont, Appalachian Gap Distillery is a solar-powered micro-distillery with an eco-friendly ethos that mirrors its home state.

RIDGELINE VERMONT WHISKEY

98 This whiskey is something of an odd duck, having a mash bill that doesn't fit with any of the major categories of American whiskey, all of which are defined by a primary grain that comprises 51% or more of the mash bill. Ridgeline uses 45% malted barley, 30% corn, and 25% rye, so there is no primary grain.

Maturation is also a bit more involved than usual. After a double-distillation, the new make is entered into three different types of wood: former bourbon barrels, new barrels, and Port wine casks. After at least two years, the whiskey is dumped, batched, and bottled.

A pour is golden with orange highlights, while a swish and coat of the glass stream with leaf vein–style legs and a heavily beaded crown.

Taking in the nose yields a strong current of wet cedar and cereals with a pinch of raisins thrown in.

The flavor continues to deliver that woody aspect up front, more in line with oak than cedar now, along with a bit of leather and a bit of dry tobacco leaf. Altogether, the initial experience of a sip of Ridgeline is something like walking into a tobacco barn with a pile of horse tack lying by the door. After some additional air and a bit of time, notes of butterscotch arose, followed by a dash of pepper. That touch of pepper rolled into the finish, which was warm and lingering.

— WHISTLEPIG FARM —

When WhistlePig got started, it was as a bottler of sourced whiskey with an excellent stock of 100% rye made in Alberta, Canada. To this, they add some of the nigh-omnipresent MGP 95% rye, which was used in limited-edition whiskeys like the Old World 12-Year-Old. The company opened a distillery on their farm in 2015.

WhistlePig FarmStock Rye Whiskey

86 FarmStock rye represents WhistlePig's transition from relying on sourced whiskeys to their own spirits. The first Farm-Stock batch was a blend of three distinct whiskeys: one-fifth of it was an in-house 1½-year-old rye, the rest was drawn from 95% rye whiskey made by MGP in Indiana and the Canadian 100% rye used in their main expression. The second batch, released in 2018, nudged the in-house content up to two years old and about a third of the blend. Successive batches of Farm-Stock will increase both the age and proportion of WhistlePig's own in-house rye whiskey used in the blend, until the company is ready to put a mature whiskey made wholly by them on shelves.

SOUTHEAST REGION

ALABAMA

— CONECUH RIDGE DISTILLERY —

Although by Act of Alabama 2004-97, "Conecuh Ridge Alabama Fine Whiskey" (the forerunner of Clyde May Whiskey) is the "official state spirit" of Alabama, Conecuh Ridge is a producer of sourced whiskeys. Such sourced and bottled brands are sometimes called "non-distiller producers" or NDPs.

The company announced plans to build a $13 million distillery in 2017, but those plans were long stalled by reported permit and planning issues, as well as pandemic-associated difficulties. Finally, Alabama newspaper The Messenger reported in February 2021 that the first substantial step in seeing Conecuh Ridge Distillery get off the ground had been made: construction of the roadway to the distillery property had begun. That was followed by a formal ground-breaking attended by the Governor in January 2022.

CONECUH RIDGE CLYDE MAY'S ALABAMA STYLE WHISKEY

85

This whiskey is inspired by the practices of Clyde May, an Alabama moonshiner who matured corn whiskey in oak barrels with dried apples tossed in. This entry-level Clyde May is six to seven years old.

It has quite a fruity scent, although not apple fruity, and a nose of mixed brown sugar and vanilla coupled to lemon zest and cherries.

The flavor is cherries, vanilla, and cinnamon, transitioning to cinnamon and a bit of oak in the finish.

It's a tasty, simple, easy-drinking whiskey. Although fruity sweet, it's not quite as fruity as a flavored whiskey would be. By that, I mean it still tastes like what an American whiskey ought to taste like, rather than being a youngish spirit smothered in flavoring. Even so, that fruity current will make it very approachable to the non-whiskey drinker, and if it's simple stuff to the aficionado, it's nice all the same.

110

The Special Reserve is the high-octane version of the basic, 85-proof Alabama Style Whiskey. Otherwise, it's also a six- to seven-year-old expression, drawing on the same sourced whiskey and finishing it with apples.

The higher proof pushes the fruitiness more directly onto the apples. A warm base of caramel and vanilla is joined by notes of leather, the aforementioned apples, and cinnamon. The flavor sits in your mouth like a rich caramel-and-butterscotch candy brushed with an apple glaze. The sweet, fruity character and thick coat it leaves on your tongue make it a natural for drinking on the rocks, but it doesn't actually require them, being quite smooth for a 110-proof whiskey.

DELAWARE

— PAINTED STAVE BOTTLED — IN BOND RYE WHISKEY

PAINTED STAVE DOUBLE TROUBLED

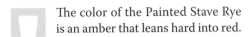

100 Painted Stave started out with a rye named Diamond State and with a similar label to this bonded whiskey, the name paying tribute to the last brand of whiskey produced in Delaware before Prohibition. The original Diamond State was a Maryland-style rye. So inspired, this whiskey comes from a 70% rye, 25% corn, 5% malted barley mash bill. It is entered into 30-gallon new oak barrels charred to level 4 at 120 proof, aged for four years, and bottled at the proof mandated by the Bottled in Bond Act.

The color of the Painted Stave Rye is an amber that leans hard into red.

The scent shows a foundation of molasses and toffee, accented by a leathery, pumpernickel character.

On the palate, that pumpernickel side lightens up quite a bit, but the toffee and molasses are still there, along with some vanilla. On the back end, a little ash is stirred into the flavor. The finish takes that rising, closing note and runs with it, turning to dry and toasted wood. This Delaware-made, Maryland-style rye is an easy drinking whiskey, and one that shows some complexity. Rye fans in particular should enjoy the fact that it is a full step removed from the sweeter Kentucky-style ryes or the overtly dry MGP-derived products.

GEORGIA

— GHOST COAST DISTILLERY —

This distillery went operational and opened its doors in 2017, in the shadow of Savannah's Talmadge Memorial Bridge. Their riverfront district site in that trendy town (lately as much the possession of the Savannah College of Arts and Design as it is Tidewater blue bloods) is so new and growing that when I visited in early 2022, I found the distillery's immediate neighbors to be a pair of not quite-finished, fashionable apartment buildings.

Ghost Coast follows what is now the standard format for new, small distilleries: produce a wide range of spirits and associated products. Many of them are strongly oriented toward cocktails, and feature prominently in the city's signature cocktail menus. Also among the offerings is a blend of four different bourbons they make at the distillery, and those four bourbons drawn on mashes using corn, rye, wheat, oat, and malted barley. To add a Four Roses layer of complexity to those grain recipes, the distillery also uses traditional distiller's yeast and Saison yeast in fermentation.

GHOST COAST MASTER STRAIGHT BOURBON WHISKEY

86

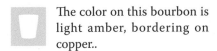

The color on this bourbon is light amber, bordering on copper..

The nose smacked of a baked apple dish, prepared with molasses and a vanilla drizzle, then finished with crushed walnuts. In fact, I'd say some walnut shell got in there as well, since a trace of nondescript wood hovers about that dish.

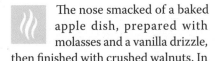

The flavor was not as sweet, but still sat inside traditional bourbon territory. A sip serves up light helpings of caramel, rye spices, and oak. For a three-year-old whiskey, I found it on the mellow side, and quite subdued. The finish ran light as well, with a current of dry oak.

KENTUCKY

Before Prohibition, Kentucky was America's foremost whiskey state, but not in the way it has been since the end of that great fiasco in social engineering. Before the dislocations caused by Prohibition, Kentucky was first among (near) equals. It outproduced all the other states, but not by a huge margin, and the biggest distillery in America was in Illinois. The commonwealth had a reputation as the originator and national leader in bourbon, but other states made bourbon as well, while rye whiskey was much more popular than it is today and stood a solid second in esteem.

The return of the whiskey industry after Prohibition saw Kentucky become first in the industry by a mile, and the state's dominance has only grown with the passage of time. In terms of production, if I were to call on hard figures and my own estimates (where there are no hard figures) to draw up a list of the top 10 whiskey producers in the country, nine of them would be in Kentucky, with Jack Daniel's as the only exception. Kentucky has gone from being known as the best producer of bourbon to being synonymous with it, giving rise to the myth that bourbon can be made only there (it can be made anywhere in the United States, as this book proves).

In global terms, the Kentucky whiskey industry is more or less equivalent in value to the Scotch whisky industry, these two peers being head and shoulders above the other three traditional and major whiskey makers: Canada, Ireland, and Japan. That is Kentucky alone, excluding Tennes-

see and the biggest brand in American Whiskey, Jack Daniel's.

Kentucky also has an outsize presence in rye whiskey. My educated guess is that the Kentucky style of rye (with a rye content hovering close to the 51% minimum required by law) is equal to or a close second to the 95% rye made by Indiana's MGP in terms of public familiarity. Beyond that, the state has a sizable and vibrant craft scene, the country's largest slate of medium-size producers (those too big to be called craft distillers, but too small to be counted among the truly large plants), and has put at least a toe in every style of American whiskey being made today.

The state's whiskey industry has even reasserted its past dominance in the realm of contract distilling. Leading the way is Bardstown Bourbon Company, whose business model is currently built around contract production, with three dozen distinct mash bills in use for their clientele. Some of Kentucky's other midsize distilleries also make whiskey under contract for outside clients.

I'm a Kentuckian, and my interest in whiskey began as a teenager with urban exploring in the ruins of shuttered distilleries in the Bluegrass State (back then, it was called trespassing). It's not sentiment that gave Kentucky such a large block of space in this book, however. The simple fact is this section is about as concise as I could make it while still giving proper recognition to the giant of American whiskey.

— ANGEL'S ENVY DISTILLERY —

ANGEL'S ENVY STRAIGHT BOURBON WHISKEY

86.6 Angel's Envy was the first major example of an American whiskey finished in Port barrels, and although the company opened a distillery in 2016, at the time of writing, the whiskey going into bottles is still entirely sourced. It's aged a minimum of four years, with five to seven years being the norm, before being given three to six months in the Port barrels.

The nose carries a sweet scent, full of maple and vanilla, with a sprinkling of nuts and a drizzle of berry syrup.

The liquid has a light texture on the tongue, and the flavor moves farther into Port wine territory. Sweet corn, maple, and caramel run like a current through the middle, underscored by nuttiness and plump raisins. The finish runs down on those raisins before turning a little dry.

Angel's Envy Cask Strength Straight Bourbon Whiskey

First introduced in 2013, this is the annual limited edition from Angel's Envy. When it started, the expression was based on barrels chosen by the Hendersons (at first Wes Henderson and his father, Lincoln; since Lincoln's passing, that has become Wes and his sons), and they told me these were four to seven years old. The whiskey would then go into the Port pipes for approximately two years of finishing. Starting in 2017, the family decided that this was too long and was putting too much of a Port influence into the bourbon; so, they cut the finishing period. Starting in 2017, releases became noticeably less "Porty." As a cask-strength whiskey, the potency of the bourbon is somewhat variable, but it is usually above 120 proof.

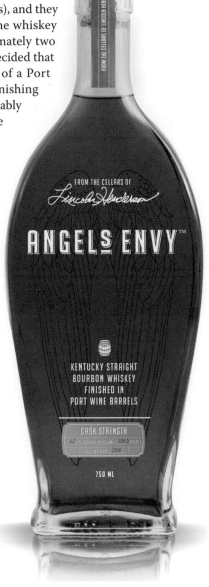

The color of the liquid is dark amber, roughly akin to a dark brew of tea. It is quite viscous, with the coat of the glass dropping just a few reluctant, molasses-like legs.

The nose was a touch too hot, so right from the start I splashed my dram with water. That done, the scent was heavy with melted brown sugar, caramel, and woody spices, accented by berry wine. It is a big, brazen, heavy aroma, something that has so much body that while finding it is easy, it also does not want to rise very far above the rim of the glass.

The flavor is a jam of black grapes and currants, woody spices plus a current of oak tannins, coated in vanilla syrup. By contrast, the finish was much lighter, just brushing you with a little spiciness and some nuttiness.

Angel's Envy Straight Rye Whiskey

When Angel's Envy decided to release a rye whiskey in 2013, they went with rum barrels for the finish. As with the bourbon, the whiskey is sourced; in this instance, it's the ubiquitous 95% rye stock from MGP. The whiskey is aged for at least six years before being finished for 18 months in barrels that were employed to age Cognac before being used to age Caribbean rum.

The nose comes across like being handed a plate of ginger and molasses cookies. Add a hint of maple and you've got it down.

A sip shows the whiskey to be even sweeter than that, very sweet for a rye whiskey. It's almost sickly sweet. Almost, but not quite. The ginger and molasses notes from the nose are joined by a cotton candy aspect that is damn near overpowering, with the semidry rye spice that so often characterizes MGP's rye standing as scarcely a hint in the background. The sweetness of the whiskey is what lingers on in the finish. It's sticky stuff, and lasts from start to finish.

This is truly an instance of the finishing cask overpowering the spirit that was put into it. For all that, being so sweet also makes it very approachable, especially for those turned off by a big-bodied, boldly spicy rye.

FROM THE CELLARS OF
ANGELS ENVY™
KENTUCKY STRAIGHT
BOURBON WHISKEY
FINISHED IN
PORT WINE BARRELS
750 ML
FROM THE CELLARS OF
ANGELS ENVY™
KENTUCKY STRAIGHT
BOURBON WHISKEY
PORT WINE BARRELS
43.3% ALCOHOL BY VOLUME [86.6 PROOF]
750 ML

BARRELL
BOURBON®

CASK STRENGTH   031   BATCH#

a blend of straight   27,585 BOTTLE#

bourbon whiskeys   6yrs   AGE

750ML

1112   55.6%

PROOF   ALC/VOL

— BARRELL CRAFT SPIRITS —

BARRELL BOURBON BATCH 031

121.2 Like all Barrell Bourbons, the thirty-first release is uncut, unfiltered, and skillfully blended. This one is drawn from 6-, 7-, 10-, 15-, and 16-year-old barrels sourced from Kentucky, Indiana, and Tennessee. The company says the 6-, 7-, and 10-year-old bourbons comprised two distinct groups, a wheated bourbon and a 99% corn bourbon, and this served as the foundation. The older whiskeys were used to tie it all together.

Keen observers invariably believe the Tennessee casks used by Barrell Craft Spirits have been sourced from Cascade Hollow (formerly called and still the makers of George Dickel), because previously they were specifically identified as having come from Tullahoma. Nowadays, that is less certain, both because the Tullahoma has been dropped as a reference and because some of Tennessee's craft distillers have been around long enough to furnish barrels that could now be six and seven years old. Indiana, however, undoubtedly continues to mean MGP, as they are the only open source of a mature 99% corn bourbon. As for Kentucky, that has always been anyone's guess. My notes reflect the inclusion of a splash of water.

The look of this bourbon is light amber, bright enough to verge on copper.

The nose delivers a current of tropical fruit salad, well-coated with brown sugar and caramel drizzle, and atop that coating is a sprinkling of crushed, green pine needles.

The taste turns slightly dry, with a fruity side of papaya and lemon drops balanced against a light gloss of peppery oak. The finish grows drier turning earthier and more peppered.

This one has about as exotic a C.V. attached to it as a blended rye whiskey can have. The sourcing draws on Indiana, Poland (!), Tennessee, and Canada. That is everywhere I could imagine picking up a consignment of mature rye whiskey, excepting Kentucky, and that Poland had that mature rye is a real surprise. Speaking of age, the barrels used here range from 4 to 14 years.

116.7

The liquid has a deep coppered appearance

The nose reminded me of ginger cookies and vanilla, with a sliver of woodiness.

The taste followed along in that vein, coming on thick with cookie spices and vanilla-brown sugared sweetness, while also coming across as a little peppery and a touch hot. Those were two distinct aspects, quite separate from each other, and I got that heat despite adding a generous splash of water. So, this whiskey has a little bite to it however you take it. The finish, however, had no trace of that heat, and that is an interesting twist to be sure. The final stanza opens with the cookie sweetness and spices, but these fade fast and leave a lovely, modest note of barrel char on the tongue.

Barrel Craft Spirits has addressed a gap in their repertoire in creating the Stellum line. Whereas Barrell Bourbon, Rye, Whiskey, and other offerings are always one-shot affairs, never to be repeated, Stellum whiskeys are in regular release, a brand created to deliver a consistent flavor profile and reliably (one hopes) occupy space on shelves. But like the aforementioned Barrell brands, Stellum is also uncut and unfiltered.

Stellum Bourbon

114.98 Stellum Bourbon is sourced from the familiar sources of Tennessee, Kentucky, and Indiana, although in the latter case drawing on a few separate mash bills from the MGP repertoire. The Kentucky and Tennessee stocks were said to be older and used to round and smooth out the profile, but no age statement or specific indication was made for this bourbon.

This dram has a dull amber look in the glass.

The smell comes across as toasty, musty oak seasoned with some clove and allspice.

Sipping on this bourbon reveals a light texture on the tongue, with a sweetness based on marshmallow and caramel, accented by that musty, toasty wood and a dash of black pepper. The finish rolls out of that spicy end, winding down as a sprinkle of cinnamon and pepper.

Stellum Rye

106.2 Insofar as sourcing goes, Stellum Rye is "rooted in a tried and true 95% Rye Indiana mash bill," with some rounding out by additional barrels from Kentucky and Tennessee.

This pour has that typically rye-style, coppered look to it.

I found the nose a touch hot, and that was despite the splash of water I added. The scent has a base of musty stout and butterscotch, enhanced by a whiff of mint.

The flavor, on the other hand, drew sweetness from candy corn, with a thick coating of spices in the form of cinnamon, nutmeg, and cloves. Unlike the nose, the palate was not hot at all. The finish rolled off that spiciness, growing a touch woody as it lingered.

— BARREL HOUSE DISTILLING CO. —

When it opened in 2008, Barrel House was not just one of the first craft distillers in Kentucky, but also the first distiller to resume work in Lexington's old James E. Pepper Distillery. The Pepper brand itself followed suit almost a decade later. Barrel House's initial products were moonshine, vodka, and rum, but it was making bourbon in its Portuguese-made Hoga still from the very start.

BARREL HOUSE ROCKCASTLE STRAIGHT BOURBON WHISKEY

118.1 Its first bourbon release, RockCastle, came out in 2015. This is a two-year-old wheated bourbon, aged in 25-gallon and 53-gallon barrels of Virginia-sourced oak. It's bottled at cask strength.

The nose delivers those core bourbon values of sweet corn and caramel, seasoned with a sprinkling of cinnamon.

Following that pleasant but simple nose, the flavor is surprisingly sophisticated. It is honey, almost malty sweet, smacking of toffee and seasoned with cinnamon and a bit of sandalwood. The woody tinge has the character of toasty pine. The finish is very much on the light side, especially for a cask strength.

THE ELKHORN TAVERN

Barrel House Distilling Co. features a separate taproom and cocktail lounge. The bar is named after the Elkhorn River, which runs through town, and showcases inventive cocktails made from Barrel House products. It also has a local beer list and a nice wine list. The bar features a rustic decor that has a historic touch to it, highlighted by lots of wood and copper.

— BEAM SUNTORY —
(JIM BEAM DISTILLERY, BOOKER NOE DISTILLERY, AND MAKER'S MARK DISTILLERY)

Headquartered in Chicago and owned by a Japanese holding company, the multinational Beam Suntory is the world's third largest producer of distilled beverages behind Diageo and Pernod Ricard. Three notable Kentucky distillers are numbered amongst its flock.

BAKER'S 7–YEAR–OLD STRAIGHT BOURBON WHISKEY

107 In the early 1990s, Jim Beam released a group of four premium bourbons called the Small Batch Collection: Knob Creek, Basil Hayden's, Booker's, Baker's. Of that four, each one became popular in its turn and saw changes to cope with demand. Most famously, Knob Creek went from being a 9-year-old to a no age statement (NAS) and then back to a 9-year-old again between 2016 and 2019. Basil Hayden lost its age statement and, to date, has not gotten it back. Baker's was the last brand from that seminal collection to change with the times, but in Baker's case it was to take a clear step up. The bourbon remains a 7-year-old bottled at 107 proof, just like it has been from the first day, but it is a small batch whiskey no longer. From 2019, Baker's became a single barrel expression.

The color took a middle amber look, while swishing the glass left a bright sheen behind, along with ample tears.

The nose on this single barrel version of Baker's was squarely in traditional bourbon territory, with oodles of vanilla and brown sugar, accented by lemon zest and cinnamon, and a hint of toasted nuts hovering in the background.

The flavor brings the sweetness forward, putting candy corn and vanilla firmly at center stage. A generous pinch of spiciness plus a smaller chip of wood, followed finally by a dusting of nuts to round things out. The finish turned to those latter elements, starting off with sweet cinnamon spiciness before fading down to a faint trace of oak. Sipping on Baker's is therefore a lot like going to your favorite diner: wholesome, nourishing, wonderful, old fashioned, but ultimately special only because it does those four things so damn well.

BASIL HAYDEN'S STRAIGHT BOURBON WHISKEY

When Basil Hayden's was first introduced, it was an eight-year-old, premium spin on Old Grand-Dad, Jim Beam's high-rye bourbon (27% rye). It's since lost the age statement, the first of the Small Batch Collection bourbons to do so. Basil Hayden's reputation was as the light member of the group, and it is certainly the lightest in terms of alcohol content.

The whiskey has a golden copper coloring, while the swish of the glass leaves it streaming with tears.

A sniff shows that dry, high-rye character. It's spicy, a dryness that comes across as black-tea tannins, and what little sweetness is present is more honey than caramel.

It's sweeter on the palate, more honeyed than the usual bourbon vanilla and brown sugar, but also mildly spicy and a little dry and leathery. The finish is sweet, but dry, and runs through quick.

Basil Hayden's became popular in recent years, and in my opinion many casual drinkers have been drawn to it because of its light, easy-drinking qualities. It's easy to see why.

 From my very first sip of Booker's some 25 years ago, I've called it a sucker puncher of a bourbon, because you can have a double at the bar and have no idea how strong it is until you stand up. As originally conceived, it's an unfiltered and uncut whiskey aged between six to eight years. These days, batches of Booker's tend to be closer to six years than eight. Another change in the expression is that those batches now all have individual titles, such as "Kathleen's Batch" and "Backyard BBQ," drawn from the colorful life of the brand namesake, Booker Noe (father of the current master distiller, Fred Noe).

The new titles tend to play up that individual batches are a little different from one another, but as a rule Booker's tends to be big, assertive bourbon without being hot enough to require water. Its color is dark amber and, being uncut, it forms a viscous, sticky coat on the inside of the glass.

The nose has a heavy presence of rich vanilla and brown sugar, accented with an earthy whiff of wet clay, roasted sweet corn, and a current of cedarwood.

It's a straightforward, unsubtle whiskey, so the flavor mirrors the scent almost perfectly, with a note of butterscotch added for good measure. The finish is substantial and lasting, running with caramel and toasty oak.

Jim Beam Straight Bourbon Whiskey (White Label)

80   Jim Beam Straight Bourbon Whiskey needs little introduction, as it is one of the best-selling whiskeys in the world and an iconic brand. The whiskey is aged for four to six years.

In the glass, the whiskey has the mid-amber coloring of the stereotypical bourbon.

The nose is like thinned, sweet vanilla syrup with some mild oaky notes. While not complex, it is not altogether dull either.

On the palate, the flavor continues as a sweet syrup of caramel and vanilla, with just a touch of rye spice. The finish is sweet, but not especially long or deep. Basically, Jim Beam looks, smells, and tastes like a youngster, which is exactly what it is.

Jim Beam Black Extra—Aged Straight Bourbon Whiskey

86   Beam Black is another expression that lost its age statement; once it was eight years old, but now it's merely Extra-Aged. Compared to Jim Beam White, it's said to be aged closer to six years than to four.

It has a deep copper coloring in the glass.

The nose is light and airy. It carries caramel with a brushing of cinnamon and oak.

On the palate, the liquid thickens up a bit to a more middling body, tasting of caramel, soft cake spices, and a little charred oak. The finish, though, is long, lingering, and runs with candy corn and vanilla.

Jim Beam Bonded Straight Bourbon Whiskey

When Jim Beam Bonded was introduced, for me it captured perfectly what a romantic anachronism the bottled in bond designation is today. Jokesters labeled it "Baby Knob Creek," because it too was 100 proof, less than half the age of what was then Knob Creek Nine-Year-Old (see page 155), and coming from essentially the same stock. The comparison illustrated how much better modern bourbon is compared to what it was in 1897, when the bottled in bond standards were necessary to protect the category.

It has a pleasant mid-amber, caramel coloring in the glass.

The nose packs candy corn, toffee, and caramel sweetness balanced against an earthy woodiness and rye spice.

The palate follows in that vein: core, simple bourbon values of corn sweetness seasoned with vanilla and caramel, but with a current of old, leathery wood. Compared to some of the other expressions bearing the Beam name, it is a richer bourbon with a dry and woody aspect all its own.

Jim Beam Pre–Prohibition Straight Rye Whiskey

90 Once upon a time, Jim Beam rye was almost indistinguishable from Old Overholt, being bottled from the same stock at the same strength. But then rye became more popular and the company decided to build on its brand by making its rye a little beefier. They added the "Pre-Prohibition" to the label and upped the proof from 80 to 90. Beam's rye whiskey mash bill isn't public knowledge, but it is known to be in the Kentucky style, with a rye content just barely over the minimum 51% requirement.

The nose smacks of green rye, with some nuttiness and some vanilla.

On the palate, the whiskey is spicy for sure, but it has equal measures of rye and oak spice rather than rye-forward, undergirded by vanilla. A certain dryness rises on the back end, which allows a little nuttiness to come out. The finish lingers and runs a little spicy, but mostly dry.

Once one of the premier whiskey brands in America and a standard-bearer of Pennsylvania whiskey, a combination of Prohibition, the Depression, World War II, and changing tastes reduced Old Overholt to bottom-shelf status at Jim Beam. Thus, it is a sweet Kentucky rye instead of a bold, spicy Pennsylvania rye, and bottled at a modest proof. Even so, it remains a favorite, thanks in part to its low price tag.

On the nose, its scent has a current of dry pepper and herbal spiciness, which is quite evened out by dollops of vanilla and fruity sweetness.

The flavor leads with cloves and pepper, but also drips with crème brûlée. The finish is all sweet, like a caramel candy.

Since the Rye Revival began in 2010, Jim Beam has introduced (rī) and Knob Creek Rye, and revamped Jim Beam Rye. Finally, they did something with Old Overholt by introducing Old Overholt Bonded in 2018. As a bottled in bond whiskey, it's four years old and 100 proof.

In the glass it has a light copper look. It leaves a viscous coating on my glass, one that forms a beaded crown and takes its time in dropping a few tears.

The nose smacks of toasted nuts, citrus, mint syrup, and cedar. As far as those scents go, it is very straightforward, being neither bold nor subtle, while offering enough variety to make things a little interesting.

My taste buds find it more restrained than does my nose, but still not light or faint. The flavors are roasted sweet corn, spearmint, and oak. The finish brings the nuttiness back up, which turns over into peppermint, and then back to nuts for the final fade.

Upping the age and the proof improves Old Overholt, but not dramatically. I find the results much in keeping with the numbers concerned.

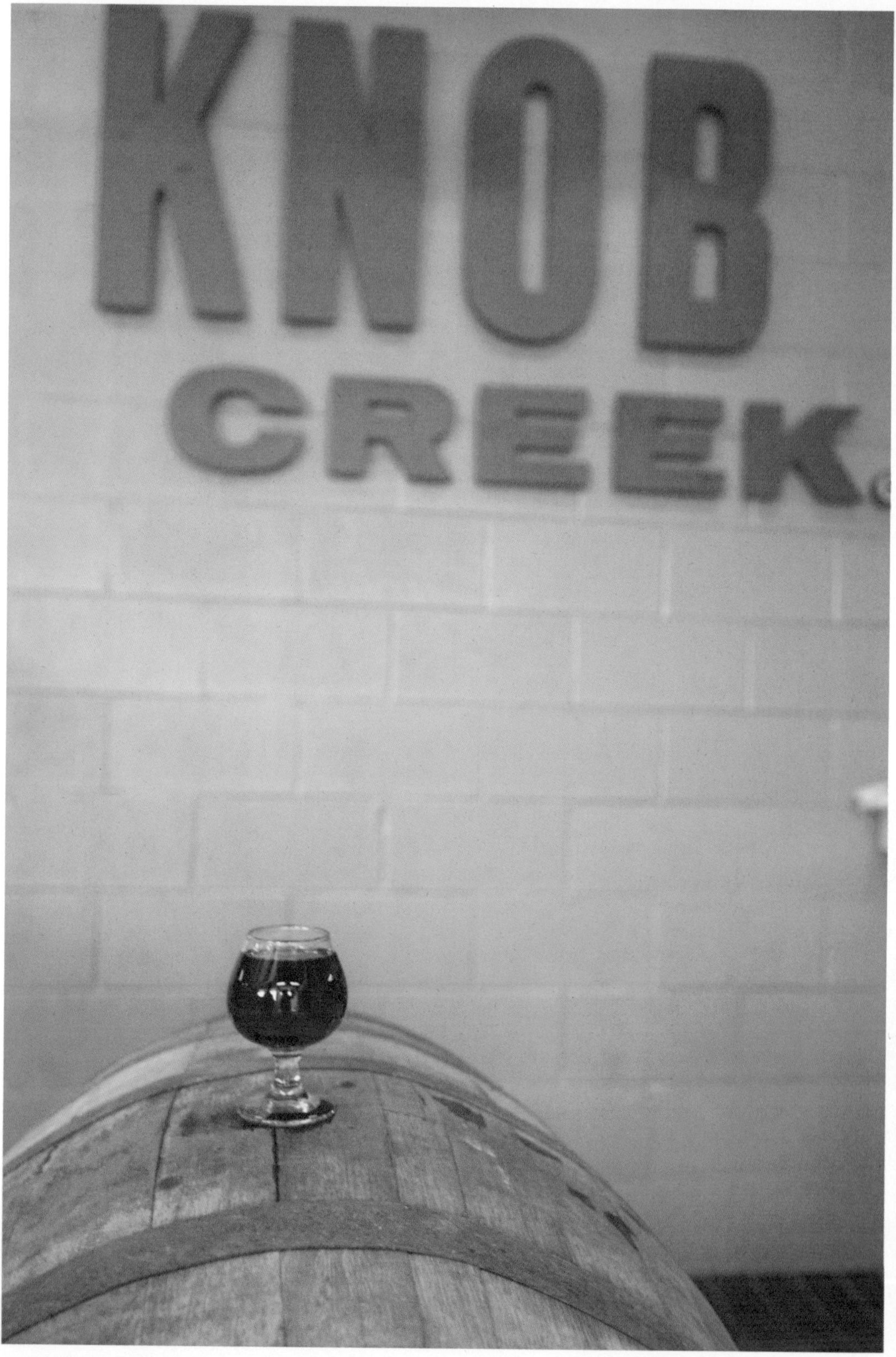
KNOB
CREEK

KNOB CREEK SMALL BATCH STRAIGHT BOURBON WHISKEY

Knob Creek Small Batch, the flagship of the Small Batch Collection, is one of those key expressions that led the way into the modern Bourbon Boom, helping to make whiskey popular again. It was originally a nine-year-old, but this was replaced by a no-age-statement version in 2016. It's made from the Beam low-rye mash bill.

The aroma coming off of a pour is quite potent, with a scent that has heaps of candy corn and vanilla sweetness, but with a current of spiciness and a rough barrel-char edge that form Knob Creek's identity.

With the loss of the age statement, the flavor has gotten spicier and a little rawer than was previously the case, but this has always been a big whiskey, even more so than the 100 proof suggests. However, the foundation of sweet corn and deep caramel is still there, as is the note of earthy barrel char hovering in the back. The whiskey goes down sweet and just a touch hot.

Knob Creek Single Barrel Straight Bourbon Whiskey

People who miss the nine-year-old Knob Creek need look no farther than the extremely high-octane Knob Creek Single Barrel. When it was first released in 2011, it took much of what made Knob Creek good a step further. It was a single barrel instead of a small batch; it's strong, but didn't need water or ice (or at least not that much of it). Nowadays, it's still nine years old. There are even plenty of private barrel bottlings for major liquor retailers and prominent bourbon bars.

The distinctive, fiery bite of Knob Creek starts nibbling on you with the nose of the whiskey. The high alcohol content really comes across from the scent alone, but the heat isn't overpowering. The woody vanilla from nine years of aging is strong, mixed with hints of orange and cinnamon. What is missing is the barrel-char note, but you can get it back by adding a generous splash of water.

On the palate, the bourbon's high-octane heat is mixed with cinnamon, nutmeg, and orange spice. The finish comes down with plenty of glowing warmth.

I think Knob Creek Single Barrel is best taken with a minimum of adulteration, especially if you have a taste for bourbon with 60% alcohol content. However, another way to take it is to get back to the original Knob Creek. To do that, water your pour down by about one-sixth.

Kentucky distilleries (indeed, distilleries in general) tend to have a single, standard rye mash bill, and Jim Beam is no exception. So, even though the company has a handful of rye whiskey brands, these are all essentially variations on the same stock. They may come from different floors in different warehouses, be bottled at different strengths, or be aged for varying lengths of time, but they all have the same roots. At Jim Beam, Knob Creek Straight Rye is the strongest of the lot, a no-age-statement whiskey.

As a Kentucky rye, the whiskey smells at least as oak spicy as rye spicy, coming across as ginger and peppermint, with a hefty dollop of caramel for good measure.

The texture here is a little buttery, and the spiciness leans more toward traditional rye territory on the palate than on the nose, joined by a very bourbonesque mix of brown sugar and vanilla. It's on the finish that the whiskey finally turns into full-on, full-bodied rye whiskey: it's dry, starts off peppery, then winds down into a softer, more herbal spiciness.

LITTLE BOOK BLENDED WHISKEY

This whiskey gets its name from its creator, Freddie Noe, son of current Beam master distiller Fred Noe and grandson of the famed Booker Noe. "Little Book" is Freddie's childhood nickname. He started working at Beam in 2013, and his official title is Fermentation Manager, but all things considered it is best to view him as the master's apprentice.

To create Little Book, Noe gets to draw from the diverse palette of whiskeys available through Beam Suntory. Each installment is a unique, one-time creation. The only thing binding them together is a name, a maker, and that they have all been bottled at cask strength. If you like your whiskeys strong and a little odd, Little Book has something for you.

The first Little Book, released in 2017, was a blended American whiskey, made from 13-year-old corn whiskey, 4-year-old bourbon, straight rye, and American malts of undisclosed age. This was followed a year later by Chapter Two, which went north of the border and utilized 13- and 40-year-old stocks of Canadian whiskies, plus some 8-year-old bourbon.

The third installment represented a showcase of the stock used to make the classic Jim Beam Small Batch collection, drawing on bourbons of the type used to make Knob Creek, Baker's, Booker's, and Basil Hayden, albeit all older and stronger than usual. Little Book has continued since then as both a showcase for the whiskeys Beam Suntory (not just Jim Beam proper) has in its inventory and the blending skill of Freddie Noe.

To create Little Book, Noe gets to draw from the diverse palette of whiskeys available through Beam Suntory. Each installment is a unique, one-time creation. The only thing binding them together is a name, a maker, and that they have all been bottled at cask strength. If you like your whiskeys strong and a little odd, Little Book has something for you.

The first Little Book was a blended American whiskey, made from 13-year-old corn whiskey, four-year-old bourbon, straight rye, and American malts of undisclosed age. They bottled it at 120.68 proof. It came out in autumn 2017 and was followed a year later by "Chapter Two." That Little Book leaned toward north of the border, utilizing 13- and 40-year-old stocks of Canadian whiskeys, plus some eight-year-old bourbon.

FREDDIE NOE

The Beams have the dynasty in an industry that is the family business for so many families. Not only can they mark their stewardship of Beam bourbon back to Jacob Beam and the late 18th century, but members of Kentucky's most illustrious bourbon family have worked for other brands and run other distilleries as well. Despite all that, Freddie Noe insists that no one pressured him about the family business.

That included his dad, Fred Noe, the current master distiller at Jim Beam. "My dad always told me the decision was up to me," says Noe. Freddie studied business in college, not chemistry as many eyeing a future in the distilling industry do. He didn't give much thought to it until his grandfather, Booker Noe, passed away in 2004.

"About eight years ago," says Noe, "my dad came home and said, 'the folks at work asked me if you were interested in joining the business.' By that point, I didn't hesitate one bit. I said yes. He continued by asking me what at the distillery I wanted to do, and I said 'everything.'"

Thus began Freddie Noe's practical education in bourbon. Starting in 2013, he had hands-on training in every aspect of the distillery: the lab, bottling plant, rickhouses, shipping. He rotated from one department to another, learning every job. It was in research and development that he discovered his passion for blending. That led to his first solo project as his father's apprentice and heir apparent, Little Book.

If one has a thing for blending, then having the palette available for Little Book must be a dream. The two releases ("chapters") made thus far have spanned what Beam Suntory can draw upon throughout North America. Of the two, it was the second release, Noe Simple Task, that proved more daunting. "The 40-year-old extra-aged Canadian whisky could easily overpower the flavor profiles of the other liquids," says Noe, "so I needed to be very careful with the proportions to get it just right." He created 32 variants before he settled on the one he wanted.

Noe also had a hand in the recent Booker's 30th Anniversary Bourbon, which sounded a little intimidating because instead of the usual Booker's Roundtable making selections for batching, it was just Freddie and Fred. The first installment of Little Book came out in mid-2017, so that is three major releases in less than two years either by Noe or with his participation. Based on the success of those, I'm sure we can expect many more Beam releases with Freddie Noe's fingerprints on them in the near future.

90 All the hype surrounding Pappy Van Winkle has brought a lot of attention to Buffalo Trace's wheated bourbon, but it's Maker's Mark that is the modern classic in that department. After all, wheated bourbon is the only thing they do down there in Loretto, Kentucky. Well, that and dip bottles in red wax and spend a lot of time moving barrels around.

One of the signatures of Maker's Mark is barrel rotation. Whereas most big distillers let their barrels sit in the same location in the rickhouse for years and rely on the well-established characteristics of that warehouse and its floors to tell them how things will turn out, Maker's moves their barrels around to ensure every one of them turns out more or less the same.

The nose is soft and sweet, loaded with candy corn and vanilla, with just a hint of wood spice. And even this is balanced out by a mild strawberry note.

A sip shows the liquid to have a creamy texture, and a flavor profile that is just as sweet as the nose. Oodles of melted brown sugar and vanilla are underscored by a helping of citrus zest and berries. The middling finish turns a little oaky, but this is subdued and balanced by a little fruitiness as well.

STEVE NALLY

Maker's Mark has a reputation for being the wellspring of the expertise behind several prominent small and medium-size distilleries, and Steve Nally is a big part of the reason why. That is because Nally is one of a couple of former master distillers from the house that the Samuels clan built to enjoy a follow-up career in consulting.

Nally grew up in rural Kentucky, near Loretto. After finishing high school, he took some vocational training in welding and electrical work and went to work on the farm. His entry into Maker's Mark and his distilling career were humble and straightforward: it was 1972, he needed extra money, and the distillery was in the area, so he went over to see about a job. He was hired and started out growing yeast.

Over time, Nally moved from one facet of operations at Maker's Mark to another. In 1978, he became an assistant warehouse manager, which included tracking Maker's famous barrel-rotation scheme, a key element of how they mature their whiskey. But this also included shipping, reports for the federal Tax and Trade Bureau (TTB), and bottling line operations. In the mid-1980s, he went back to the stillhouse as assistant distiller, and by 1988 he was running the stillhouse.

Nally retired from Maker's in 2003, having spent over three decades at the distillery, from the Whiskey Crash of the 1970s to the cusp of the modern Bourbon Boom. After leaving Maker's, he began his distilling consultancy, working on four different projects, and spent four years delivering grain to different Kentucky distilleries. Then he got a call from "three lawyers in Jackson, Wyoming," says Nally, who asked him "to come out to Wyoming, build, and start a bourbon whiskey distillery." With Nally's help, Wyoming Whiskey was born in 2009.

Nally is proud of his work at Wyoming Whiskey. First, making whiskey at 4,200 feet above sea level presented him with new and interesting challenges. Almost everything in the production process, from cooking time to maturation, required some adjustment. He considers Wyoming Whiskey's Small Batch Bourbon as his best achievement thus far, saying: "It is a product that I made on my own, starting with the recipe all the way through aging and packaging."

After helping Wyoming Whiskey get started, Nally returned to Kentucky and his next big project: Bardstown Bourbon Company. Opened in 2016, this distillery was started from the ground up as a contract producer for other brands. The demand for those services has been strong; just a year and a half after starting production, they found it necessary to install a second, 50-foot-tall column still. Managing that growth, as well as the complexity of contract distilling for so many different clients, has been challenging. "We've grown from producing custom whiskey and bourbon in our Collaborative Distilling Program for just a few customers to 22 with nearly 30 different mash bills," says Nally.

Maker's Mark 46 Straight Bourbon Whisky

94 This bourbon was Maker's Mark's first major brand extension, using a finish based on seared French oak staves inserted into the middle of the barrel. This idea was first employed by the independent Scotch blender-bottler Compass Box in their expression The Spice Tree; they were subsequently told to cease and desist by the Scotch Whisky Association and forced to find a workaround to continue the expression.

Maker's Mark had no such obstacle, so they set about dumping mature barrels, placing the inserts, refilling the barrels, and giving their wheated bourbon a short finish. In experimenting with Maker's 46, the distillery learned that the finish achieved its best results during the cooler winter months, and eventually they built a cellar to create optimal year-round aging conditions.

The look in the glass is what you can see in the bottle: light, coppered amber. I've always thought Maker's coloring was a bit lighter than many bourbons of similar age (approximately six years) and bottled at the same proof, and this is no exception. The coating of the glass was quite viscous, though, dropping just a few moderate tears.

The nose is classic Maker's, but with a solid twist. The deep vanilla, sweetness, and toasty white bread are there, with the expected floral softness, but now with toffee, a little extra spicy cinnamon, and a certain dry quality.

The tasting keeps on in the vein of Maker's plus something else. It's a creamy bourbon with a soft profile, predominately sweet and caramel in the main. But that current of cookie spices is there too, like someone put a bit too much cinnamon into the spice mix. The flavor is a bit oakier than the nose suggests, and the touch of dryness comes on at the end. From there the finish is light and soft, a bit oaky and a bit dry and spicy. As that fades away, I was left with a little dried grassiness. Overall, this final stage is modest and wraps up quickly.

— BROWN-FORMAN CORPORATION —
(BROWN-FORMAN SHIVELY DISTILLERY
AND WOODFORD RESERVE DISTILLERY)

Brown-Forman takes a considerable amount of pride in being the only one of the big Kentucky whiskey companies, also known as the "Kentucky majors," to own their own cooperage.

COOPERS' CRAFT STRAIGHT BOURBON WHISKEY

82.2 This bourbon, the first entirely new brand created by Brown-Forman since Woodford Reserve was introduced in 1996, is one of the rare charcoal-filtered bourbons. Such bourbons are distinct from Tennessee Whiskeys (such as Brown-Forman's own Jack Daniel's) in that the filtration takes place *after* barrel maturation, not before. Also, the charcoal in question doesn't need to be made from sugar maple. In this instance, after the barrels are dumped, the whiskey destined for Coopers' Craft is filtered through beech and birch charcoal.

The nose on this copper-colored bourbon is a light one, which isn't too surprising for a fairly low-proof whiskey. The scent is that of cornflakes, a little tropical fruit and vanilla, and just a hint of oak lurking in the background.

It's an easy sipper, straightforward and uncomplicated to drink. The flavor comprises corn sweetness and a little orange rind, plus a sliver of charred oak and a pinch of pepper. The finish is more interesting, starting sweet, and then kicking with a little spicy heat, before finally winding down with a little leather.

80 The reason Early Times is called "Kentucky Whisky" is that it's aged in used barrels, as opposed to the new white oak barrels required for bourbon under federal law. Otherwise, it shares the same roots as a handful of Brown-Forman bourbons made at their Shively distillery. Fun fact: exported Early Times is often labeled as a bourbon.

The used barrel is instantly obvious in the glass, as Early Times has a thin, semitranslucent amber appearance that is just a shadow of what bourbon aged a little more than three years in new oak would have.

In light of its look, the nose comes as a surprise: fragrantly corn sweet with a nice current of vanilla and a touch of rye spice.

On the palate, the whiskey has surprising weight. The flavor balances corn sweetness, dry oak, rye spice, caramel, and vanilla surprisingly well. That said, the whiskey is rather flat, despite having all the core elements, and is tinged with a bit of a mineral spirits bite.

OLD FORESTER BOURBON WHISKEY

The basic iteration of Old Forester is a classic among budget bourbons—the stuff looks, smells, and tastes like a benchmark bourbon. Old Forester has been in continuous distillation since before Prohibition (thanks to some "medicinal whiskey" licensing) and is made to specifications that are practically archetypal for bourbon; it is made from a mash of 72% corn, 18% rye, and 10% malted barley, and aged in #4 alligator char barrels.

It's sweet on the nose, with a dollop of vanilla, a bit of fruit jam, and a pinch of pipe tobacco, accented by peppermint and a whiff of pine.

From there, the flavor moves into traditional bourbon territory: sweet corn, a little rye spice, a zip of citrus zest, plenty of vanilla, and a hint of oak. The finish is long and dry.

90

Brown-Forman launched its Whiskey Row series to celebrate the brand's historic ties with Louisville's Whiskey Row, a stretch of Main Street that used to be (and is fast again becoming) bourbon central. Each is named for a particular date of importance to the Old Forester brand. In this particular expression, 1870 was the year it was launched, right there on Whiskey Row.

The original Old Forester was blended from bourbons made at three different distilleries, and 1870 consciously mirrors those roots. Although all the bourbon is made from Old Forester's standard mash bill, the selected barrels come from three distinct batches, each from a different production season, entered into the barrel at a different proof, and aged to a different degree in separate warehouses. The second point, entry proof, is the most interesting in my mind, since it means at least two of the constituent bourbon stocks used in making Old Forester 1870 differ from what is used to make the staple Old Forester, which uses a standard entry proof of 125.

The liquid has a dark brown amber coloring, but looks thin in the glass, and the latter point reflects a general lightness on the nose and palate.

The scent is driven by citrus sweetness. It's quite floral, accented by a generous helping of vanilla and a teaspoon of cloves.

The flavor is very much in tune with the nose. It opens with baking spices, which are balanced by rising citrus sweetness. A little oak rounds it out. The finish has more body on it, starting with spiciness before fading down to a trace of oak.

OLD FORESTER 1897 BOTTLED IN BOND BOURBON WHISKEY

For whiskey history buffs, the significance of 1897 ought to be obvious: it was when the Bottled in Bond Act was passed. In keeping with that, this is a bottled in bond version of the standard Old Forester. Old Forester Signature is also a 100-proof whiskey, so it's worth noting what separates the two expressions. In accordance with regulations, this was made at a single distillery (Brown-Forman's Shively plant) in a single distilling season and aged for at least four years under government supervision.

A pour comes across as dark amber in the glass, while the swish and coat yield some hefty tears.

The nose is a touch hot, but bursts with sweet honey and vanilla nonetheless.

The palate is a well-balanced mix of the sweet and the spice. On the one hand it carries plenty of caramel and coconut, but on the other it's got gobs of oak-driven spice. The finish runs with both aspects, starting with melted brown sugar before turning oaky and spicy.

93 The fourth installment in Old Forester's Whiskey Row series, released a year after the first three, is a "double-barreled" bourbon. This is a style of secondary maturation (finishing) that uses new white oak instead of used casks, such as Port, Sherry, beer, rum, and so on. Drawing on a fresh, second round of oak, whether toasted or charred, doubles up on the sweetness provided by American oak.

In modern times, this began with Woodford Reserve's Double Oaked. However, according to Brown-Forman, the story reaches back farther, to 1910.

A fire shut down the bottling plant and some already vatted bourbon needed to be transferred to indefinite storage, so they put it into a new set of barrels.

This double-barrel bourbon differs from Woodford Reserve Double Oaked because whereas the latter uses new, toasted barrels for the second round, Old Forester 1910 relies on heavily scorched barrels. The char time is implied to be above that of the #4 "alligator char," the usual maximum. Regular Old Forester goes into those barrels for another six to nine months. The result is bottled at 93 proof.

A pour in my glass holds a dark, rusty amber liquid. It is thick, and the coating of the glass leaves a thin crown that dropped tiny, slow-moving tears. The look of it is like that of reddened maple syrup.

I find the nose light, leading with oak and a bit of leather, with mild touches of vanilla and citrus behind it.

That light, airy scent gives way to something more substantial and chewy on the palate, and sweeter to boot. This bourbon really sticks to your mouth. Also, the sweetness drawn from the heavily cooked second set of barrels comes out much more with a sip than with a sniff. Brown sugar, caramel, and a pinch of lemon zest are rounded out by a light dusting of spice and just a hint of oiliness. The finish eventually becomes the oakiest part of all. It starts by continuing to run sweet, and turns quite woody before finally turning to a moderately dry spiciness.

OLD FORESTER 1920 PROHIBITION STYLE BOURBON WHISKEY

115

This Whiskey Row expression represents what Old Forester was up to during Prohibition, when it was one of the few brands still in production. The company was one of six distillers to secure a license to make "medicinal whiskey," and thus remained in business. A person could get a prescription to buy a pint of medicinal whiskey every 10 days, and doctors prescribed 64 million of those pints in Prohibition's first year alone. As you can imagine, writing those prescriptions was a lucrative business for many a physician.

Much of that medicinal alcohol was bottled at 100 proof, but Brown-Forman's master distiller Chris Morris decided that Old Forester bottled at 115 proof replicated the Prohibition-era product better. Thus, Old Forester 1920 is the high-octane entry in the Whiskey Row series, and my favorite bourbon out of Old Forester as a whole.

This strong bourbon is a looker in the glass. A pour has a brown amber coloring, with copper highlights when you hold it up to the light.

The scent has oodles of brown sugar and caramel, accented by oak and earthiness, and with a light touch of raisins.

As one might expect from so potent a bourbon, it's got a big and bold flavor profile. Thick caramel and crème brûlée predominate, but not so much that you cannot easily get at hints of nuts, cocoa, and barrel char. The finish starts peppery before mellowing out and returning to the earthy traces that have been present throughout.

OLD FORESTER BIRTHDAY BOURBON

101

Introduced in September 2002 to mark the brand's second anniversary, the theme of Birthday Bourbon is to draw on a single day's production. That day has usually been 12 years prior, so although the bourbon lacks an age statement, 12 years is the norm. They also adjust the strength of the bourbon to best suit that year's batch. It often is in the mid- to high 90s proof, but 2018's edition was bottled at 101 proof.

The 2018 batch has a dusty auburn look, and a swish yields a curtain of skinny legs.

The nose has a surprisingly tropical aspect to it, with nuts sharing center stage with vanilla and brown sugar, and bananas joining cake spice and wood among the more modest notes.

Once this goes from nose to tongue, the oak moves from a very modest background note to occupying center stage. It's not actually oaky, though, but more of a pleasant mix of vanilla, wood spice, and oak. The spiciness develops in a modest kind of way, transitioning into the finish.

OLD FORESTER STRAIGHT RYE WHISKEY

100   Released in February 2019, this rye is a remarkable departure for Brown-Forman in two respects, both stemming from the 65% rye, 20% malted barley, and 15% corn mash bill. First, that mash bill is separate from the one used to make Woodford Reserve Rye. Also, that mash bill is more in the Maryland approach to rye whiskey than the low-rye Kentucky style, or would be were it not also a malted barley-forward recipe. As opposed to merely being there for the enzymes that help convert starch to sugar, enough malted barley is in this whiskey to count it as a flavoring element.

A pour reveals a light amber coloring. A swish and coat of the glass leave a typical coating, not particularly thin or viscous, except that it dropped very few, quite small tears in its wake.

The nose leads with generous helpings of brown sugar and vanilla, and behind that comes sassafras and baking spices, tinged with just a little citrus zest.

This profile evolves on the tongue, leading with ginger and a pinch of pepper instead of sweetness. That comes on later, but with a more floral and fruity aspect, so that by the time the whole thing has developed in your mouth, it's like having a spicily seasoned, boozy bite of baked apples. The finish is less distinguished, running spicy with a hint of vanilla.

Overall, it's a mighty nice sipping whiskey. The palate was a little more complex than I was expecting, in fact. For the price point, it's well worth having.

King of Kentucky Bourbon

PKing of Kentucky is a bourbon brand that dates back to 1881. That was only a decade after George Garvin Brown introduced Old Forester and laid the foundation for Brown-Forman, and his company scooped up the rights to King of Kentucky after Prohibition, in 1936. The mid-1930s was a time when distilleries shuttered by Prohibition and the brands they once produced were being traded about like so many baseball cards. Brown-Forman took King of Kentucky and brought it back as a cheap blended whiskey, which it remained until it was discontinued in 1968.

Brown-Forman dusted off this venerable brand name in 2018, reintroducing it as a middle-aged, single barrel, cask strength annual limited-edition bourbon. Thus far, King of Kentucky releases have been 14 or 15 years old; have consistently clocked at much higher than 120 proof; and been produced in runs of 2,000 to 3,000 bottles (only the inaugural 2018 release was less). The new make is the same as Early Times, but the standard Early Times is matured in used barrels, whereas all the stock going into King of Kentucky was (as per federal law) aged in new oak.

This is both an annual limited edition and a single barrel, so individual lots could vary quite a bit. That said, this is what I got to try from the 2021 release.

A sniff (with water) smacked of rich, deep caramel and toasted graham crackers, dusted with cinnamon and brown sugar. Rounding out the picture was a note of charred, leathery oak.

The flavor followed through with an almost stereotyped bourbon base: brown sugar, vanilla, some dried red fruits, but with a current of sharp, distinctive spices running right through the center. That spicy aspect is a mixed bag of the dry, oaky, and peppery and rye-driven cake spices. It's the former that carries on into the finish, though.

Jackie Zykan

A major misconception about making whiskey is that to do it right, one absolutely must come from either an engineering or chemistry background. Although a chemistry degree actually is a good base to start from, much more important than engineering is having a palate and a keen understanding of how that palate works. Although training helps, some people really are born with better senses than others. These distinctions are noticeably clear in the Scotch industry, where the person who works the stills is usually called the distillery manager, but the person with the word "master" in their job title is the master blender.

Another thing often not understood about the industry is what the time split is between making whiskey and public relations. In modern times, anyone in the whiskey business with the word "master" in their job title spends a large chunk of their time engaged in the business of selling, not making, whiskey.

Jackie Zykan brings those threads together in a way that few other people in the business do. While she went to college for a chemistry and biology degree, the whiskey business was not her objective at the time. Instead, her initial intent was to go into medicine, with a particular eye on pathology.

Her introduction to the industry came from working as a bartender. She continued to work in the bar business after moving to Louisville, but it was in the Derby City that the bourbon bug bit her. Making her way up the bar ladder to bar manager and beverage director acquainted her with a lot of people on the brands and marketing side of the whiskey trade, and those folks in turn became very much aware of her science background and formidable palate.

As Zykan herself put it, "I did not consider making the complete change until I had my son, which made unorthodox hours and lack of benefits a challenging place to remain. The timing worked out for Old Forester to have an interest, right as I was looking for something more grounded on the brand team side of the business." That was in 2015, when Brown-Forman asked her to come aboard as a bourbon specialist.

Even today, it is still (and strangely) unusual for someone to jump from the bar business into a major whiskey company, but Zykan's credentials should have made (and probably did make) that hire a no-brainer: I can affirm from first-person experience she is a personable storyteller; she understands the needs and interests of bar people in a way only one of their own can; she has the science background; and she has the sensory side of things nailed. Her reputation in the industry on that last point, and this after only half a dozen years, is formidable. By 2017, she was named Master Taster for Old Forester.

As described above, anyone in the whiskey business with the word "master" in their job title spends a good deal of time on the road, serving as ambassador for the brand and product. But some bourbon fans make the mistake of assuming that anyone without the word "distiller" in their title is peripheral to the production process, which is rarely the case and especially not for Zykan. "[My] responsibilities gear more toward post-distillation liquid," says Zykan. "Quality assurance, new product development, as well as blending all fall under this umbrella, alongside ambassadorship and marketing duties."

In other words, she plays a lead role in deciding what to do with Old Forester bourbon when it comes time to dump the barrels. Zykan has introduced the Old Forester 117 Series, which is entirely her own; she leads the single barrel program; and her fingerprints were on all three versions of the Old Forester 150th Anniversary Bourbon. It's only been four years since her appointment as Master Taster, and as time grows, that C.V. will continue to lengthen.

— WOODFORD RESERVE —

WOODFORD RESERVE DISTILLER'S SELECT
STRAIGHT BOURBON WHISKEY

90.4 Woodford Reserve has its own distillery, but the bourbon is made with the same tried-and-true mash bill as Old Forester: 72% corn, 18% rye, and 10% malted barley. There is a good reason for that. The brand was introduced in tandem with the 1996 reopening of the historic Labrot & Graham Distillery as the Woodford Reserve Distillery. The timing meant that all the bourbon in those mid-1990s bottles were made at Brown-Forman's Shively plant, and even today what goes into Woodford Reserve is a blend of the bourbon made at both distilleries. Consistency demanded staying on the same mash bill.

Even so, Woodford Reserve has a singularly distinctive characteristic: the distillery has an Irish-style, triple set of copper pot stills. When it first opened, Woodford was the only distillery making bourbon with pot stills. Today it remains the only distillery in Kentucky making it with triple distillation in copper pots. That unique approach has gone a long way, as this is the distillery's flagship product.

It pours as a mid-amber colored whiskey.

The nose sits squarely in the middle of the traditional bourbon profile. It has a candy corn and vanilla scent, underscored with graham crackers and a trace of oak. I've also found Woodford Reserve to have a rather boozy scent for a 90-proof whiskey, although it's not hot in any way.

This light-bodied, flavorful bourbon tastes of vanilla, sweet corn, and orange zest in the main, with a hint of cinnamon and oak. The finish starts off peppery, before turning to earthy oak and drying tobacco leaf.

Beyond being a nice dram in its own right, what makes it noteworthy is the example it provides. The bourbon made at Woodford Reserve itself shares some characteristics in common with Old Forester, and the expression has a good deal of actual Old Forester in it. Yet if you try the two side by side, you'll notice the differences far more than the similarities.

WOODFORD RESERVE DOUBLE OAKED
STRAIGHT BOURBON WHISKEY

90.4 When it was first introduced in 2012, Double Oaked was a noteworthy release for two reasons. First, for a decade and a half the brand's regular lineup had consisted solely of Distiller's Select, and this was the first permanent addition. More importantly, it was the first double-barreled bourbon, a whiskey finished in new white oak barrels, of the modern era.

Bottled at the same proof as Distiller's Select, it has a deeper, darker coppery color, reflecting the extra new oak aging.

On the nose, the extra oak finishing comes across in the smooth scent of honey-sweet caramel, with earthy and woody notes resting just beneath.

The woody quality of the bourbon comes forward more strongly on the palate, still blending in fully with the sweet caramel candy flavor. It's a bit leathery, with a hint of raisins. Notably absent from both the nose and the palate is even the slightest hint of char smoke. The finish is smooth, mellow, and understated, with a lingering touch of earthy leather.

Elizabeth McCall

Perhaps it's a sign of the times that one rarely meets a Gen Xer or Millennial making American whiskey who says, "Yes, my family worked in the business and I wanted to do that too, so I went to school and studied chemistry so I could get into fermentation and distilling." They usually follow a much more roundabout path. Elizabeth McCall is a good example. The Kentucky bourbon industry is the only work she's done since graduating from college, but if you had met her on the University of Louisville campus in 2005, you probably would not have guessed her career trajectory.

McCall's mother was in the business for a time from the late 1970s to early 1980s, managing bottling at what is now MGP. Elizabeth enrolled at the University of Louisville in 2004, and came out the other side with a BA in psychology and an M.Ed in counseling in 2009. From there, she went almost straight to work for Brown-Forman, taking a post as a sensory technician. Insofar as making the transition from psychology to whiskey, the lesson seems to be science is science. "The research methodology, statistical analysis, and the human interaction piece to each is what makes someone with a psychology background a good fit for sensory work," says McCall.

Mastering the skill of picking out defects in the company's products fostered a curiosity of how those defects arose in the first place. Following that curiosity in its turn led her to becoming master taster at Woodford Reserve in 2016 and then assistant master distiller in 2018.

Becoming Chris Morris's deputy at Woodford Reserve means that McCall has implemented the experimentation found in the Distillery Series and the Master's Collection to ensure the quality of Woodford's regular expressions. One of the personal projects she has undertaken delves into heirloom and exotic grains and terroir; she has had a bourbon made using red corn grown on a farm near the Woodford Reserve property (McCall says she even rode on the combine while it was being harvested). This whiskey is currently resting in a Brown-Forman warehouse, waiting for a future Master's Collection or Distillery Series release.

Something that will reach bottling sooner is an accident McCall has been keeping an eye on since 2012. That was when some of the grain recipe used to make a Master's Collection whiskey carried over into a regular production batch of Woodford Reserve that immediately followed. "It was my job to understand how many batches were impacted by the carryover character from the Master's Collection batch," says McCall. Now she will continue to monitor it, working with Morris to turn it into a happy accident. For now, she says that mistake is delicious.

WOODFORD RESERVE MASTER'S COLLECTION

The Master's Collection is an annual series of releases, each being a unique, one-shot whiskey made at Woodford Reserve. It was launched in 2006, with a four-grain whiskey (and keep in mind that was before craft distillers started their own work with four-grain whiskeys). In this respect it is similar to the Parker's Heritage series from Heaven Hill, except sometimes Parker's Heritage releases some well-chosen, middle-aged but otherwise normal bourbon. Until this year, everything from the often overlooked Master's Collection represents interesting tweaks in making the whiskey.

The Master's Collection had a landmark year in 2018, because it saw three separate releases instead of just one. First was the Batch Proof Bourbon, which was a cask-strength release of normal Woodford Reserve. Later in the year came a pair of additional Master's Collection releases, the Select American Oak and Oat Grain Bourbons. The former was aged in oak harvested from the Ozarks, while the latter is a four-grain bourbon with oats added to the traditional Woodford Reserve/Old Forester mash bill, while cutting back on the rye content.

WOODFORD RESERVE STRAIGHT MALT WHISKEY

90.4

This straight malt whiskey is Woodford's fourth and most recent brand extension, one building on the limited-edition malt whiskeys that came out in their Master's Collection and Distillery Series. I wonder what took them so long; having a set of triple, Irish-style copper pot stills practically screams for a regular malt whiskey release.

It's made with 51% malted barley, 47% corn, and 2% rye, so it's not a single malt. The mash bill is just equal to the legal minimum requirement of malt content.

A pour of this is on the line between dulled gold and light amber. A swish of the glass leaves behind a curtain of skinny tears.

The scent is like a caramel-coated nut and apple bar, sweetened with a little brown sugar and a tinge of cocoa.

The fruity side comes forward in the flavor, with apples and cherries riding over the notes of caramel and nuts. After opening with this sweet profile, a dry peppermint note rises up, serving as a nice complement. The finish starts out light and fruity, but this evaporates quickly, leaving a dot of spicy mint behind.

ERSARY
2016
Y-52
BOURBON WHIS
RC 53 6
FILL DATE
LOT NO
DISTILLERY
WOODFORD RESERVE DIS
DSP-KY-52
BOURBO
RC 53
CHINKAP
FILL DATE 06

BOURBON WHISKEY

RC 53 G

04-114

FILL DATE   17 D

LOT NO

WOODFORD RESERVE DISTILLERY

DSP-KY-52

BOURBON WHISKEY

RC 5

CHINKAPIN

FILL DATE   06 16

OT NO   16

90.4

Woodford's third regular release whiskey was, like their later malt whiskey, built on experience from previous limited editions. It's a Kentucky-style rye, made with 53% rye content (just over the minimum requirement), plus 33% corn and 14% malted barley.

It's a light copper whiskey, with a nose that is just as light, teasingly so, in fact.

It takes some direct nosing to take its measure, but the rye spice, a little fruitiness in the form of Granny Smith apples, and some green oak are definitely there.

Once on your tongue, the rye spice turns more to pepper and hot cinnamon, and it's balanced out by apple and pear sweetness and vanilla. The finish, which is more pronounced than any part of the tasting experience before it, rolls off the pepper, before fading to apples and a trace of cocoa.

WOODFORD RESERVE FLAVOR PROFILES

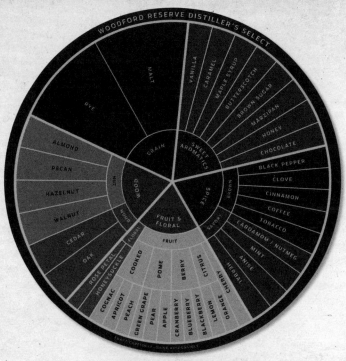

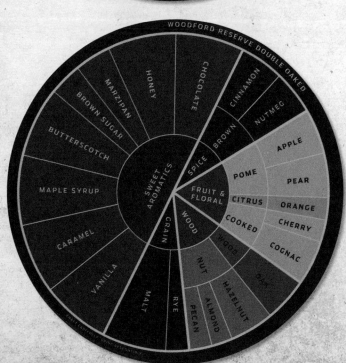

— DIAGEO —
(INCLUDES BULLEIT DISTILLING)

BLADE AND BOW STRAIGHT BOURBON WHISKEY

91 Two things set Diageo's sourced Blade and Bow Bourbon apart. One is the use of a solera system of five tiers. Batches are made by draining the oldest tiers, which are then refilled from the next oldest, and so on. The youngest tier is then refilled with new whiskey. Solera systems are used in making bourbon, but they remain uncommon. The other special part is that the solera was "charged" with 23-year-old bourbon from the Stitzel-Weller Distillery, birthplace of the famous Pappy Van Winkle Bourbon.

The nose is sweet with candy corn and pear, with a teaspoon of vanilla stirred in for good measure.

The taste follows very much from there, adding some light spices into the mix. The finish has a fruit candy character, with a touch of woodiness.

Bulleit Straight Bourbon Whiskey

90 Bulleit is a bourbon brand in transition. For many years the bourbon was sourced from Four Roses, albeit blending those bourbons in a way that made Bulleit quite distinct from Four Roses Yellow Label. In 2014, the demand for Four Roses prompted them to put Bulleit on notice that their supply contract would not be renewed, as Four Roses needed all of their production capacity for themselves. Bulleit's parent company, Diageo, eventually responded in 2017 by opening a distillery in Shelbyville, and at some point in the future what is in their bottles will come entirely from their in-house production.

In the glass, the liquid has a light amber, copper coloring.

The nose smacks of oaky vanilla and a teaspoon's worth of cinnamon, plus a light trace of charcoal that comes out if you take your time with it and let the liquid catch some air.

The flavor is light on the sweetness relative to the traditional bourbon flavor profile and balanced pretty evenly off a packet of cookie spices and dry wood. The latter note is something about Bulleit that always catches my attention: this high-rye bourbon brings more of the wood out than should be the case at this age. Basically, it's woodier than I expect something like this to be, and I'm not past studying that aspect as I sip on it. The finish is just spicy and dry enough to be a little rough, but only a little, the sort of thing that gives a bourbon character without denting its approachability.

My take on this one is that it, and not Basil Hayden, is what drinkers in search of a good, spicy bourbon should be buying.

Bulleit 95 Straight Rye Whiskey

90 Thanks to its extensive presence in sourced whiskey brands, MGP's 95% rye whiskey is ubiquitous on store and bar shelves. Among the plethora of brands using the same basic, Indiana-made rye whiskey stock, Bulleit is arguably the benchmark. I say that because, in my experience, it's the one with which the largest number of people are familiar.

The scent is sweet with a mix of red berries and vanilla, accented by spicy pipe tobacco.

Those aspects invert on the palate. A taste starts out with a current of spiciness, which then evolves into that spiced tobacco note from the nose, and then comes a rising tide of red berries and orange zest. The finish runs short, but spicy.

Bulleit 10-Year-Old Straight Bourbon Whiskey

91.2 This bourbon has a lighter look than I expect from a middle-aged whiskey, with a light amber coloring. Coating the glass yields skinny legs.

The nose is what I expect from an older bourbon with a higher (if not actually "high") rye content: spicy with cloves, cinnamon, anise, and a hint of dill; a dry, tea-tannin note; and a current of barrel-driven caramel around the edges.

A sip shows the flavor follows pretty directly from there: spices, dry pepper, a little vanilla sweetness, and a touch of barrel char. The finish runs with dry pepper and barrel char.

What the additional aging does to the old Bulleit profile is bring the barrel char out more, enhancing it by adding some dryness to the whiskey. So, if you like your bourbon with barrel char, this is a bottle to keep on your shelf.

— FOUR ROSES DISTILLERY —

Fans of Four Roses wax nerdy about the distillery's famous 10 recipes. However, it would be more accurate to describe it as five spins on two recipes. Four Roses has just two mash bills in use: a normal bourbon recipe of 75% corn, 20% rye, and 5% malted barley; and a high-rye recipe of 60% corn, 35% rye, and 5% malted barley. They apply five distinct strains of yeast in fermenting each of those two mashes, thus producing 10 separate whiskeys.

FOUR ROSES STRAIGHT BOURBON WHISKEY (YELLOW LABEL)

This is Four Roses' flagship bourbon, and is the only one that ever, though not always, blends together all 10 of those whiskeys.

On the nose, Yellow Label has a foundation of citrus blossoms and caramel, with a layer of crisp, green apples and pears lying on top.

Despite using one of the highest of high-rye bourbons around, the palate is soft and silky, and the flavors are balanced and not overtly spicy. Corn and citrus sweetness are supplemented by fruitcake spices and a dash of barrel char. It's on the finish that the high rye shows itself. It's a lingering conclusion, one that starts off fruity before turning to a light dusting of cake spices that take their time in fading away.

Four Roses Single Barrel Straight Bourbon Whiskey

100

Ostensibly, the single-barrel expression of Four Roses should grant access to a sample of each of those 10 bourbon recipes. In practice, this is only possible by seeking out private barrel bottlings. The normal single-barrel whiskey is from Four Roses' OBSV recipe, a 60% corn mash bill whiskey fermented with a yeast noted for being delicate and somewhat fruity, but also spicier. Four Roses Single Barrel starts by delivering on the OBSV bourbon's reputation.

The nose is light and airy, but nonetheless delivers the redolence of raisins, vanilla, and wildflowers with a soft but spicy current washing over them.

Taking a sip, however, delivers a crack of cookie spices up front. A second sip allows that spiciness to yield to sweeter flavors: cherries, peaches, and brown sugar seasoned with vanilla. A hint of oak makes itself felt on the back end. From there, the whiskey winds down on notes of peppermint and earthy cocoa.

Four Roses Small Batch Limited Edition Straight Bourbon Whiskey

105+

Like the regular small batch, this annual limited-edition version is made by blending four of the distillery's 10 recipes. The difference is that the stock chosen is rarified. The 2018 installment, which also honored the 130th anniversary of the brand, was made with a 10-year-old OBSV (30%), a 13-year-old OBSF recipe (40%), a 14-year-old OESV (20%), and a 16-year-old OESK (10%).

Another difference between the normal small batch and the limited edition is that the latter is bottled at cask strength. This is not the rocket fuel that some cask-strength bottlings can be, however. Four Roses Small Batch Limited Edi-tion usually comes in the 105- to 110-proof range, and if it is higher than 110, it is not much higher (2016's was 111.2 proof).

Single barrels and many of these annual limited-edition whiskeys aren't noted for their rigid consistency. Instead, their flavor profile sits on a spectrum, with some differences between individual batches or barrels.

With Four Roses Small Batch Limited Edition, I've found the palette of recipes and ages that Brent Elliott, the master distiller, and his team can draw upon widens that spectrum quite a bit, so much so that no example is typical of the whole. It's a reliably good bourbon, but each year should be taken as a creature entirely unto its own.

Four Roses Small Batch Straight Bourbon Whiskey

90 This small-batch bourbon is made with four of the 10 Four Roses recipes, but those four draw from both the normal and the high-rye mash bills. The proportions used from those four recipes aren't known, but the object is to achieve a consistent flavor profile in any case. The barrels chosen are usually six or seven years old.

Taking a sniff shows a light, airy scent with a foundation of caramel with a decent sprinkling of winter spices and a lighter dusting of orange zest.

The palate proves more substantial than the nose, with a buttery mouthfeel and the same foundation of caramel. Over the top are the familiar winter spices, now joined by orange blossom honey, cherries, and barrel char. The winter spices come forward on the finish, which runs long and deep. At the start, the notes of fruit and barrel char are there, but these fade away, leaving a warm, spicy glow.

FOUR ROSES SMALL BATCH SELECT

In 2019, Four Roses made their first brand extension in twelve years by adding Small Batch Select. This latest bourbon draws on six of Four Roses' famous ten recipes: OBSV, OBSK, OBSF, OESV, OESK, and OESF. What makes that recipe special is how those choices mark this as the first bourbon to prominently feature Four Roses "F" yeast. Each source of stock is at least six years old, and the Small Batch is bottled unfiltered. As for why all that makes this a "select" whiskey, compare notes with the previously described Small Batch.

The whiskey takes on a dulled copper look in the glass, perhaps because the higher proof and absence of chill filtration have made it a viscous liquid.

The nose here is a strong one, loaded up with cinnamon graham crackers and ginger, plus citrus blossoms, and a hint of dill, with dry, toasty wood coming up from the bottom.

The flavor is less complex than the nose. Instead, a sip of Small Batch Select is more in tune with the typical and expected bourbon flavor profile, albeit that of a full-bodied, spicy bourbon. Elements of brown sugar and vanilla were strongly accented by ginger and that dry, toasty oak that wafted up in the nose. That carried over into a dry, toasty finish. If you want your bourbon rich and spicy, this one is a desirable choice.

— HARTFIELD & COMPANY —

Located in bucolic Paris, Kentucky, Hartfield & Company is a nano-distillery whose main claim to fame is "bringing bourbon back to Bourbon County," as they are the first distillery to operate in that famed region since 1919.

HARTFIELD & COMPANY BOURBON WHISKEY

100 Hartfield's standard bourbon uses a high-malt mash bill of 62% corn, 19% rye, and 19% malted barley. Whereas malt is typically used in American whiskey for the sole purpose of introducing the enzymes needed to convert grain starch to sugar, which is then fermented, Hartfield has upped the malt to make it a full-fledged flavoring element in their whiskey. Consequently, they distill to 115 to 120 proof, so as to retain more of the oils and other compounds coming from that high-malt mash. They aged this whiskey in char #3, 5.8-gallon barrels made in Minnesota, noted for their tight-grained oak.

It is a slightly dark, syrupy amber in the glass.

The nose shows that it's a young, small-barrel whiskey for sure, with some corn huskiness and woodiness, and running a touch hot.

The flavor is where things turn around and defy expectations. Predominately vanilla and cookie spice sweet, the bourbon has a tasty current of toasted popcorn, cooked just a hair too much, which gives the whiskey a smoky element that isn't anything like barrel char. At the same time, that smoky trace isn't overpowering like some of the smoked craft whiskeys I've tasted. This flavor profile comes out of the boosted malt count, and makes it quite distinct from other small-barrel craft bourbons. From there the finish is a touch spicy, but in a mellow way, and leaves only light warmth.

Overall, Hartfield's bourbon makes for a nice little sipper: simple, but interesting too.

— HEAVEN HILL DISTILLERY —
(BERNHEIM FACILITY)

BERNHEIM ORIGINAL 7-YEAR-OLD STRAIGHT WHEAT WHISKEY

90 When it was first introduced in 2005, Bernheim Wheat Whiskey was the only wheat whiskey in existence, making it quite an odd duck. Within a few years, several others had joined the ranks, but these were either produced by craft distillers or sourced from MGP stock. Bernheim remains the only wheat whiskey produced by a big distiller. To help it retain its unique status, the distillery added an age statement in 2014, at a time when age statements began disappearing from labels left and right.

Bernheim follows the Kentucky rye pattern to produce this whiskey, using just enough of the primary grain to qualify and putting a hefty amount of corn behind it. The mash bill is 51% winter wheat, 39% corn, and 10% malted barley.

Bernheim is in the vein of wheated bourbons, which are famous for their soft, fruitier character. Bernheim heads even farther in this direction.

A sniff of this whiskey is like sitting in a blooming cherry orchard while nipping at toasted wheat bread blanketed with cherry jam.

The liquid feels weighty on the tongue, and the flavor is very much in line with the nose—until the barrel aging makes its presence known. There is a solid current of vanilla and just a pinch of barrel char. Comparing my experience with the seven-year-old version to the notes I made when I tried the no-age-statement predecessor, I think both of these elements are now stronger. A finish of middling length carries out the candied fruit quality before fading to nuttiness.

ELIJAH CRAIG SMALL BATCH STRAIGHT WHISKEY

94 Launched in 1986, Elijah Craig was one of the premium bourbon expressions that laid the foundation for the modern resurgence of American whiskey. It came a couple years after Blanton's Single Barrel was introduced, and six years before the Jim Beam Small Batch

Collection. It's also a recent casualty of the no-age-statement trend, having lost its age statement in 2016. It's now described as an eight- to 12-year-old whiskey with a mash bill of 78% corn, 12% rye, and 10% malted barley.

The scent on the somewhat younger Elijah Craig hasn't shifted all that much: it still resides in that classic bourbon territory of vanilla and caramel, with a wash of toasted oak and nuts.

It has a light feel on the palate and a flavor profile very much in tune with its nose: vanilla and candy sweet with a current of dry oak and nuts. The finish turns a little spicy with a tinge of cinnamon, and while it is just a light jacket to warm you, it lasts for a good spell.

Elijah Craig Barrel Proof Straight Whiskey

In much the same way that the high-octane Knob Creek Single Barrel offers those who miss the original Knob Creek a way to fill that hole, Elijah Craig Barrel Proof is one way to get at the original Elijah Craig 12-Year-Old. It's still bottled with the 12-year-old age statement, so one can either imbibe it at the bracing cask-strength level (the expression sometimes clocks in at over 130 proof), or add a splash of water and bring it down to something like 94 proof. Given that this dram is often at least a little hot, some water isn't a bad idea.

For a middle-aged, cask-strength whiskey, the bourbon is not as dark in the glass as I would expect. It has a coppery look, and a swish leaves bands of tiny legs rolling down the glass.

The scent is one of spice and cedar, with a note of wet char and just a hint of vanilla-soaked sweetness. I also felt it was a little hot, so in went some water. That raises still more char, as well as additional vanilla. In other words: absolutely, splash this whiskey with water.

After that start, the flavor is a sea change. The light and creamy mouthfeel give way to brown sugar and vanilla—the sweet side of bourbon became ascendant—with notes of spicy rye, wood spice, and a sliver of cedar. The finish is modest after that one-two punch, bearing just a bit of spice.

Elijah Craig 18-Year-Old Single Barrel Straight Bourbon Whiskey

90

The Elijah Craig brand first added its 18-Year-Old Single Barrel Bourbon in 1994, at a time when there was no Woodford Reserve, and the Jim Beam Small Batch Collection was still a novelty. Regular production stopped in 2012, although a fresh batch was released in 2015. At the time, Heaven Hill said they were bringing the 18-Year-Old back on a "limited basis," implying that there will be future, periodic releases of the expression.

The 18 is a favorite among bourbon enthusiasts, and especially Elijah Craig die-hards, in large part because it's an ultra-aged bourbon that isn't aged to the point that it becomes unduly oaky. The relationship the 18-Year-Old has to its younger and older siblings is similar to the way some view Pappy Van Winkle 15-Year-Old within its lineup: it occupies the sweet spot of being more than merely mature whiskey, but not too old. Just because this whiskey is frequently described as not too oaky doesn't mean that the barrel doesn't loom large.

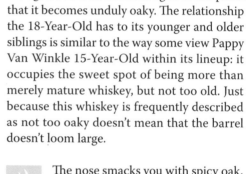

The nose smacks you with spicy oak, but not so much that the honey and candy corn sweetness and notes of cherries and blackberries are drowned out.

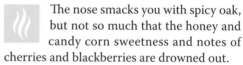

On the palate, the vanilla and caramel, which were faint in the nose, come to the front and further moderate that bitter and spicy oakiness. The result is a sophisticated, well-balanced shot of bourbon, as much fruity sweet as candy sweet, and as sweet as it is tannic and spicy. The former aspects soften the finish, at least at first. As it unwinds, the bourbon turns spicy before finally fading to leave some musty, hoary old oak on the tongue.

Elijah Craig 23-Year-Old Single Barrel Straight Bourbon Whiskey

90 The oldest Elijah Craig yet (although not the oldest bourbon from Heaven Hill) is their 23-Year-Old, with batches released in 2014 and 2015. This single barrel is considered a periodic release.

Compared to its younger siblings—the 18-Year-Old and the one-shot releases of 20- and 21-Year-Old Elijah Craig—the 23-Year-Old is a very woody whiskey.

The nose is like a trip through a furniture maker's lumberyard, coming at you with not just oak, but also mahogany and even a little cedar. A bit of cherry and apricot lurk in the background, but they are not easy to find amid all that woodiness.

It takes a sip, though, to tell you just what an oaky, barrel-driven beastie you've got in your glass. The bourbon is dry, tannic, leathery, and oaky, with just hints of brown sugar and vanilla present, mostly to remind you of what the whiskey once was. The oak only lets go in the finish, which isn't as dry, bitter, and spicy as the experience thus far would lead one to expect. In the end, the woodiness takes on a toasted oak and roasted nuts aspect, and the leathery quality is joined by a bit of tobacco.

Some bourbon fans adore very old, very oaky whiskey, and there are plenty of others who are focused only on the age statement. Then there are those (and I count myself as one of them) who think a whiskey like this is too old and too oaky. I think it says a lot, and does not speak kindly, when a 90-proof bourbon needs a splash of water to bring the best out in it, as Elijah Craig 23 does in my experience.

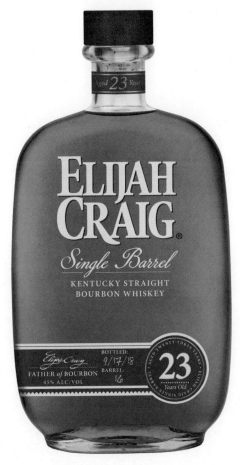

Bourbon Heritage Center

Heaven Hill built a new, lavish welcome center at its Bardstown location. The gleaming glass, steel, and oak building is a veritable Taj Mahal. At the new center, an immensely informative (even for the moderately knowledgeable) self-guided tour not only tells you about Heaven Hill, Elijah Craig, Evan Williams, and others, but also about bourbon in general. The center also offers two distinct experiences. The Mashbill Tour takes visitors on a tour of warehouse "Y," explains how bourbon is made, and ends with a tasting of three whiskeys. The Connoisseur Tour is a more in-depth tasting experience, shepherding visitors across four whiskeys.

Several times a year the center offers special events, tastings of new releases, book signings, and talks. So be sure to keep tabs on them!

Evan Williams Bottled in Bond
Straight Bourbon Whiskey (White Label)

Heaven Hill introduced "Evan White," the bottled in bond version of their staple bourbon, in 2012. Compared to the Evan Williams Black Label, the core and standard expression, this is much stronger, but also a bit younger. Despite the lack of an age statement, it's known that Evan Williams Bonded is a five-year-old bourbon.

It is a sugarloaf on the nose, full of caramel, vanilla, and candy corn, with a dash of ginger. Noticeable by its absence is any trace of oak or barrel char.

The flavor follows from there: melted brown sugar and vanilla with a trace of hot cinnamon and pepper, just enough spice to make it interesting. It is only on the finish that some oakiness rears up, just a bit of dry wood stopping by to say hello.

Evan Williams Single Barrel
Straight Bourbon Whiskey

Every year, the master distiller at Heaven Hill picks out the barrels to be bottled for this series. Although there is no fixed age statement, the bottles bear a date of distillation and a date of bottling, so you can easily do the math and determine the age. In my experience, the vintages typically range from eight to 10 years.

Of course, the thing about single-barrel expressions (and single barrels with variable aging periods in particular) is that they are all at least a little different. This is what I noted the last time I took in a pour of Evan Williams Single Barrel:

It is sweet on the nose, with the expected bursts of corn and vanilla, but a trace of butterscotch and an accent of oak add some welcome intrigue.

The taste starts with more sweet corn and vanilla and carries a hint of oakiness, followed by a rising note of cinnamon that eventually comes to share center stage. That cinnamon spiciness runs into the finish before it dissolves and leaves behind a touch of orange zest.

Evan
Williams
Bourbon
EXPERIENCE®
D.S.P. KY-1
C
Bourbon Whiskey
Serial NO. 1
O.E.D. November 14, 2013
Sour Mash
R.C. 53G.

Evan Williams Straight Bourbon Whiskey (Black Label)

This whiskey is the standard-bearer for Heaven Hill, and is the second best-selling brand of bourbon around, after Jim Beam White Label. Knowing that, a little comparison of the hard numbers is in order. The two are made from very similar mash bills (Beam is 77% corn and Evan Williams is 78% corn), and both whiskeys enter the barrel at 125 proof, whereupon Beam receives approximately four to six years of aging and Evan four to seven.

There are two main differences in production. First, Evan is stored in barrels featuring a #3 char and Beam in barrels with the deeper #4 char. Second, Beam is bottled at 80 proof, and Evan is bottled at 86 proof.

86

The color is light amber, like a coppery honey.

The scent features elements of corn- and citrus-based sweetness, with a hint of vanilla and dashes of rye spice and cinnamon.

On the palate, the bourbon has an unremarkable feel, neither thick nor thin. A solid current of oak kick-starts the taste, with a layer of that corn and citrus sweetness lying underneath. A pinch of rye spice emerges in the middle, along with a trace of oak. The finish is lightly sweet, with a moderately warm and mid-length run.

Fighting Cock Straight Bourbon Whiskey

Another casualty of the modern boom, Fighting Cock used to be a six-year-old bourbon, but since 2015 it's been a no-age-statement whiskey. It continues to be the go-to bourbon for Heaven Hill fans who want something that is stronger while still at a reasonable price point.

103

Despite being a high-octane bourbon, it has a copper, as opposed to amber, color in the glass.

The scent is quite fruity, with banana and vanilla sitting on top of a less distinct sweetness, accented by a traces of nuttiness and oakiness.

The flavor is what you would expect after such a whiff: banana-forward, fruity sweetness seasoned with vanilla, plus a touch of dry wood that turns into peppery spice on the back end. The finish continues on that peppery note, which fades with warmth until a note of leathery oak lingers on the tongue.

Henry McKenna 10-Year-Old
Single Barrel Bourbon Whiskey

This expression has gone from being the sleeper in Heaven Hill's lineup to "if you see it, buy it" status. And with good reason. After the company took Elijah Craig from a 12-year-old to a no-age-statement bourbon, this became the go-to for those who wanted something approximating the old version of Elijah Craig, both in terms of flavor profile and price. Furthermore, there were always those that preferred Henry McKenna 10, happily trading the couple of years for the double pluses of it being both single barrel and bottled in bond. My experience is that although it is increasingly scarce on store shelves, it's usually still at a normal retail price when you do find it.

McKenna 10 is made with Heaven Hill's standard bourbon mash bill, with 78% corn.

100

Amber in appearance, it drops a coat of long legs in the glass, which will cling for as long as you care to look at them.

The nose is exactly as I would expect, given its pedigree and age: sweet corn, vanilla, and caramel resting on a platter of oak.

On the palate, it's a barrel-forward bourbon, but not a barrel-dominant one. The vanilla and oak are front and center from the first sip. Upon taking another taste, melted brown sugar, a spoonful of gingerbread spices, and a drizzle of caramel syrup come into the picture, creating a thoroughly balanced drink. The finish runs for a middling length of time, starting sweet and turning spicy, dry, and a little oaky before ultimately resolving in a hint of leather.

Larceny Straight Small Batch Bourbon Whiskey

92 Most of the bourbons from Heaven Hill are based on their 78% corn, 12% rye, and 10% malted barley mash bill, which is a very traditional bourbon recipe. However, Heaven Hill also makes wheated bourbons. In 2018, the company revamped its other wheated bourbon brand, Old Fitzgerald, to favor a biannual, limited-edition series of middle-aged, bottled in bond bourbons. That left Larceny as the unquestioned standard-bearer of the distillery's wheated bourbons.

Heaven Hill's wheated bourbon recipe is 68% corn, 20% wheat, and 12% malted barley. Beyond the altered mash bill, the production process behind Larceny is similar to other Heaven Hill bourbons: the proof upon entering the barrel is 125, and that barrel is charred to #3.

This is one of those bourbons that straddle the line between copper and gold in the glass.

The nose smacks of freshly baked banana bread with a pinch of cinnamon and a teaspoon of vanilla stirred into the batter, plus hints of oak and sweet leaf tobacco.

The flavor is sweeter, with more vanilla and the floral, citrusy note wheated bourbons often have. Cookie spices rise up behind this front, ultimately turning the bourbon a little dry and oaky before it sprints to a short, simple finish.

Mellow Corn Bottled in Bond Straight Corn Whiskey

100 For a long time, this expression was the only aged corn whiskey available, to say nothing of its rare status as a bottled in bond corn whiskey. Other expressions on the market were either aged in charred new oak, as Tennessee whiskey is, or had a corn content below the 80% threshold, such as Early Times. Mellow Corn is right on the line, at 80% corn, 12% rye, and 8% malted barley. Corn whiskeys can be aged in either used or new, but uncharred, barrels; Heaven Hill chose used barrels for Mellow Corn, which makes sense given all the bourbon and rye that they produce.

The nose has plenty of candy corn, with light brushings of vanilla and oak, as well as the vegetal traces of corn husk that almost always accompany corn whiskey. The main thing about Mellow Corn's scent is how restrained both the corn husk and barrel flavors are. That is the whiskey living up to its name, since that corn husk element is usually the harshest part in an unaged corn whiskey.

That candy corn characteristic continues in the palate, which has a light mouthfeel. Modest notes of vanilla, roasted nuts, and oak round out the picture. The finish doubles down on the characteristic piece of the experience, offering one more burst of candy corn before dashing behind the curtain.

OLD FITZGERALD BOTTLED–IN–BOND
STRAIGHT BOURBON WHISKEY

In 2018, Heaven Hill revamped Old Fitzgerald Bottled in Bond, shifting it from a regular release bourbon into a biannual, limited-edition series. While it remains a wheated bourbon and a bottled in bond release, each batch is now a one-shot affair that comes out in the spring and autumn, featuring age statements (four is the minimum for bottled in bond designations, but Old Fitz releases are always much higher than that). The most recent Old Fitzgerald available at the time of writing was the Fall 2021 release, which was an 11-year-old.

The color was bronze.

The scent was not floral, in the way that so many wheated bourbons are, but herbal, spicy, and earthy, showing a good deal more maturity than its middle age might have suggested. Seasoned with cinnamon, ginger, and peppermint, with a sweet side like an ultra-dark, cocoa-rich chocolate bar with a thick caramel center balancing that out.

The palate developed out of that profile, adding a dry, woody layer into the candy bar. It is only on the finish that any fruity, floral character comes out in the bourbon, but even that is subdued placed next to its dry, earthy qualities.

Parker's Heritage Collection

This annual series of limited-edition whiskeys was started in 2007 by then-master distiller Parker Beam, who passed away in 2017. It is in the middle of the pack when it comes to annual, limited-edition releases: while popular, it is not quite as sought after by bottle hunters as Pappy Van Winkle or Buffalo Trace Antique Collection. The series is also one of the most varied in its class, and although it is a good bet that the coming year will bring enthusiasts a bottling of well-matured bourbon drawn from honey barrels, it is far from certain in this series.

Most of the releases have been bottlings of 10- or 11-year-old bourbon, carefully selected and given some special spin such as cask strength, single barrel, or a barrel finish (Cognac and Curaçao thus far). Other bourbons in the series have been ultra-aged, such as the 2008 release of a 27-year-old bourbon and a 24-year-old in 2016, which was also bottled in bond. Sometimes Parker's Heritage releases unique examples of other whiskeys made at Heaven Hill, such as 2014's 13-year-old wheat whiskey (the oldest wheat whiskey released in modern times) and 2015's American Malt. In recent years, Parker's Heritage has been exploring how its whiskeys turn out after aging in extra heavily charred oak barrels, with the 2021 release being the 11-year-old Heavy Char Wheat Whiskey.

Most of the releases have been bottlings of 10- or 11-year-old bourbon, carefully selected and given some special spin such as cask strength, single barrel, or a barrel finish (Cognac and Curaçao thus far). Other bourbons in the series have been ultra-aged, such as 2008's release of a 27-year-old bourbon and a 24-year-old in 2016, which was also bottled in bond. Sometimes Parker's Heritage releases unique examples of other whiskeys made at Heaven Hill, such as 2014's 13-year-old wheat whiskey (the oldest wheat whiskey released in modern times) and 2015's American Malt. Thus far, Parker's Heritage has not ventured into Heaven Hill's stocks of rye and corn whiskey, but that is likely only a matter of time.

122

The look of a pour of this Parker's has a bright, clear amber coloring.

The smell is a near-perfect balance of ginger, spearmint, and honey on the one hand, and oaky spices on the other. The scent was too rich and heavy to be described as subtle, but in reality, all that really means is you don't need to chase anything when you nose the whiskey. Instead, this lovely scent comes to you with its hand out, ready to give you a shake.

The taste expanded on the nose, becoming a thing of sweet, herbal, earthy, and woody beauty. The elements from the nose—sweet honey, spearmint and ginger, oaky allspice—were joined by a current that I think is best described as half-dried, still pretty green tobacco leaf drying in a barn with a damp clay floor. That new note was just too earthy to really be called tobacco, but it certainly has certain of those aspects to it. The finish closed with the woody spices in ascendance. I adored Parker's Heritage 2021, very nearly naming it my best new whiskey of the year. It stands as a marvelous example of what middle-aged wheat whiskey and heavily charred barrel aging can do. The taste expanded on the nose, becoming a thing of sweet, herbal, earthy, and woody beauty. The elements from the nose—sweet honey, spearmint and ginger, oaky allspice—were joined by a current that I think is best described as half-dried, still pretty green tobacco leaf drying in a barn with a damp clay floor. That new note was just too earthy to really be called tobacco, but it certainly has certain of those aspects to it. The finish closed with the woody spices in ascendance. I adored Parker's Heritage 2021, very nearly naming it my best new whiskey of the year. It stands as a marvelous example of what middle-aged wheat whiskey and heavily charred barrel aging can do.

PIKESVILLE STRAIGHT RYE WHISKEY

110 A revival of the last brand of Maryland rye whiskey to go under, with the distillery closing in the 1970s and the brand soldiering on using whiskey that had already been barreled for a while after that. The Maryland style bridged the gap between the bold spice available in Pennsylvania ryes and the just-barely-qualifies approach ryes receive in Kentucky, but Pikesville is made using Heaven Hill's only rye recipe: 51% rye, 35% corn, and 14% malted barley. What separates Pikesville from Rittenhouse Rye (see below) is its potency and age, as Pikesville is approximately six years old.

It's an assertive take on Kentucky rye, and it looks it. Most ryes tend to be copper, whereas this is not just amber, but a fairly dark red amber.

I found it just a touch boozy, as opposed to actually hot, on the nose. The scent is both sweet and spicy, with the sweet side showing some honey and red licorice with a little vanilla stirred in, and the spicy side featuring cloves, cinnamon, and rye grain.

The palate pretty much runs from there, with notes of cherry and apple also making an appearance. The sweet fruity quality continues into a long, contemplative landing, when it drains away to reveal a bed of dry oak.

RITTENHOUSE BOTTLED IN BOND RYE WHISKEY

100 Although this isn't the most basic version of Heaven Hill's rye whiskeys (there is an 80-proof version of Rittenhouse), I've found it's the most common on store and bar shelves, so I tend to think of this as their flagship rye.

It's a copper-colored whiskey.

The scent blends light rye bread and stone fruits with a bit of vanilla and baking spice.

The spiciness comes forward more on the palate, with pepper and baking spice climbing to stand on equal ground with the fruit and grain. The finish is signaled by a light, peachy note before turning to a trace of leathery oak.

— JAMES E. PEPPER DISTILLERY —

JAMES E. PEPPER 1776 STRAIGHT BOURBON WHISKEY

The James E. Pepper brand officially came home in January 2018, when the distillery fired up and started making whiskey. It occupies only part of the old Pepper plant in Lexington, sharing the space with bars, restaurants, a brewery, and even another distillery (Barrel House Distilling Co., which was the first tenant to move in amid the ruins, back in 2008). But it's there all the same. The whiskey they are making is described as mirroring the Pepper bourbon made before the closure of the distillery in the 1950s, but for now, what is in the bottle comes from MGP's high-rye stock.

Any fan of high-rye bourbon ought to appreciate this one, what with its whopping 38% rye content in the mash bill. In spite of those bold features, it's still quite approachable and doesn't lean quite as far into dry and spicy territory as some other high-rye bourbons do.

The nose is a little sweet and a little woody, seasoned with cookie spices, ginger, a little chili powder, and a drop or two of vanilla extract.

The flavor falls right in line, leaning just a smidge into dryness to produce a mild, easygoing, and balanced sip.

100 The Pepper Rye is also sourced from MGP, drawing on the prevalent 95% rye stock. It stands out in a crowded field of similar whiskeys, though, with its combination of reasonable pricing and bottling proof. With all the iterations of Indiana-made whiskey available on store and bar shelves today, this is one that has the attributes of a much-loved, go-to whiskey—quality, affordability, availability—pegged perfectly.

The nose is full-bodied pumpernickel with notes of dill and wood.

The flavor turns to a blend of clove, pepper, and allspice, a trio that's been sweetened by a dab of honey and dried out just slightly by the touch of the barrel.

Old Pepper Finest Oak Straight Rye Whiskey

110.7 While James E. Pepper is still years away from bottling the whiskey it produces, the company still has some surprises in store for us. Late in the summer of 2018, the company released Old Pepper Finest Kentucky Oak Straight Rye Whiskey, or Old Pepper FKO. It's another entry into the double-oaked category, meaning it has received a second round of maturation in new oak barrels. In this case, Pepper chose to heavily toast and then lightly char that second set of barrels.

In the glass, Old Pepper FKO has a murky, amber appearance. Swishing the glass left a sticky, thick coat that dropped a single, long tear.

It's an aromatic whiskey, but also a little hot, so I added a few drops of water. That toned down the alcohol and brought out the gingerbread, molasses, vanilla, and cedar hiding beneath all that heat. Behind this array are hints of toasty oak and pepper, lending a dry tinge to a thorough nosing of the whiskey.

The flavor is richly sweet, a certain product of the double barreling. Molasses, vanilla, and a touch of apricot flood the tongue initially, but eventually cede the stage to more modest notes of oak and pepper. After that, just a hint of barrel char rises on the back of the palate. With things turning tannic, the finish dawns spicy, appropriately enough. Initially that takes the form of fruit pie spices, but these slowly turn over to a lightly peppery conclusion.

— JEPTHA CREED DISTILLERY —

This distillery, located in plain view of I-64 outside Shelbyville, occupied a special spot for me for a few reasons long before I got hold of the late 2021 release of their bonded bourbon. They were the first new distillery I visited upon returning to the United States from my long sojourn abroad; they were among the first (and are engaged in a protracted argument over just who was the first distillery in America) to start using red, Bloody Butcher corn in their mash in modern times; and they are the only female-owned and -operated distillery in Kentucky.

JEPTHA CREED BOTTLED–IN–BOND RYE HEAVY BOURBON

As for their bonded bourbon, it is some delightfully good stuff, delivering on the bright promise of using something other than yellow or white or even blue corn to make bourbon. All that red corn is estate grain, grown on their own farmland within ten miles of the distillery. That mash is 75% Bloody Butcher corn, 20% malted rye, and 5% malted barley. The age on this bottle is the statutory minimum of four years.

On my nostrils, Jeptha's bonded bourbon smelled like licorice stick candy served on a platter of wet, unfired clay.

The flavor took an expected foundation—for a bourbon made with malted rye, rather than plain rye—of rich, earthy caramel and nutmeg, and sprinkled a punch of ash across the top. The finish ran on for a middling length of time, starting out with a run of the sweet side of oak (vanilla) before fading down to and out with the spicier, woodier, earthier side of oak. The surprise of this bourbon is its earthiness. That is a note I pin on the Bloody Butcher corn, and one that runs through the entire experience, but is always just a note and not an especially strong one. Even so, I had been wanting to see if Bloody Butcher corn could make a bigger deal than the more familiar blue corn, and with this expression I am beginning to think it might.

— KENTUCKY PEERLESS DISTILLING COMPANY —

Louisville's Kentucky Peerless Distilling Company is the story of a family with Kentucky whiskey business roots reviving another distillery shuttered by Prohibition. The original Peerless was located not in downtown Louisville, but in Henderson, a town down the Ohio River, about halfway between Louisville and the Mississippi.

PEERLESS STRAIGHT RYE WHISKEY

The new Peerless started distilling in 2015, and as soon as they had a batch of two-year-old whiskey in 2017, they released it as this rye.

The mash bill is undisclosed, but Peerless chose to go with a sweet-mash, rather than sour-mash process. Sour mash means a little of a previous batch's mash is held back and put into the next batch, a step that helps ensure consistency and controls the bacteria levels. A sweet mash starts over again every time. It's an uncommon choice, though far from a rare one.

This is a cask-strength whiskey, but because it's so youthful, the angel's share (what has evaporated) has little time to move the needle, and it comes out only slightly higher than the entry proof of 107.

The scent tells us a lot about the whiskey. It's too young to have much barrel on it, so the sweet corn and barest trace of corn husk tell us there is a generous helping of corn in the spirit. The spices are there, with anise, mint, and dill coming through clear, along with apple fruitiness, a modest note of vanilla, and a woodiness that is piney instead of oaky.

This is a high-octane whiskey, and it packs the flavors to match. It's much spicier on the palate than it is on the nose, with the initial spices joined by a peppery current. The sweet side of apples, sweet corn, and vanilla also wash over the tongue. However, it's also a touch hot, which isn't surprising for a two-year-old packing over 50% alcohol. The finish starts dry, but soon clears to a flavorless warmth.

MINOR CASE STRAIGHT RYE WHISKEY

90 Sometimes a whiskey-making family is so large that some members of the clan seek opportunities outside the distillery typically associated with them. This is especially true of the famed Beam family, who have had plenty of relations working outside of the family shop. In 2010, Steve and Paul Beam started Limestone Branch Distillery, and in 2017 they released a whiskey named for one of their illustrious forbearers, though you won't find their names on the dynastic list of master distillers at Jim Beam. Instead, Steve and Paul went all the way back to Minor Case Beam, their great grandfather, who got his start in the late 19th century making Early Times.

Minor Case is sourced from MGP, but it's not the usual 95% rye stock you've already read so much about. In 2013, MGP introduced several new whiskey recipes to their inventory. One of these was a Kentucky-style (51% rye, 45% corn, and 4% malted barley) rye whiskey. Limestone Branch acquired some of the 51% rye stock when it became available as a two-year-old whiskey, and finished it in Sherry casks from Meier's Winery for several months.

Despite the Sherry cask finish, it retains the copper coloring typical of rye whiskeys.

It's got a light, airy nose that starts with dried fruits and wildflowers before the spices and vanilla come forth.

The flavor opens with a layer of dried cherries and raisins, a healthy amount of brown sugar sprinkled on top, plus a pinch of light spice. As the spice fades away, the fruitiness turns drier, into something that is akin to Oloroso Sherry. The finish runs light, short, and sweet.

MINOR CASK

MADE · MARK

STRAIGHT
RYE WHISKEY
Sherry Cask
Finished

45% ALC/VOL

100 PERCENT
100% AMERICAN-GROWN HEARTLAND GRAINS

BOTTLED BY
LIMESTONE BRANCH DISTILLERY Co.
LEBANON, KENTUCKY

YELLOWSTONE SELECT STRAIGHT BOURBON WHISKEY

93 The Yellowstone brand is part of Steve and Paul Beam's heritage, since they are descended from Yellowstone creator J. B. Dant on their mother's side. Eventually, the brothers partnered with Luxco to bring Yellowstone back into the family.

In the near future, Yellowstone Select will incorporate the distillery's in-house bourbon. For the time being, it is a blend of two sourced, high-rye bourbons, one a four-year-old and the other a seven-year-old.

The scent on this one outstrips its age, with a mix of dried, tart apple slices resting on a foundation of hoary old oak. A sprinkling of black pepper sits right on the edge of the aroma.

A sip hits you with a creamy texture, and the flavor is of cocktail cherries and canned pears in syrup. But this sweetness is subsumed by rising layers of peppery spices, caramel, and oaky tannins. That spiciness and woodiness carry over into the finish, and linger for a good long while.

LUX ROW DISTILLERS

Both the Ezra Brooks and Rebel Yell brands are owned by Luxco, a company that has been in the business of sourcing and bottling alcoholic beverages for decades. Luxco opened a whiskey distillery in Bardstown in 2018, but it will be several years before their in-house whiskey is ready to replace sourced stock.

EZRA BROOKS STRAIGHT BOURBON WHISKEY

90 The Ezra Brooks brand was created in the late 1950s, with the intention of following the path Jack Daniel's had used to dominate the market, a legacy that continues in the square bottles and black labels that Ezra Brooks utilizes, as well as in the production process. Ezra Brooks is filtered through charcoal, but this is done after barrel aging. In Tennessee Whiskey, the charcoal filtration (always using sugar maple charcoal) is done before the whiskey is put into the barrel.

The nose sits comfortably inside the classic bourbon zone: sweet corn, vanilla, and a hint of toasted, nutty oak.

The taste follows accordingly, once again bringing on the sweet corn and vanilla, but with a fuller woody note. It's a mellow whiskey, so much so that its profile is unremarkable.

Sourced from MGP's popular 95% rye stock, Ezra Brooks put its characteristic spin on the familiar spirit to create something a little different than what you would expect. Like the Ezra Brooks bourbon, the rye has been filtered through charcoal after two years of barrel aging, which turns this youthful take into something almost bourbonesque.

This is a golden whiskey.

It presents a bed of wildflowers sprinkled with pepper, crushed vanilla beans, and citrus zest for its nose.

The charcoal mellowing is likely the reason that peppery quality is more subdued on the palate. It is quite barrel-forward with flavors of vanilla, caramel, and oak. The conclusion is clear and short, allowing you to sit and reflect upon the unexpected trip this young rye just took you on.

90

As mentioned on the facing page, Luxco sources the whiskey for its ryes from MGP's 95% rye stock. The important thing to realize about the numerous whiskeys sourced from that common stock is that they aren't necessarily alike by the time they get to the bottle. Some are aged on the bottler's site, not at MGP in Indiana. Some are older or younger. Some are stronger or weaker. This one is at least four years old, because the law says a straight whiskey less than four years old must have an age statement, and this doesn't.

The color is a light, bronzed amber.

The nose is floral with citrus and herbs, sweet and spicy with a hint of vanilla.

On the palate, it has a light texture but solid flavor, combining rye spice with vanilla-flavored sugar cookies. It goes down a little hot, the one time the youth of the spirit comes out, but that fades quickly, making for an undistinguished finish.

This take on the MGP rye produces a youthful whiskey, but a surprisingly nice, tasty one.

Rebel Yell 10-Year-Old Single Barrel Straight Bourbon Whiskey

This is the premium, annual, limited-edition offering of the Rebel Yell line. Although Rebel Yell is largely known for producing bottom-shelf standbys, this amazing stuff has attracted quite a following. It's presumably the same wheated bourbon stock used to make the two other Rebel Yell bourbons, except it's 10 years old and given a single-barrel spin. The source for that stock is assumed to be Heaven Hill, but when Luxco is asked, the answer has sometimes been "yes" and other times been "we can't say."

It has a look of rich yet light amber, with more gold and red in the mix than brown.

The nose has a strong current of caramel and vanilla, garnished with a woody nuttiness on one side and tobacco leaf on the other.

The flavor again leads with sweetness, candy corn, and vanilla with a floral aspect, before turning earthy and woody. The latter point is where the age really becomes evident, and it leads into a long, running finish that turns tannic.

Certainly the barrels chosen for Rebel Yell 10 are being bottled at just the right time: a few more years and they would likely be too oaky.

Rebel Yell Straight Bourbon Whiskey

80 From its very beginning, Rebel Yell has been a wheated bourbon, and so it remains to this day. As mentioned in the review for the Rebel Yell 10, what is currently in the bottles is said to be sourced from Heaven Hill.

What this bourbon really yells at you, once you pour it anyway, is its youth. In the glass, it has a light copper appearance that just barely scratches the bottom of the amber range.

The nose is light and dominated by a very sweet citrus and caramel scent, though it's not quite one-dimensional, as it has a leathery aspect as well. This is also a bit harsh, however.

The flavor is very straightforward, and dwells on the rough side of the core bourbon territory. It is corn-sweetened caramel and vanilla, with a little earthiness, but also a certain harshness. The finish is undistinguished, with the flavors evaporating rapidly to leave only a solid ball of warmth sitting in your center.

— MICHTER'S DISTILLERY —

MICHTER'S US*1 SMALL BATCH SOUR MASH WHISKEY

86 Michter's is a revival of an esteemed Pennsylvania whiskey brand that went defunct in the late 1980s, and one of the beloved creations of the original was the Sour Mash Whiskey. Then and now, it's called a sour-mash whiskey because it is indeed made using the sour-mash process, but from a mash bill lacking in a dominant grain. So it's not a bourbon, rye, or malt whiskey. It's not known what the modern version is made from, but the original was 50% corn plus loads of rye and a little malted barley, intentionally done to produce a not-quite-bourbon, high-rye whiskey.

It is caramel colored in the glass.

Its nose smacks of that coloring, coming on strong with caramel and vanilla syrup, poured thickly over nondescript fruits seasoned with a pinch of baking spices.

The palate is better defined, with the fruitiness turning to dried apricots, the baking spices gaining a larger foothold, and the caramel and vanilla changing over to crème brûlée. The finish turns boldly spicy over fast-fading traces of stone fruit, ultimately dissolving into a long-lasting afterglow.

MICHTER'S US*1 SINGLE BARREL
STRAIGHT RYE WHISKEY

84.8 This is a surprisingly robust whiskey for one bottled at just a little above the minimum strength.

It has an even and bright copper color in the bottle and glass.

The nose is packed with fruity, spicy rye notes and strongly belted with an earthy, artisan caramel candy quality, minus the saltiness.

The liquid has a creamy texture on the palate, but in contrast to the nose it delivers a more standard mix of rye flavors, albeit with a formidable woody twist. The taste is citrus and rye spice sweet, rolled up with a pinch of wet tobacco, and a distinctly dry and woody stripe running from start to finish. That finish is mild, but endowed with a lengthy, spicy afterglow.

Michter's US*1 Small Batch Straight Bourbon Whiskey

The company plays their contract production cards so close to the vest that there really isn't much to say about how this whiskey is made, other than it has the required 51% or greater corn content.

91.4

The color is full-on copper.

The nose is classic bourbon territory: sweet and a touch floral, a dollop of vanilla, a spoonful of butterscotch, and a burst of barrel char.

The flavor is quite creamy and thickly sweet, almost too syrupy with corn sweetness. Every decent bourbon needs a strong caramel current, and this one has it, rounded out with a dab of rye spice and a minor note of dry wood.

This isn't a complex bourbon, demanding an hour of study per dram. Instead, it's pleasant, easy drinking, and thoroughly approachable.

MICHTER'S US*1 SMALL BATCH UNBLENDED AMERICAN WHISKEY

83.4

Figuring out what goes into this expression is a popular game among whiskey nerds. The label refers to "bourbon-soaked barrels," a clear reference to the used bourbon barrels. The whiskey is "unblended," so there can't be any neutral grain spirits in the mix. Also, it may or may not have a dominant grain in the mash bill. So, it could be akin to Early Times (a bourbon mash bill aged in used barrels) or it could share the same roots as Michter's Sour Mash Whiskey, except aged in used barrels.

The liquid has a dark cast in the bottle, and retains it in the glass. Its amber runs far into the brown end of that spectrum, lending it the look of viscous iced tea.

The nose is a molasses-and-caramel bomb that is so thick, it almost physically sticks to your nostrils. Brushed on top of that shellac is a thin coat of timber and just a trace of ginger.

The flavor is just as sweet, think candy made from buckets of butterscotch and caramel with a handful of dried fruits thrown in. The spiciness starts soft before becoming more prominent than in the nose, and growing peppery over time. A current of toasty wood throughout keeps things from becoming too sugary. The finish is defined by a lingering vanilla aftertaste and the mildly prickly afterglow.

Michter's US*1 Toasted Barrel Finish Bourbon

91.4

Introduced in 2014, this bourbon is a limited-edition whiskey, but unlike some others, it is periodic rather than annual. Short supply halted production after the 2015 batch. Michter's brought it back in 2018, although at present it remains unclear if they have committed to putting the whiskey out annually.

Toasted Barrel is a double-oaked bourbon, made by taking Michter's standard bourbon and finishing it in barrels made from air-dried staves that are toasted rather than charred.

In the glass, the bourbon has a bright and clear amber appearance.

The floral nose carries a hefty dollop of sweet vanilla and caramel, placing it firmly within the oak-drawn flavors zone, but without being overtly woody.

The flavor has a distinctly candied character, like a whiskeyed candy corn, really. It is very caramel and corn sweet in a medium-light body. A tingle of cookie spice on the palate unrolls into the finish, which has a light but lasting touch.

MICHTER'S 10-YEAR-OLD SINGLE BARREL
STRAIGHT BOURBON WHISKEY

94.4 The 10-Year-Old Single Barrel Bourbon is one of three annual, limited editions released by Michter's, the others being a 10-year-old rye and a 20-year-old bourbon. Although they ostensibly come out every year, Michter's operates under the belief that no bourbon should be released before its time, a practice former master distiller Willie Pratt started and that his successor, Pam Heilmann, has continued. If the bourbon is deemed not quite there yet, they wait until it is. As such, this expression doesn't have a hard-and-fast release date. For example, the release of the 2015 installment was delayed, so it came out only four months before the 2016 edition.

In the glass, the color is a clear, coppery amber.

The nose is thick and sweet, a concoction of corn syrup heavily enriched with vanilla bean, plus pinches of cinnamon and clove, with a trickle of wet tobacco leaf running through it all.

On the tongue, the liquid is a bit lighter than the nose suggests, with a slick, almost slinky character. Caramel, orange cream, and now double pinches of cinnamon and clove lie at the core, fringed with traces of cedar. The finish starts off caramelized before turning dry and making a long run into some woody territory.

Michter's 10-Year-Old Single Barrel Straight Rye Whiskey

92.8 The other 10-year-old annual, limited-edition offering from Michter's is a rye whiskey, and of the two it's my favorite. Because Michter's is secretive about their sourcing/contract production, and their in-house whiskey is years away from being 10 years old, all the available data for this rye are on the label.

A pour of the 2017 iteration has that reddened copper look so common to aged rye whiskeys.

The scent contains brown sugar, vanilla, and baking spices, but there is also a current of dryness, more so than I recollected from previous installments of this expression. A little more nosing gives the impression of a toasty aspect, not entirely unlike barrel char meeting up with a large helping of wood-driven spice.

That richness follows into the palate. A smooth, creamy liquid, the whiskey is a full step further toward warm and dry than I thought it was in the past. That might not be indicative of the entire 2017 batch, but it certainly was for the bottle of this single-barrel release that I tasted. The flavor is filled with brown sugar and vanilla, which are met in the middle by spices that are equal measures grain- and wood-driven, and accented by a little toastiness and a little tobacco leaf.

NEWPORT KENTUCKY
NEWPORT, KENTUCKY
NEW RIFF DISTILLING, LLC
DSP-KY-20016
FILL DATE:
NEW RIFF DISTILLING,
DSP-KY-20016
FILL DATE:
NEWPORT KENTUCKY
NEWPORT KEN
NEW RIFF DISTILLING, LLC
NEW RIFF DISTILLING, LL

— NEW RIFF DISTILLING —

NEW RIFF BOTTLED IN
BOND BOURBON WHISKEY

100 When Newport's New Riff began operations in 2014, they turned out a batch of 65% corn, 30% rye, and 5% malted barley new make, barreled it, and settled in to wait. Four years later, the result was released, without chill filtration, as a bottled in bond bourbon. What is most interesting about how New Riff's first bourbon turned out is how different it is from other high-rye offerings.

The scent combines demerara sugar, vanilla, and butterscotch with a strong current of cinnamon and nutmeg.

The flavor moves a step forward in intensity while remaining quite smooth, with the sweet side staying just ahead of the spiciness. It's like a spicy herbal tea with a few cubes of the demerara and half a teaspoon of vanilla extract stirred in. The spice from the high-rye content kicks with full force at the finish, before eventually turning minty.

— OLD POGUE DISTILLERY —

OLD POGUE MASTER'S SELECT
STRAIGHT BOURBON WHISKEY

91 When the Pogue family decided to get back into the bourbon business in 2004, it was with this bourbon, made and aged under contract. The offering was well received, and was eventually distributed to 18 states and overseas. Unfortunately, as the Bourbon Boom began, sales soon outstripped supply. The limitations on Old Pogue's contract production meant they could only dump and bottle 20 to 30 barrels a year, and distribution has been contracted to the point that most of their whiskey is now sold out of the distillery.

Old Pogue opened their own distillery in 2012, and with it production expanded to support the dumping of 50 barrels per year. However, Master's Select is a nine-year-old bourbon, meaning the in-house whiskey won't be ready until 2021.

It has a nose of candy corn, red berries, honey, and vanilla, as well as a hovering note of juniper and spruce.

The flavor is less candied, but still lays on plenty of honey and vanilla, along with spearmint and a dash of pepper. The full flavor carries over into the finish, with the sweetness fading first, then the spices, and finally the wood until all that is left is a trace of dark, supple leather. It's not hard to see why people travel to Old Pogue to lay their cash on the counter and bring home a bottle: this is a flavorful, complex whiskey.

Whereas Old Pogue's bourbon is presently sourced, their rye whiskeys have always come out of their own distillery. Old Maysville Club is 100% malted rye whiskey, and an evolution of a previous brand, Five Fathers. Compared to Five Fathers, Old Maysville Club is two years older and bottled at a lower proof—100 instead of 110. The result is a much mellower whiskey.

In the glass, it cuts a very light amber look, like gold with a copper wash. That said, a swish puts a thick, sticky coating on the inside of the glass, one that drops heavy legs so reluctantly that it is more of a crown.

The nose is akin to toasted pumpernickel bread, with a whiff of the mustiness one would find in an old grain bin and a sweet, fruity note.

A sip grants a current of rye spiciness that is restrained by a wallop of toasty grain, with a nibble of dried apricot coming up at the end. The mouthfeel on this one, as suggested by the coat in the glass, is quite thick and oily. The finish is a touch spicy, but overall, it's a gentle and lasting experience.

— RABBIT HOLE DISTILLERY —

Rabbit Hole's distillery only became operational in 2018, and what is in their bottles at the time of writing was produced under contract by "an undisclosed distillery in northern Kentucky" that could only be New Riff Distilling in Newport. New Riff and Rabbit Hole share the same consulting Master Distiller, Larry Ebersold, formerly of MGP.

RABBIT HOLE STRAIGHT BOURBON WHISKEY

95 Rabbit Hole went with a four-grain mash bill that is self-consciously different from the norm in Kentucky, using 70% corn, 10% malted wheat, 10% malted barley, and 10% malted honey barley. Although there is no age statement, this is a five-year-old whiskey.

This bourbon has a clear, middling amber color in the glass, and absolutely runs with its legs after a swish.

The nose is very grain-forward and decidedly toasty, as one would expect with 30% malted grains in the mash bill. This is so much the case that I even picked up a note of dry grass on top of the toasted graininess. A current of vanilla runs underneath all that farmer's field scent.

The flavor is inside the profile of a spicy, peppery bourbon, which is odd considering that there is no rye in the mash bill and the whiskey is relatively young. Sweet corn meets with some vanilla and a note of sun-scorched grass, but right through the middle is a strong, spicy current. That fades rapidly, however, leaving the grassiness and a warm touch to wind it all down.

The Rabbit Hole Rye is a **95** 95% rye, 5% malted barley mash bill, just like what Larry Ebersold made when he was at MGP. But there is more to a whiskey than its mash bill. Anyone who has ever tasted several iterations of ryes sourced from MGP already knows that, and that just accounts for aging, blending, and bottling. Ever since I first came into contact with Rabbit Hole's rye, I've always been more taken with the differences than the similarities between its MGP-made cousins.

The look is similar enough, though. In the glass it has a light copper coloring with thick, healthy legs.

The nose has that classic cinnamon, licorice, and just very slightly peppery spiciness, with a bit of an earthy, woody note, much like an old log.

It has a light mouthfeel, and a flavor that is predominately dried fruit sweetness, supported by notes of caramel and a lighter spiciness than is present in the nose. The finish runs long and middling warm, with the spiciness fading into an herbal aftertaste.

Rabbit Hole Straight Bourbon Whiskey
Finished In PX Sherry Casks

93 This whiskey takes Rabbit Hole's bourbon and puts a Pedro Ximénez (PX) Sherry finish on it. Oloroso casks are usually more common for finishing whiskeys, as that type of Sherry is noted for its fruity and nutty flavors. PX Sherry is sweeter, but even darker. This is bottled at 93 proof.

This sherried bourbon has a medium amber color that is more coppery than red. A coating of the glass prompts plenty of thick tears to roll down the sides.

The Sherry cask sits on top of the nose of this whiskey, with the aromas of rich wine and raisins hitting my nose, and a trace of musty wood. The customary caramel becomes apparent only with air and study, and is attended by some cherry sweetness.

The flavor is like a handful of trail mix containing lots of raisins, dried cherries, and dried currants, with just a couple roasted almond slivers. As on the nose, there is a thick and dominant Sherry influence that elbows aside the native bourbon flavors, leaving just a note of vanilla. It's also just a touch oaky. The finish is light, with the slightest touch of dryness, and fades away quickly.

— SAZERAC —

(INCLUDES BARTON 1792 DISTILLERY AND BUFFALO TRACE DISTILLERY)

1792 SMALL BATCH STRAIGHT BOURBON WHISKEY

93.7 As a distillery, Barton 1792 is very much a throwback. The control panels for the equipment look cobbled together from components originating in different decades, and coal-burning boilers fire the stills. They make a number of whiskeys at Barton 1792, including Very Old Barton, but it's the 1792 brand that is currently the flagship. The mash bill is unknown, and it's a no-age-statement whiskey.

A pour is somewhere between gold and copper.

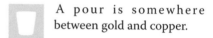

In terms of the tasting experience, this is a mature, straightforward bourbon, flavorful but uncomplicated. The scent carries a hefty load of caramel and vanilla, coated with rye spices and a trace of oakiness. Add some brown sugar to what's available on the nose and you've got the palate. Shift the emphasis to the rye spice, and you've got the finish.

80 This brand has been around since just after the Second World War, and for a long time it was the entry-level whiskey, and best seller, produced by the George T. Stagg Distillery, now known as Buffalo Trace. As recently as the early 1990s, Stagg was occasionally referred to as the Ancient Age Distillery.

Ancient Age is made from the distillery's #2 mash bill, which is the one with the higher rye content; however, neither bourbon mash bill at Buffalo Trace actually qualifies as a high-rye recipe in anyone's mind. As with pretty much everything in regular release that is made at the distillery, Ancient Age is aged in barrels with a #4 char.

That this is a young, straight bourbon is plain to the eye, as the coloring is a pale amber, golden with a little copper mixed in.

Keeping that in mind, the nose is surprisingly rich and floral, thick with corn sweetness and orange zest, with a teaspoon of vanilla added for good measure. From a sniffing point of view, this is actually quite a good bourbon.

On the palate, it veers back to meet expectations. The whiskey offers the core bourbon flavors—corn sweet, a little spice, caramel, vanilla—with a touch of dry wood, but the texture is much too thin to progress beyond these standards. Following that young and thin trend, the finish is nice and warm, but otherwise undistinguished.

BLANTON'S ORIGINAL SINGLE BARREL BOURBON WHISKEY

93 Introduced in 1984, Blanton's was the first step in bourbon's comeback from its nadir in the 1970s. Elmer T. Lee, the master distiller at what was then the George T. Stagg Distillery, noticed the growing popularity of single malt Scotch and decided that the single-barrel concept was a way for bourbon to grab some of that burgeoning market. Named after Col. Albert Blanton, head of the distillery during the Prohibition era, it was both the original single-barrel bourbon and the first premium brand of the post-bust era.

As a single barrel, some variation is to be expected in the profile, but this expression is made from the distillery's #2 mash bill and is always bottled at the same proof.

The reddish amber liquid has a scent thick with vanilla syrup that has been seasoned with citrus zest.

The nose is both floral and spicy, and tinged with oak. While the oaky vanilla and floral sweetness are on the bold side, there is enough sophistication there to make this bourbon a real sniffer, the sort you'll want to nose over and over again.

The flavor is heavy and chewy, with fruits like apricot and peach taking the place of the citrus that was in the nose. The vanilla sinks to a minor note, subsumed by a rich mixture of baking spices. Throw in notes of dry, toasty wood and earthy chocolate, and you have a sophisticated, potent sipper. In a startling contrast to the nose and palate, the finish starts off very warm and in a spicy, dry, and woody spot before winding down quickly.

When Sazerac rebranded the George T. Stagg Distillery as Buffalo Trace in the late 1990s, they launched a new bourbon to go with it. In the 1990s, small-batch bourbons were all the rage, so Buffalo Trace was modeled accordingly. They chose to go with mash bill #1, their lowest-rye bourbon recipe, with barrels drawn from the middle floors of their various warehouses, the areas that see the sharpest temperature changes over the course of the year.

Although there is no age statement, whenever I've asked about the age of Buffalo Trace, the answer has been either "about eight years" or "several years old."

It has a clear, orange amber appearance in the glass.

The nose is clear and crisp and quite vanilla-forward, with touches of honey, orange zest, licorice, and oak sitting underneath.

The flavor follows along similar lines. It's sweet and mellow, with the only difference being the growth of the orange zest from just a touch to a good-size pinch. The finish places things on different ground, starting with a little pepper before fading to a mild oakiness.

Colonel E.H. Taylor Small Batch
Bottled in Bond Bourbon Whiskey

The Colonel E.H. Taylor line of whiskeys started in 2011 as one-shot, premium, limited-edition whiskeys. The series got to its sixth installment in 2012, before its standard-bearing, regular release came out, which is this Small Batch version.

Usually the Taylor bourbons are made using the distillery's #1 mash bill, aged in the Colonel's own Warehouse C, and bottled in bond, and this Small Batch carries all of those characteristics. That the series is almost entirely composed of bottled in bond releases is a nod to Taylor's role in lobbying for the Bottled in Bond Act of 1897. At the time of its initial release, the Small Batch was said to be seven years old, despite being a no-age-statement whiskey.

The liquid has a syrupy, copper and amber look, which turns out to be suggestive of the whiskey's scent.

It has a sweet nose, thickly inlaid with caramel, and just a tiny bite for its strength.

A taste reveals a sweet but well-balanced bourbon, syrupy and caramel candy sweet, with a hint of butterscotch. Offsetting that candy store side of the taste is a dollop of woodiness and just a dash of pepper. It's thick, flavorful, and delicious. The finish is a long, lingering one. It starts out soft and somewhat warm, and then drifts into a prolonged and somewhat peppery close.

I think of this bourbon as a conversational whiskey, because it's great stuff, but not so complex that it requires your complete attention to get the most out of it.

Colonel E.H. Taylor Bottled in Bond Rye Whiskey

Although it's made in Kentucky by one of the state's core distilleries, Colonel E.H. Taylor Rye isn't a "Kentucky rye." That style calls for a mash bill with scarcely enough rye to qualify, and a high, secondary amount of corn. The rye mash bill used here, however, is a two-grain recipe consisting of just rye and malted barley. The proportions are unknown, but the main thing is the lack of corn. The rye is another bottled in bond whiskey in the Taylor series, meaning it is at least four years old.

Ryes tend to have a lighter color than bourbons, and this one is no exception, bearing a deep golden look in the glass.

The nose explodes with a blend of cardamom, peppercorns, dill, rich caramel, and earthy cocoa.

A taste proved as flavorful as the scent is potent, with raspberries and blackberries, toffee, and caramel graciously sharing the stage with the spicy kick from the nose. The finish grabs the cardamom and berry elements and takes them both on a long ride.

Eagle Rare 10-Year-Old Straight Bourbon Whiskey

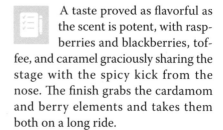

Eagle Rare underwent a labeling change in 2014 that caused a panic among bourbon enthusiasts. First, the label lost the term "single barrel." At the time, the distillery said this was because Eagle Rare had moved to an automated bottling line, and because of the equipment, Buffalo Trace could no longer guarantee that each bottle did not contain a mixture of the whiskey from two barrels. The other change was moving the age statement to a discrete place on the back of the bottle, which caused widespread speculation that said statement was soon to be removed altogether.

It's been more than four years, and Eagle Rare remains a 10-year-old bourbon. It's also often categorized as a single barrel, although unofficially. It's made from the distillery's #1 bourbon mash bill.

It is a dark copper in the glass, resembling the hue of a much-utilized tea kettle.

The nose is barrel-forward, full of caramel and char that appears in the form of an almost scorched, campfire-roasted marshmallow. This strong current of toasted sugar is supplemented by a healthy dollop of orange blossom honey and the faintest trace of hoary old oak.

A sip starts with a wave of melted brown sugar and molasses slapping down on your tongue, which gives way to vanilla, cinnamon, cloves, and some tannic oak as it recedes. The finish winds down slowly with traces of spice and old oak.

EAGLE RARE 17–YEAR–OLD STRAIGHT BOURBON WHISKEY

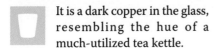

90 Part of the Buffalo Trace Antique Collection (BTAC), this offered enthusiasts a much more mature take on Eagle Rare 10, albeit not as a single barrel. Yet, despite not being a single-barrel bourbon, the expression has the variance in flavor profile you would expect of one. Each year's batch is a little different from those that came before, and in that respect the 17 is very much like its younger sibling.

BTAC whiskeys are among the most sought-after of the annual limited editions, right behind those expressions bearing the name "Van Winkle." The rule is that they are either very well aged or bottled at cask strength, with the exception of George T. Stagg, which is both. Eagle Rare 17, being quite old, is bottled at a modest proof. Given the variability, I went through my notes and compiled something that comes close to a general description of the 17.

Expect a bright, middling amber color that becomes downright scintillating when you give it a swish.

Taking in the scent, I found deep vanilla, with thick notes of corn and orange zest for sweetness, bringing to mind an upscale experiment in ice cream. This image was altered just slightly by the dash of barrel char.

The flavor turns things upside down. First, the creamy nose shifts to a lighter mouthfeel. Also, the rye spice and barrel char are on top, with the latter acquiring a toasty, dry aspect. Finally, the bourbon becomes a bit earthy and chocolaty. The finish is light and a little spicy, and wraps up promptly.

GEORGE T. STAGG STRAIGHT BOURBON WHISKEY

Introduced in 2002 as an ultra-aged, cask-strength bourbon made from the distillery's low-rye (aka #1) mash bill, George T. Stagg—although not the first expression of the BTAC line—has grown to become its crown jewel. It is arguably the most sought-after annual, limited-release American bourbon that is made from a rye rather than a wheated mash bill (i.e., the Van Winkles).

Each batch of Stagg is unique, but the age is always in the middle to upper teens, and the alcohol content is usually above 60%, sometimes above 70%. It's also always unfiltered.

Again, because every Stagg release is different, I reviewed my notes of various installments and cobbled together a description featuring the typical features.

The color is deep, royal amber, and by that I mean a color fit for the tsar's Amber Room. It's dark, but with a gorgeous jewellike quality.

The aroma is thick with caramel and dried, dark fruits such as raisins and figs. Yet a balancing and quite crisp note of wood walks hand in hand with these aspects.

The palate is where the big payoff is with this bourbon.

The liquid reveals more complexity, with a toasty oak underpinned by spices like ginger, cinnamon, and cloves, and mixed into a concoction of vanilla and chocolate syrups. The finish is moderate, and somewhat understated compared to the taste, but the warmth goes on and on.

Kentucky Gentleman Whiskey

The phrase "Kentucky Gentleman" implies a certain Southern genteelness, and frankly, no one possessed with such grace and class would ever stoop to drinking anything resembling Kentucky Gentleman whiskey. It's a blend of bourbon and neutral grain spirits made at Barton 1792, and intended to be cheap enough to occupy a dusty corner of the bottom shelf.

In the glass, as in the bottle, the whiskey is an amber that is more brown than copper, and looks like watery iced tea.

The nose and flavor carry on this watery quality, with equal measures of caramel and corn sweetness, coupled to a nauseating astringency. The finish does nothing to salvage the proceedings, being reminiscent of a cheap, knockoff cough syrup.

90 The only outfit in Kentucky that plays its mash bills closer to the vest than Buffalo Trace is Michter's, and this secrecy really shows when it comes to the rye whiskeys Buffalo Trace produces. We know the Taylor Rye has no corn in it, and that it is a separate entity from the other Buffalo Trace ryes, but only because the company told us at the time of release. Sazerac 6-Year-Old is presumably in the Kentucky style of having scarcely enough rye to qualify, but we cannot really be sure. What we do know is that the whiskey in the bottle is at least six years of age.

In the glass, it has a golden brown appearance, akin to iced tea that has been watered down just a bit.

The nose is built on a foundation of caramel, dried apricots, and baking spices, and on top of this platform your nostrils are struck first by a handful of mixed citrus zest, followed by a smack of pepperiness.

The flavor is directly in line with the scent, with the finish landing on the same foundation as the nose: caramel, dried apricots, and baking spices. It's a simple, easy-drinking rye, and quite flavorful and full-bodied considering the proof.

Sazerac 18–Year–Old Straight Rye Whiskey

In 2003, a large quantity of 18-year-old rye whiskey was transferred to stainless steel containers, effectively freezing its maturation. That whiskey became Sazerac 18-Year-Old, and Buffalo Trace steadily drew down this reserve until it had sufficiently aged replacement stock. In 2016, that transition was made, and now Sazerac 18 is like its BTAC stablemates: every year, two to four dozen barrels are chosen from the warehouses and dumped. And, as with other BTAC whiskeys, there is some variance in the flavor profile. Although I was familiar with the tanked Sazerac 18, I've been able to get a handle on just one of the few releases to come out since the BTAC shift, that being the 2017.

It has a scent redolent of warm graham crackers and ginger cookies that have been sprinkled with cinnamon and placed on an oaken platter.

A sip starts out dry and spicy, but further sipping brings out a maple syrup sweetness that balances the baking spice and pepper nicely. The finish, though, turns dry again, and quite oaky.

Stagg Jr. Straight Bourbon Whiskey

This appropriately named whiskey is exactly what it is billed as, a younger version of the George T. Stagg that occupies a seat in the highly esteemed and much sought-after Buffalo Trace Antique Collection. Both Staggs come from the distillery's low-rye, #1 bourbon mash bill, and both are bottled at cask strength. The only difference is that Stagg Jr. comes in at eight or nine years of age (as a no-age-statement whiskey), while George T. Stagg bottlings are at least 15 years old. Stagg Jr. routinely clocks in at over 130 proof, and it's a whiskey that needs a splash of water to bring out the best in it.

The color in the glass is a bright, shining middle amber that is lovely to look at.

It carries a rich and caramel-coated vanilla scent, with a sweet, floral citrus note.

On the palate, Stagg Jr. explodes: a zesty citrus tang, bourbon spiciness mixed with vanilla, and a hefty bit of oak to provide balance. It's not subtle or complex, but it's certainly yummy. The finish is much more restrained, imparting a mild, lasting warmth and a light vanilla and oak aftertaste.

Thomas H. Handy Sazerac Straight Rye Whiskey

120+ Where Sazerac 18-Year-Old is the ultra-aged rye whiskey of BTAC, Thomas H. Handy is the cask-strength entry. The expression is usually six years old, and the cask-length bottling comes in above 60% alcohol content.

A pour is reddish copper, very bright with barely a nod toward brown.

Despite being a high-octane whiskey, nosings of Handy usually don't torch my nostrils, but instead give a pleasant, restrained sensation of a thick slice of coconut cake. It's a little floral and a little vanilla, but the seasoning is really heavier with clove and nutmeg, all undergirded by a creamy richness.

Likewise, tasting this big and bold whiskey usually stays just inside the boundary: it's challenging, but not quite too hot. The flavor packs on oodles of marmalade, vanilla, red fruits, and baking spices, a combination that smacks of a heavily seasoned, liquor-soaked holiday fruitcake. It's not subtle, but it is delightfully yummy. The finish is moderately warm, leaving only the slightest hint of a sweet tobacco flavor on the tongue, and it lingers for a considerable amount of time.

William Larue Weller Straight Bourbon Whiskey

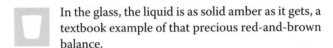

This expression started in 2000 as an ultra-aged wheated bourbon. In 2005, it was revamped as a mature, but not old, cask-strength version of the same wheated bourbon stock. By that time, the rest of the whiskeys in what would make up BTAC had come around, too. Thus, Weller became the wheated bourbon of the collection, as well as the one that is cask strength, but not old (Eagle Rare 17 is old, and George T. Stagg is both cask strength and old). A bottling of Weller is usually 12 years old and is over 60% or even 70% alcohol content.

In the glass, the liquid is as solid amber as it gets, a textbook example of that precious red-and-brown balance.

On the nose, the bourbon is surprisingly mild for something that is sometimes so strong you could pour it in your gas tank and run your car off it (albeit with a little knocking).

The scent is thick and powerful, though, dominated by surging currents of citrus flowers and vanilla, with a column of leathery wood and barrel char. It reminds me of nothing quite so much as some of the rustic cabins I've been in, the sort with no running water or electricity. Picture that setting, add a wood fire on an iron range and some kind of fruit cobbler coming out of the oven, and you can approximate the feeling of nosing a glass of Weller.

On the palate, the Weller reverts to exactly what I would expect from a monster, high-proof bourbon: it is simply too hot to drink neat and straight. At any rate, it is for me. I always have to put water in, and not just a couple of drops, but closer to 10. This is the kind of bourbon for which drinkers will need to find the appropriate amount of water for them, putting it in the category of "self-cut whiskey." That said, once you dial it in, it's very enjoyable, if still big, bold, and potent. Baking spices and syrupy vanilla join a dry, toasty wood in a bourbon-fueled rush. The mouthfeel is thick without being creamy, rich, or oily. Instead, it is simply dense. The finish is very long and very warm, as one might expect from such a hot bourbon, but the light oak and spice aftertaste isn't burned off by the heat.

W.L. Weller Antique 107
Straight Bourbon Whiskey

The Weller line is made from Buffalo Trace's wheated bourbon mash bill, and this occupies the midpoint of that collection. Although it lacks an age statement, it's known to average about seven years, and the "107" in the name refers to the proof. That relatively high proof adds a bit of bite to the whiskey, which is something I've always liked about this iteration of Weller, since one shouldn't consume such a bourbon while worrying about the heat.

The scent is sweet and floral with notes of orange blossom honey and vanilla, but cinnamon and nutmeg are underneath, and if you go chasing after these underlying elements, the heat will get into your nostrils.

The flavor offers caramel and dark berries, followed by a hard alcoholic bite. This is a whiskey that may force a wince but will not overtly burn you. The finish turns fruity and oaky, with the fruit eventually fading to make way for the dry oakiness.

W.L. Weller Special Reserve Straight Bourbon Whiskey

90 This is the entry-level bourbon of the Weller line, and it's similar to the Weller Antique 107 bottling, except that it weighs in at a much lighter proof.

On the nose, the floral citrus, honey sweetness, and vanilla qualities of the 107 really shine now that the added heat is not lurking behind them.

Ditto for the berry and apple fruitiness and the caramel on the palate. The lack of bite also allows the finish to develop into a leathery oakiness, as opposed to the drier and more tannic ending in the 107.

90

Nothing encapsulates the hothouse absurdity of bourbon's modern boom quite as much as W.L. Weller 12-Year-Old. I think of it that way because it went from being a largely overlooked bourbon to a very difficult-to-acquire (aka expensive) one almost overnight, attaining "chimera bottle" status all because the late Josh Ozersky wrote a piece in 2014 labeling it "baby Pappy Van Winkle." Other writers repeated the claim and the obsession has now grown to the point that the other, cheaper Weller expressions have also become hard to get. The Pappy comparisons aside, Weller 12 deserves a good deal of the acclaim it receives.

The liquid has a bronzed look in the glass—it's not quite copper and not full-on amber. A coat drops a few tears, meaning this bourbon resides just shy of viscous.

The scent combines thick vanilla and caramel with blackberry jam fruitiness and an accent of leathery, hoary oak. The aroma would come across as older than the age statement suggests were it not for the berry current, which is an oddity in and of itself. Usually the fruit in a wheated bourbon comes across as citrusy, but with Weller 12 it has always struck me as berries.

The flavor profile runs the same exact lines as the scent, with just one exception. Once off your nostrils and on your tongue, the woody element turns a bit dry, a dryness that runs into a soft but spicy finish.

Balanced and flavorful with a charming amount of sophistication, Weller 12 is an outstanding example of how a bourbon needs to merely be middle-aged to hit its sweet spot.

— TOWN BRANCH DISTILLERY —

N ative Irishman Dr. Pearse Lyons, the founder of animal feed giant Alltech passed away in 2018, but he began his career working in distilleries, and for most of his adult life wanted to make whiskey. He acquired a brewery in Lexington, then expanded it into a distillery in 2008 (making it a very early example of a brewstillery, incidentally). Appropriately enough, given Lyons's Irish roots, the first production run done there was a malt whiskey.

PEARSE LYONS RESERVE WHISKEY

80 Pearse Lyons Reserve was the first American malt made in Kentucky since 1919. It comes from a mash of 100% malted barley, distilled in a Scots-style pair of copper pot stills, and is aged in former bourbon barrels that were also used to age the brewery's Kentucky Bourbon Barrel Ale. This is one reason the expression is merely "whiskey" and not "malt whiskey," because under federal law an American malt must be aged in new oak barrels.

The nose of the Pearse Lyons Reserve is sweet like molasses, topped by a raisin-like note. It also has a distinct malty strand, as well as some minor notes of vanilla and oak. It's a mellow nose, and is very suggestive of what follows.

The taste carries all of the same characteristics, although the woody vanilla and oak flavors come a bit more to the forefront. Overall, it's a balanced and subdued whiskey, with just a bit of complexity to it. The finish starts with a spicy bite, which is kind of a shock given how mellow the whiskey has been up until this point. It then winds down quickly, but warmly, ending on a woody note.

Town Branch Straight Bourbon Whiskey

80

The distillery was named for the Town Branch Creek, which has been buried underneath Lexington for over 100 years, and a bourbon was released under that name in 2012. Initially this was sourced, but in-house production of the bourbon began in tandem with the product launch. Starting in 2016, the distillery's in-house production took over. The mash bill is 72% corn, 13% rye, and 15% malted barley.

Once in the glass, the whiskey has the color of brightly polished copper.

The nose is clear, and distinctly corn syrup sweet with a dash of a citrus zest in there, as well as a hint of caramel and oaky woodiness.

The flavor is not quite as sweet as the scent, and is actually a bit dry. It's light and almost balanced, but I found that the dry quality makes it too crisp and throws it off just a bit. The taste remains corn sweet, but not predominately so, with minor notes of caramel, dried fruit, and brown sugar, a heftier helping of oak than the nose might suggest, and a dash of pepper. The finish springs off a continuing bite of pepper, and the woody astringency into a rising but short wave of warmth.

Town Branch Straight Rye Whiskey

100

When I got my first crack at Town Branch Rye, it was still under development. It was eventually released as an approximately four-year-old, Kentucky-style rye whiskey, made from a mash bill of 55% rye, 30% corn, and 15% malted barley. The distillery bottled it at a substantially higher proof than its other regular-release whiskeys.

In the glass, the whiskey has a bright copper coloring.

The nose carries notes of sweet tobacco and a little musty wood, but only the tiniest hint of rye spice.

The flavor follows from the nose, with sweet tobacco and woody flavors, plus some spice that mixes together into something reminiscent of a thick cookie with a bit of ginger. Just as those flavors come across the threshold and become familiar, the whiskey delivers a solid, spicy kick. The finish is spicy, warm, and lingering, winding down with a tobacco barn-like aftertaste.

— WILDERNESS TRAIL DISTILLERY —

WILDERNESS TRAIL SINGLE BARREL BOTTLED IN BOND STRAIGHT BOURBON WHISKEY

100 The first time I met Shane Baker, already an industry veteran when he cofounded Wilderness Trail with Pat Heist, he told me their goal was to make the kind of whiskey they liked drinking. Among the things they liked were wheated bourbon and some combination of bottled in bond, single barrel, and cask strength. You can see how

that ambition turned out in their Single Barrel Bottled in Bond, made from a high-wheat mash bill of 64% corn, 24% wheat, and 12% malted barley. They entered it into #4 char oak barrels at 110 proof and aged it for the bonded minimum of four years. In an interesting twist, Wilderness Trail joined Maker's Mark in adopting barrel rotation; every year, their bourbon is aged in a two-story rickhouse, and every year they shift the bourbon up or down a floor.

The bourbon has a brown-tinted amber appearance in the glass.

The nose is honey sweet with touches of apple blossoms and wildflowers, seasoned with ample caramel and vanilla.

The flavor oozes more honey and apples off a foundation of an earthy cocoa and caramel candy, plus a dash of peppery spice to give it some character. On the finish, that pepperiness transitions to hot cinnamon, and runs hand in hand with caramel until both fade away.

WILDERNESS TRAIL SETTLERS SELECT SINGLE BARREL BARREL PROOF STRAIGHT RYE WHISKEY

The Wilderness Trail Rye is made in the Kentucky style with 56% rye, 33% corn, and 11% malted barley. They put the whiskey into the barrel at an unusually low entry proof of 100. At the time of writing, that was the lowest entry proof in use in the state. Barrels chosen for this expression are aged for three or more years and come from the upper floor of both their A and B warehouses. Finally, Wilderness Trail has released the whiskey as a single barrel and at cask strength. Although being both a single-barrel and a cask-strength release means one should expect some variation in alcohol strength, the very low entry proof and relatively short aging period mean a given barrel should come out as scarcely higher than 100 proof for bottling.

It's a fruity rye, leading with tropical fruits and orange zest on the nose, undergirded by cinnamon and nutmeg plus a touch of sweet tobacco leaf.

The flavor grows spicier and brings out more of the barrel. The sweet tobacco is there, with the seasoning turning to allspice, on top of a foundation of caramel and maple. The finish is spicy and citrusy, a bit like the Bigelow Constant Comment tea.

PAPPY VAN WINKLE

If you are looking for notes on the Van Winkle whiskeys in this book, you will look in vain. The reason is that the bottle of Pappy Van Winkle 15 Year Old I acquired in 2009 was the last I ever expect to own. Because Julian Van Winkle III, president of Old Rip Van Winkle, doesn't give out samples, and I don't pay three-digit bar bills for 1½ oz. pours of whiskey under any circumstances, I have no recent experience with Pappy Van Winkle. When it comes to unicorn bottles, my attention is fixed elsewhere. (For example, I think W.L. Weller 12 is a much better buy, even at its real market price of $150 a bottle, never mind if you can get it at its official retail value of $40.)

Thus, I don't feel qualified to discuss the merits of Van Winkle whiskeys as they are presented today, because recent experience is crucial to doing so. Like many brands discussed in this book, Van Winkle is based on sourced whiskey and contract production, and the stock behind the brand has changed over time.

Since the early 1970s, Van Winkle bourbon has been a brand without a distillery to call its own, initially made under contract for family patriarch Julian Van Winkle II (Pappy's son) at the Stitzel-Weller Distillery in Shively, the Louisville suburb that is home to so many bourbon distilleries. This timing coincided with the world whiskey bust, which left traditional producers sitting on an ocean of whiskey nobody wanted to buy. Stock sat in the rickhouses for longer, including the Van Winkle stock, which would lead to many of the age-statement whiskeys that emerged a decade or more later.

When Julian Van Winkle II passed away, his son Julian III took over, and Stitzel-Weller was shuttered in 1992. New production for Van Winkle bourbon was primarily sourced through the Bernheim Distillery (owned first by Brown-Forman and then Heaven Hill during that time), until the brand found its current home at Buffalo Trace in 2002.

A lot of happy accidents had to come together to make Van Winkle whiskey the superstar it is today, and that reputation was built on the Stitzel-Weller stock the brand had at the outset. A combination of production factors (mash, yeast, warehousing, and so on) enabled Stitzel-Weller to produce excellent wheated bourbon, one that continues to be (ever more) dearly prized by bourbon aficionados to this day. Next, wheated bourbon is thought to bear longer aging periods better than bourbon made with rye, and that Stitzel-Weller bourbon aged well. Finally, the world whiskey bust ensured there would be enough sitting on the ricks year after year to start bottling very old expressions.

Pappy Van Winkle 20 Year Old was introduced in the early 1990s, around the same time as the Jim Beam Small Batch Collection. Ultra-aged American whiskeys existed in the 1990s, but nobody was releasing them with any regularity. I recall well enough that if you wanted to reliably find a bourbon with a 20-year-plus aging statement in the 1990s, Pappy Van Winkle was the brand you put your name on the waiting list for (or just bought off the shelf).

The Van Winkle name has risen to such heights that, at the time of publication, Wine-Searcher.com listed Old Rip Van Winkle 25 Year Old Bourbon as having the dearest price tag of all bourbon whiskeys, at an average of $20,160. That expression is the oldest release to date, and made entirely of Stitzel-Weller stock. That last bit is as important, perhaps more important than the age statement, because a simple math exercise tells us that Pappy Van Winkle cannot be using much Stitzel-Weller whiskey anymore.

When I interviewed Buffalo Trace master distiller Harlen Wheatley about Old Rip Van Winkle 25-Year-Old, he confirmed that some Stitzel-Weller–made bourbon had been stored in stainless steel tanks and (at that time) continued to be used in Pappy Van Winkle expressions. That said, it is a good guess that the older Van Winkle whiskeys are now based squarely on the Bernheim-made whiskey, with Pappy Van Winkle 15 and the other middle-aged expressions drawing mostly on Buffalo Trace–made stock.

Bernheim and Buffalo Trace produce excellent whiskeys, but they don't have the legendary cachet of Stitzel-Weller wheated bourbon, and that was the stuff that I knew so well. One of the ironies of Pappy Van Winkle is that as its fame exploded into the mainstream and made the brand a virtually unobtainable luxury, the very stuff that made it such a cult favorite in the first place began to dwindle. Now that Stitzel-Weller whiskey is the stuff of ultra-aged, one-shot releases and vintage collectables, not the backbone of any annual release.

— WILD TURKEY DISTILLERY —

WILD TURKEY LONGBRANCH SMALL BATCH
STRAIGHT BOURBON WHISKEY

86 When a booze brand reaches a long-term marketing arrangement with a celebrity, typically it's just an advertising deal. But when Wild Turkey and actor Matthew McConaughey got together, it was bigger than that. McConaughey became the creative director for his ads, and some collaboration with Master Distiller Eddie Russell yielded a new expression too. To give the whiskey a little bit of McConaughey's Texas identity, it is filtered after aging through oak and mesquite charcoal. Although it is a no-age-statement whiskey, at the time of its spring 2018 release, it was officially said to be about eight years old.

The post-aging charcoal filtration doesn't seem to have done anything to the look of the whiskey, because it is very much in tune with the reddish amber appearance of Wild Turkey 101.

The aroma is light but manages to carry a lot despite being airy. Caramel and nuts are seasoned with cinnamon and nutmeg, and rounded out with a touch of barrel char.

Despite the light nose and the filtration, the liquid retains a creamy mouthfeel. The bourbon tastes of candy corn and caramel with a spoonful of orange zest stirred in and cinnamon sprinkled on top. The flavor and texture are such that I wouldn't guess it had been charcoal-filtered—quite the opposite. That comes back on the finish, however. The caramel fades away, leaving a dry note of barrel char to linger on the back of the tongue.

Wild Turkey Rare Breed Barrel Proof
Straight Bourbon Whiskey

110+ Wild Turkey Rare Breed is sometimes seen as the step up on the distillery's ladder from the Wild Turkey 101 (their top regular bourbon) into the premium stuff. First, it's bottled at barrel proof, so it's stronger than WT101. As Eddie Russell's role at Wild Turkey grew, the proof on Rare Breed seems to have inched up. His father, Jimmy Russell, preferred stronger-than-average whiskey, but not too strong, so Rare Breed was batched in such a way that it often came in at below 110 proof. Nowadays it seems to come in at well over 110.

Rare Breed is also a blend of 6-, 8-, and 12-year-old stock, making it a bit older than the 101. It also shares a couple of characteristics all Wild Turkey bourbons have in common. They all come from the same distillate, made from 75% corn, 13% rye, and 12% malted barley. Also, Wild Turkey bourbons are, as a rule, aged in new oak barrels charred to Level 4, the famed "alligator char." The distillery distills its whiskey and enters it into the barrel at a somewhat lower proof than is usual among the major Kentucky distillers (although nowadays there are folks in the state who both distill and enter into the barrel at a lower proof than Wild Turkey).

It has what I consider Wild Turkey's trademark appearance: a strongly coppered amber, where red and orange are more prevalent than brown.

The nose has the waft of rich citrus zest and creamy vanilla, tinged with cedar.

On the palate, it's noticeably woodier and spicier than Turkey 101, with those two notes predominating over the orange-and-corn sweetness and vanilla flavor. The finish is clear, leaving a simple, warm afterglow that just lingers on and on.

My view on Rare Breed is that it's a close, but more sophisticated cousin of WT 101.

90

The factor that distinguishes Russell's Reserve 10 from other Wild Turkey bourbons is that it raises the floor on the age above that of their flagship expression, Wild Turkey 101. The latter is about six to eight years old, and their other premium expressions in regular release tend to at least start by drawing on the same six-year-old whiskeys as WT101, whereas everything in a bottle of this stuff is aged a minimum 10 years. Although older, it's also lighter than WT101.

The scent packs on the vanilla and marzipan and covers it in a glaze of cherry and orange.

The flavor profile builds off that by sprinkling earthy cocoa and cinnamon on the top, and serving it on an oak plate. The finish kicks off a touch spicy, but winds down on a trickle of maple syrup.

RUSSELL'S RESERVE SINGLE BARREL
STRAIGHT BOURBON WHISKEY

110

Two characteristics separate Russell's Reserve Single Barrel from the rest of the Wild Turkey lineup. The first one is right there in the title: single barrel. This is one of two single-barrel expressions in regular release from the Lawrenceburg distillery (the other being Kentucky Spirit). The second point is that, while not a cask-strength bourbon, it is a high-octane one: they bottled this whiskey at 110 proof. So, what you get out of a bottle of this bourbon is whiskey coming from a "honey barrel," chosen by Eddie Russell, and cut with little

more than a splash of water. As befits a strong whiskey, it isn't chill-filtered.

As a single barrel, there is some variation between individual barrels, and thus one should not expect every bottle to be the same. As a rule, though, it's surprisingly mild for a bourbon of this strength. You can usually nose and sip on a pour of Russell's Reserve Single Barrel without adding a drop of water.

When I last had some, the nose was a little like tea time: the orange and spices reminded me of Constant Comment tea, and in this instance it was served with a slice of angel food cake done up with vanilla.

The flavor was quite a contrast, leading as it did with big oak and hot cinnamon, but this was soon buried by candy flavors: a big caramel with minty stripes covered in nut shavings. The finish turns oaky and spicy again, and lingers for a lengthy spell.

RUSSELL'S RESERVE SINGLE BARREL STRAIGHT RYE WHISKEY

104

Wild Turkey has just two mash bills. Their bourbon grain recipe was discussed earlier, but this is my first mention of their rye mash bill. It's a Kentucky rye, made with just enough rye to count as a rye whiskey: 51% rye, 37% corn, and 12% malted barley. Like its cousin, Russell's Reserve Single Barrel Bourbon, Eddie Russell picks out choice barrels from that rye stock and bottles them at high proof. In this instance, that is 104 proof, only slightly higher than the flagship Wild Turkey 101 Rye.

Like many ryes, this one has a lighter color than a bourbon, straddling the line between copper and amber. That is just about the only fully stable characteristic for Russell's Reserve Single Barrel Rye, however, because in a single barrel one must expect a little variability.

The scent of this whiskey is like someone took a cinnamon graham cracker and sprinkled it with both freshly ground pepper and vanilla and cherry syrups.

The palate builds on that, bringing on ample red fruit and vanilla balanced against robust spiciness. The conclusion opens with that full-bodied spiciness, but as this fades out, one is left with traces of vanilla and orange zest.

Among the mass-market, flagship bourbons, Wild Turkey 101 occupies a special place. A quick look at the bottle will tell you why. First, whereas most mass-market products are bottled at 80 proof, and a few are a notch stronger at 90 proof, the classic Wild Turkey expression is 101 proof. Another point you can see by looking at the bottle is the very reasonable price point, and many fans point to it as one of the best bang-for-the-buck bargains in bourbon. Not on the label is that Wild Turkey 101 draws on six- to eight-year-old stock; much of the expression's competition comes from four- to six-year-old stock.

In the glass, it has the benchmark mid-amber coloring.

The nose has a crisp character, in keeping with the bad boy reputation this bourbon often carries. A vanilla and citrus zest sweetness balances evenly against the scent of cedar, with just a pinch of spice.

This isn't fancy bourbon, so the flavor follows from there. The woody side spreads out to embrace oak and cedar, with thick corn and vanilla sweetness. Once again, that dash of spice is there, just within reach. The finish has a very light bite to it, a fair reminder of the high alcohol content. The vanilla lingers in the aftertaste, but otherwise the wind-down is simple, warm, and lasting.

Back in the days when rye whiskey was moribund and selection was narrow to say the least, this whiskey was much loved by rye whiskey fans, in part because it was stronger and had a fuller body than Old Overholt and Rittenhouse. During the height of the Rye Crunch of 2011–12, when a surprise spike in demand for rye whiskey far outstripped supply, Wild Turkey's stock of rye whiskey was put under enough strain that they introduced an 81-proof version, and the original WT101 Rye all but disappeared from store shelves. After that brief period as a unicorn bottle, this rye has slowly made its way back to having a general presence on liquor store shelves. And despite buyers today having a lot more options available when it comes to rye, Wild Turkey 101 Rye has remained quite popular among rye lovers. The 101 proof is only part of why this whiskey enjoys such a good reputation. For my part, I have long thought it was the best example of how balanced a Kentucky-style rye whiskey can be.

A sniff tells you why on the spot, balancing a eucalyptus and mint herbal spiciness against caramel and honey sweetness.

A sip of the whiskey comes forward with more of the same notes from the nose, pauses on them for a moment, and then shakes an oaken baton at you for good measure. That oakiness follows through on the finish, growing larger if anything, and joined by hot cinnamon.

— WILLETT DISTILLERY —

For many years, the Willett Distillery was known as Kentucky Bourbon Distillers (KBD), and they were one of the top bottlers of sourced bourbon in the state. In 2016, they began to release their in-house offerings.

Johnny Drum Private Stock
Straight Bourbon Whiskey

101 Johnny Drum is a legacy of the KBD era, before the company made a drop of whiskey themselves. The label says it is made by "Johnny Drum Distilling Company" (KBD has tended to do that with their sourced brands), but there is no such distillery. The brand continues to be sourced to this day, although from whom isn't known.

The scent is a bit like a plate of boozy baked apples. A hint of ethanol is the first thing to hit the nostrils, but behind that are cooked apples, brown sugar, and vanilla.

The flavor is richly sweet, bringing on ample vanilla and caramel, while the apple note from the nose turns over to tobacco leaf. Some toasty oak comes up on the back end, and this carries over into the finish before ultimately turning spicy.

WILLETT DISTILLER
DSP-KY-78
SOUR MAS
RYE WHISK
RC-5
SERIAL NO
FILL DATE
BARDSTOWN NELSON COUNTY KY

114.3

This bourbon used to be one of my favorites, because it was 15 years old, high octane, and quite reasonably priced. Changing times and changing sources of stock compelled KBD/Willett to drop the age statement some years ago, and I don't think the brand has been the same since. It's still pretty good, but it lost that special something that made it a staple for me. For one thing, I used to be able to sip on Noah's Mill neat, but now it's hot as is (for me, anyway) and requires a good-size splash of water.

This is a bright amber bourbon.

It has a nose of melted brown sugar, vanilla, walnuts, and that mix of wood and tobacco that reminds this farm boy of standing in a tobacco barn.

It's a viscous liquid with a creamy mouthfeel, a flavor that brings that vanilla and nuttiness forward again, but also with a hefty helping of gingerbread spices. The palate is also a touch acidic on the back. That acidic note is there just long enough to be noticed however, with the finish running pretty much the same notes as the palate. Noah's Mill isn't what it used to be, but it's still a big-bodied, flavorful bourbon.

OLD BARDSTOWN BOTTLED IN BOND
STRAIGHT BOURBON WHISKEY

Willett opened their distillery in 2012, and as soon as they had the whiskey to do it (four years later), they released a bottled in bond bourbon. Old Bardstown Bottled in Bond is made using the old Willett family grain recipe: 72% corn, 13% rye, and 15% malted barley. That is a somewhat odd way to go, what with the malted barley being a slightly bigger component than the rye, thus becoming a full flavoring element rather than just there for the enzymes. This break from tradition means that this bourbon heads in a much lighter direction than most.

In the glass, the whiskey has a light copper coloring. It's sharp, clear, and pretty to see, but at the same time one might wonder why a four-year-old bourbon bottled at 100 proof isn't a little darker.

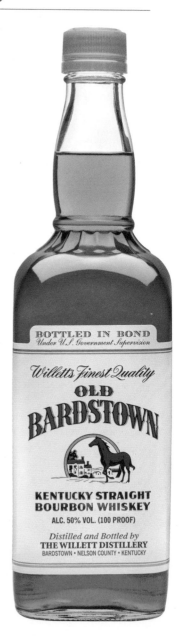

The nose has a light, airy, and slightly floral character to it as well. The scent of brown sugar and vanilla lies in the main, but is seasoned with a toasty cereals note that puts the heightened malt content on display. Behind that is a slight spiciness, like cinnamon and anise. In fact, the aroma reminds me of a plate of warm, well-done cinnamon toast.

The lightness carries over on the palate. It's all sweetness and vanilla up front, with a spoonful of dry wood and barrel char on the back. The finish is a little dry and spicy, leaving some nice warmth.

WILLETT POT STILL RESERVE
STRAIGHT BOURBON WHISKEY

94 Back when I was living in Europe, I used to curse this expression as that damned thing I didn't dare buy. This was because the iconic pot still-shaped bottle was too damn difficult to pack in a suitcase! I would look at it, eye-catching as it was, and it would say to me, "I'm going to soak your clothes in bourbon." When it was introduced in 2008, Willett Pot Still was a single-barrel expression, but it has since dropped that. At the time of writing, it was still a sourced bourbon.

The bottle is also an awkward one to pour, but once you've managed to fill your glass, the bourbon has a mid-brown amber look.

The scent carries candy corn, a pinch of citrus zest, and toasty wood.

A taste yields caramel, a more generous helping of that citrus zest, a dash of peppery spice, and now a leathery wood note. The finish carries on in the same vein, with each aspect drifting off on a trace of dry woodiness.

MARYLAND

BALTIMORE

EPOCH

POT DISTILLED · SMALL BATCH

STRAIGHT RYE WHISKEY

750 ML

— BALTIMORE SPIRITS COMPANY —

Baltimore Epoch Rye Whiskey

100 Made in Baltimore, the first batch of this whiskey was received with rave reviews in the blogging community, getting marks as one of the best whiskeys of its kind (approximately two years old). I'm sure that it was helped by the fact that American whiskey enthusiasts tend to favor stronger whiskeys.

Taking in the nose shows a spicy whiskey with notes of caramel, oak, and a hint of that molasses that seems to always accompany malted rye.

Once you take a sip, the spiciness turns to cinnamon, which is sweetened by vanilla and honey, and supplemented by a little oak. The woody side isn't the harsher, green oak one often encounters from a younger whiskey. The finish escalates the cinnamon to hot, as in Red Hots, and runs long and warm.

— SAGAMORE SPIRIT —

Sagamore Spirit Cask Strength Straight Rye Whiskey

112.2 Also found in Baltimore, Sagamore Spirit opened their distillery in 2017, with the intent of pursuing the big-bodied, floral, Maryland style of rye whiskey, but at present their offerings are sourced. To achieve the desired flavor profile, for the time being they are blending the classic 95% rye from MGP with their newer, low-rye mash bill rye whiskeys. The batch of Cask Strength I tried was 2E.

In the glass, it had a light copper look. Giving the glass a swirl to coat left behind a curtain of tears.

The nose was pleasant enough, imparting gingerbread, citrus oil, and vanilla.

Although my first sip wasn't too hot for tasting, I found myself thinking the whiskey was too bundled up, so I put in a splash of water despite having no bite to mediate. Doing so allowed a tart, berrylike fruitiness to come out, accompanied by cookie spices and woody notes of both cedar and oak. On the finish, a brief current of vanilla gave way to a dry, spicy woodiness.

CASK STRENGTH
112.2 PROOF
750 ml
56.1 ALC/VOL
HAND BOTTLED
SAGAMORE
SPIRIT
Spring Fed
RYE
STRAIGHT WHISKEY
AMERICAN MADE
STRAIGHT
RYE WHISKEY
BALTIMORE, MARYLAND
BATCH 2E
BOTTLE 449
BOTTLER CAM

BLUE RIDGE DEFIANT SINGLE MALT WHISKY

82 Once the Bourbon Boom was underway and the craft distilling movement took off, folks began looking for ways to shortcut the maturation process. It's easy to understand why: socking away even just hundreds of 53-gallon barrels of whiskey to age for the four to six years needed to achieve even basic maturity is a very capital-intensive investment. Most chose to follow the small-barrel route, but even that takes at least several months.

Blue Ridge Distilling Company, an outfit founded by commercial divers, came up with a different solution. They took new white oak staves and cut them into spirals, thereby greatly increasing the surface area, and inserted these into their aging whiskey. With that extra step, they got the results they desired in 60 days.

In my experience, the problem with such tricks is that while they can greatly speed absorption of certain flavors from the oak, like vanilla, they don't accelerate some of the other processes that take place during maturation. Also, like small barrel–aged whiskeys that were aged for too long, they tend to be over-oaked while remaining raw, like white whiskey.

Defiant Single Malt is a case in point. It oozes with malty honey and vanilla, and a spicy note reminiscent of Irish whiskey. It would be a candy bomb of a whisky were it not for the green, astringent, woody edge present in every sip.

— SOUTHERN GRACE DISTILLERIES —

When it comes to hooks, Southern Grace Distilleries certainly has a good one, so much so it may even remain unique well into the future.

Located about 20 minutes from Charlotte, Southern Grace set up shop in an old prison, formerly the Cabarrus Correctional Center.

SOUTHERN GRACE CONVICTION BOURBON WHISKEY

Conviction is made from an 88% corn and 12% malted barley mash bill, enough to be corn whiskey were it not for what the whiskey was aged in. Recall that aging a corn whiskey requires used oak; if a distiller uses new oak, the result is bourbon. Southern Grace uses a mix of 10- and 15-gallon barrels, and the aging period ranges from 7 to 10 months. They bottle at cask strength, which in practice runs between the high 90s and just across the 100 mark in terms of proof.

A sniff reveals an unsurprisingly young whiskey, a scent packed with green oak, but also with some fudge and vanilla.

The flavor is bold and brash, full of vanilla and brown sugar, while the finish turns to coffee and wet leather.

⊰ TENNESSEE ⊱

America's second-ranking whiskey state is Tennessee, a status it has occupied without real dispute since the 1950s, and that status is due entirely to the success enjoyed by one distiller: Jack Daniel's. As strange as it might seem today, the Volunteer State suffered under statewide prohibition for almost 30 years, far longer than the country as a whole. That proved a major hurdle for the return of the state's whiskey industry, so it's paradoxical that one brand in particular was so successful. Jack Daniel's took off in a big way in postwar America. It was so successful that the family that owned the distillery, the Motlows, was unable to fund the necessary expansion, pressuring them to sell the distillery to current owners Brown-Forman.

Jack Daniel's looms so large in Tennessee whiskey that its sale actually prompted the revival of the state's second distillery, George Dickel (as it was known until 2018; it is now called Cascade Hollow Distilling Company, which is featured on the facing page). Dickel was revived near the site of the original Cascade Hollow Distillery after a failed bid by Schenley Industries to buy Jack Daniel's in the mid-1950s. Schenley's owner, Lewis Rosenstiel, was so enraged by the Motlows' refusal to sell the company to him that he invented a rival for Daniel's out of spite. The first bottle of George Dickel Tennessee Whiskey made at this new distillery didn't go on sale until 1964.

It was just these two distilleries until the 1990s, when craft whiskey forerunner Prichard's Distillery opened. Nowadays, Tennessee hosts a substantial small distilling sector, but its claim to being America's #2 whiskey state is still based squarely on Jack Daniel's. Tennessee's stature couldn't be described any other way, as Jack Daniel's is America's best-selling whiskey by a wide margin.

— CASCADE HOLLOW DISTILLING COMPANY —
(FORMERLY GEORGE DICKEL DISTILLERY, DIAGEO)

GEORGE DICKEL NO. 8 TENNESSEE
SOUR MASH WHISKY (BLACK LABEL)

80

Dickel relies on a high-corn mash bill, even higher than Jack Daniel's, at 84% corn, 8% rye, and 8% malted barley. Their approach to the Lincoln County Process involves first chilling their new make to 40°F before pouring it into a vat of sugar maple charcoal to sit for a few days. Dickel No. 8 is aged about five to seven years in new oak barrels with #4 char. Despite the minimum strength and the charcoal mellowing, it's a surprisingly bold whiskey.

No. 8 is quite crisp on the nose, with honey and corn sweetness accented by a slice of Granny Smith apple, caramel, and a sprinkling of mint and cinnamon.

The flavor follows pretty much directly from that, although the apples turn into apples and peaches. The conclusion is caramel sweet and mint spicy.

GEORGE DICKEL BOTTLED IN BOND TENNESSEE WHISKEY

100

In the past, I have found efforts by George Dickel to release older whiskeys disappointing, which goes to underline that who is blending and batching the juice is sometimes as important as the juice being used. Nicole Austin wasn't at the helm down in Cascade Hollow, Tennessee, when any of the whiskey used in making her Bottled in Bond series was barreled, but I don't feel that really matters: George Dickel Bottled in Bond is her creation all the same, and a wonderful creation it is.

Introduced in 2019, the releases in Dickel Bonded greatly are middle-aged, greatly exceeding the statutory four-year minimum of the Bottled in Bond Act. The inaugural release was 13 years old, 2020 was 11 years, and 2021 again 13 years old. There are many whiskeys coming from Jack Daniel's and George Dickel these last few years that should change the minds of all but the most blinkered and hidebound drinkers as to what Tennessee Whiskey can be, but this expression takes the cake. I named the 2021 release as the Best New Whiskey of that year.

A pour comes across as middle amber, not too dark considering its age.

The nose takes Dickel's sweet side, with its vanilla and maple, and endows it with a Life Saver's orange-like citrus scent, and an earthy, woody current that is best described as freshly split pine and oak logs dropped on an earthen shed floor.

The flavor takes that profile and veers off toward the earthy, woody side some more, but not so far that it loses its sweet side. The logs turned to charred, dry oak staves, and the earthy side complements the vanilla and maple more by becoming an especially thick nougat. The finish leaves the char behind and rolls off that dry, spicy oak

George Dickel Superior No. 12
Tennessee Sour Mash Whisky (White Label)

This is the older, stronger cousin of the No. 8. It's the same production process and stock, just aged six to eight years and bottled at a higher proof.

90

A pour reveals an orange and amber liquid.

It has a scent that is very much in tune with Dickel No. 8, but Superior No. 12 has a current of sweet butter smeared thickly across the top.

The palate has the same corn and honey sweetness, but the caramel has risen from a modest note to an almost equal partner. The spiciness is now in the vein of cinnamon, nutmeg, and anise, and a little oak has joined the mix. The finish rolls off the palate, extending it in a straightforward fashion.

The bottom line on this expression is that it's a simple, mature, and flavorful sipper of a Tennessee Whiskey, noticeably more so than the respectable No. 8.

NICOLE AUSTIN

It's rather a coincidence that the two people I consider the brightest of the young, rising stars in the whiskey trade are both working as master distiller at the major Tennessee distilleries. In Lynchburg at Jack Daniel's, you've got Chris Fletcher. At George Dickel, you've got Nicole Austin.

Austin followed the tried-and-true path for many distillers in going to school for chemical engineering, graduating from Manhattan College in 2006. Out of college, she worked as an environmental specialist, but as she herself puts it, she found no great love for that line of work.

As Austin tells it, she discovered her love of whiskey one night while out on a date; a bartender, doing what many bartenders do and telling the story of whiskey, left her spellbound. She did not need to look far to break into whiskey, either: just across the East River to Kings County Distillery in Brooklyn, in fact. Austin became master blender there in 2010, joining the company on an unpaid basis only a few months after it started production.

In November 2012, she left the environmental stuff behind and started work as a chemical engineer and apprentice to the Johnny Appleseed of modern American whiskey, Dave Pickerell. This seminal consultant, provided the expertise that went a long way to making names like Corsair Artisan, FEW Spirits, Garrison Brothers, Whistlepig, and many others what they are today. All of this was while she continued working as a de facto volunteer at Kings County.

After leaving Pickerell's consultancy in 2015, she did some consulting on her own for a while. She then took a staff role at her first big whiskey company, becoming project commissioning engineer at Tullamore Dew in Ireland. She held that job for less than two years, having been offered the master distiller slot at Cascade Hollow, home of George Dickel. When she took charge, Dickel had been adrift for a couple of years. Austin put the brand's product line back on track in record time.

Austin continues to remain an admired figure in craft distilling and returns that sentiment with interest. That is best illustrated by 2021's release of the staggeringly good George Dickel x Leopold Bros. Collaboration Blend Rye. "It really was a phone call from Todd [Leopold]," says Austin, "who was looking for some help sourcing column-distilled rye that could be blended with his Three Chamber Rye to recreate that historic style. I've been following his Three Chamber project for years and was thrilled at the opportunity to work with him. The Three Chamber Rye is so unique, and his work as a distiller has always been so inspiring. We worked together on every aspect of the finished product, and I am so pleased with how it turned out."

George Dickel Barrel Select Tennessee Whisky

86 Each year, the master distiller at Cascade Hollow chooses several barrels of 10- to 12-year-old whisky and makes a small batch. This becomes George Dickel Barrel Select.

The nose is thick with corn and honey sweetness that has been spiked with a hefty dollop of vanilla, yet remains subtle and restrained. The almost syrupy sweet side leaves plenty of room to pick up on the notes of leather, floral citrus, cinnamon, and ginger.

The flavor is more subdued than the nose suggests. It has corn and vanilla sweetness balanced against delicate woodiness, with a moderately spicy kick at the end. Despite that last part, this is still a very mellow whisky, a point that plays out in the finish. The wind-down is light, only slightly warm, and just a little spicy, but despite the light touch it just lingers on and on.

Those looking for big, bold flavors should look elsewhere, but drinkers seeking mellow restraint and balance will love this stuff.

90 This one is unique among the plethora of rye whiskeys drawing on MGP's pervasive 95% rye stock, as it was made, in a sense, under contract. Dickel required MGP to make rye using their particular version of the Lincoln County Process. So, unlike all the other sourced 95% ryes that crowd store shelves, this one was chill and sugar maple charcoal-filtered prior to aging.

As for why Dickel would outsource their rye when they have a perfectly functional medium-size distillery, what they told me is that mashes with a high-rye content are sticky and difficult to work with (one distiller who wishes to remain anonymous once told me he was convinced the active ingredient in rye grain was Gorilla Glue), and Dickel wasn't set up to handle it. They aged it for about five years, and it's among my favorite variations on the MGP 95% rye.

The coloring is that of bright, polished copper.

On the nose, the rye smells of toasty oak, floral citrus, and sweet tobacco with drops of vanilla and caramel. As with everything from George Dickel, mellow is a defining characteristic here.

The flavor has a little bit of everything, coming out in a nicely balanced and supremely restrained package. There is a little oak, a little bundle of ginger, vanilla, and cinnamon, and some sweet tobacco. It's spicy, but sweetly so and without being corny or fruity. Above all, it's silky smooth. The finish is spicy and dry, but still mellow, leaving a moderate and lingering warmth.

— CORSAIR DISTILLERY —

Started in Bowling Green, Kentucky, in 2008, Corsair has expanded with locations there and in Nashville, producing absinthe, gin, and rum along with whiskey. Corsair is one of the Four Kings behind the first collaborative whiskey bottling (see page 39), and the subsequent series.

CORSAIR OATRAGE WHISKEY

100

Oat whiskeys are still rare enough that I don't believe you would need all the fingers on one hand to count them. Corsair's version is all-malted and heavily reliant on barley, using just 51% malted oats and the rest coming from a mix of six-row malted barley and coffee (roasted to a dark color) malted barley. They describe it as a "breakfast whiskey," and although Corsair isn't a brewery, it's easy to see the similarity this mash bill has to certain oat stouts. It's aged in small barrels for several months.

The scent is spicy, and was in fact the inspiration for the way I season my son's oatmeal: cinnamon, ginger, and cloves, plus a little maple syrup. The thing in the nose that isn't in the breakfast I make is a sprinkling of nuts.

The palate is a full-bodied one, with a sweet flavor full of maple syrup and the aforementioned spices, predominately cinnamon, joined by earthy cocoa and green oak. The finish runs a bit hot and packs on more of that slightly astringent green oak.

CORSAIR QUINOA WHISKEY

Strictly speaking, this is an American malt because its mash bill is 80% malt, a mix of roasted and unroasted malted barley; only a fifth of the content is quinoa. Even so, it's the only whiskey I'm aware of that even uses quinoa, never mind as a flavoring grain.

I think if there is a reason no one else has released a quinoa whiskey since this one came out several years ago, it's the light but solid current of chemical solvent running right through the nose. It comes nowhere close to dominating the scent, but it's there and impossible to ignore. With it comes a pretty generous helping of orange zest and pineapple, with a dash of cinnamon. However, having an open jug of paint thinner in the room tends to be what you pay attention to, whatever else might be there, and so it is with this exotic whiskey.

The palate shifts sharply, turning to buttery wheat toast with walnuts, accented by cinnamon and ginger. The finish picks up those spices and carries on with them.

DAREK BELL

Whenever I'm asked to name influential figures in craft whiskey, Darek Bell always comes to mind. He started Corsair Distillery and has grown it to where it can straddle two states. He has written two books, *Alt Whiskeys* and *Fire Water*, cataloging his numerous experiments in making whiskey with unorthodox grains and smoking them.

This wasn't the most likely outcome for Bell. Bell studied computer graphics, but was an avid home brewer and winemaker, along with Corsair cofounder Andrew Webber. It was Bell's consuming hobby. "I would carefully gather all my ingredients during the week, prep everything on Friday night, and spend all Saturday brewing," says Bell. However, the idea of starting a commercial distillery only sparked after the biodiesel plant he and Webber were working on hit a snag. Webber quipped that making whiskey would be better, the idea stuck, and they started distilling batches of beer. Corsair grew out of that.

Bell was one of the early craft whiskey distillers who hit upon what seems like a no-brainer now: going where the big distillers weren't. Yet if you look back at the trailblazers of those initial years of the ongoing boom in small distilling, this wasn't a path that many of them followed. That, coupled to his love of peaty Scotch and the Southern tradition of smoked meats, is what drew him to smoking his whiskeys, as well as using nontraditional grains.

Following that path was not a guaranteed route to success. Bell struggled with raising money, citing the regulatory hurdles and the necessity to spend time aging whiskey before a product is ready. "There is no quick, two-year breakeven like in, say, a tech stock," says Bell. "The time span is very long and you have to have very patient investors." Initially, Corsair was turned down for funding and had to bootstrap it.

The bootstrapping worked, and unlike so many outfits that try to do a little bit of everything, Corsair does its spirits well (I cannot speak about the beer yet, but I'm confident). Bell's experiments aren't always the sort of thing you would want to buy on their own; I tried his olive-smoked malt whiskey once; it might make a marvelous blending component, but I would never pour it as an evening's sipping whiskey. For his part, from a technical standpoint, Bell is most proud of his 12-grain bourbon, Insane in the Grain. "So many grains are so different and require their own cereal mashes," says Bell, who has in fact pulled off a 12-grain mash bill of yellow corn, blue corn, two different types of barley, millet, oats, quinoa, rye, sorghum, spelt, triticale, and wheat. But, as a smoke lover, he is also quite fond of the whiskey that started everything at Corsair, Triple Smoke.

This is the best known and most well regarded of Corsair's whiskeys. The company calls it "the whiskey that put us on the map." The "triple" refers to their use of three separately smoked malts: cherrywood, beechwood, and peat.

In the glass, it has a color that is (and I write this without a trace of irony) very much like a smoke-stained copper pot. Coating the glass leaves behind a sheet of tears.

The scent yields a butterscotch-and-cherry candy served on an oaken plate, with just a hint of charcoal and a trace of citrus.

The flavor is like having two very different barbecues running side by side, because one current of smoke is fruity and the other is earthy. This cloud of smoke is thin enough to not overpower, but it's very much a constant presence on the palate, hovering atop a foundation of oak, and this despite the buttercream texture. The smoke fades away on the finish, leaving behind traces of oak.

Triple Smoke came along early in the craft whiskey movement, at a time when genuinely smoky American whiskeys were nonexistent, and if you wanted that sort of thing you were forced to reach for a bottle of Scotch. In today's context, it's a quite easy-drinking smoker of a whiskey. It's not a beast, nor is it overly light. It also isn't sophisticated. It's just simple, flavorful, and approachable.

— JACK DANIEL'S DISTILLERY —
(BROWN—FORMAN CORPORATION)

In the course of my long vagabondage, I discovered a hard-and-fast internationally applicable rule about booze. You could be in a bar with a dirt floor and a single dingy lightbulb hanging from a half-stripped wire, and you would still have a choice of two whiskeys: Johnnie Walker Red and Jack Daniel's Old No. 7.

That is no accident; those two are the world's best selling whiskeys. For its part, Jack Daniel's got there because its production process, and its reliance on the Lincoln County Process in particular, is designed to produce a consistent, mellow, easy-drinking whiskey in the most direct way possible.

JACK DANIEL'S OLD NO. 7 TENNESSEE WHISKEY

Made from a high-corn mash bill of 80% corn, 8% rye, and 12% malted barley, it's intended to be sweet, not spicy. The fermentation period runs for six days, and anything above 60 hours is creating flavors rather than alcohol. Finally there is Jack Daniel's approach to charcoal filtration: drip-filtering through a vat of sugar maple charcoal.

JD Black, as it's sometimes called, has a quite sweet corn and brown sugar-forward nose, with plenty of mint and vanilla to sweeten things up further, plus a little banana.

A sip reveals an uncomplicated, pleasant whiskey that delivers along that same profile: corn and sugar sweet with vanilla and even more banana, a hint of mint, and a sprinkling of barrel char. It's light, supremely mellow, and goes down smooth, without much in the way of a finish.

Jack Daniel's 10—Year—Old

97 Historically, Jack Daniel's has not been fond of age statement expressions. Although the distillery made it a practice over the years to generally describe how old their products were (their flagship Old No. 7 is four or five years old and Single Barrel is five to seven years), they rarely put that information on their labels... until late summer 2021. In an early statement of the direction he wanted to take, Chris Fletcher set aside approximately 3,000 barrels of Tennessee Whiskey for extra aging shortly after coming to Lynchburg to become assistant master distiller. Now he is master distiller, and those 3,000 barrels have become the first age statement whiskey Jack Daniel's has done in a century.

The nose is recognizable as Jack Daniel's, but richer and deeper than Old No. 7. It is led by brown sugar, caramel, and fried plantains, but enhanced by a spiciness of cinnamon, peppermint, and wood..

The palate is noticeably drier compared to the predictably mellow Jack Daniel's standard, developing much more character. The sweet side deepens with notes of mixed dark, dried fruits (think raisins and cherries), but the dry spices and wood come much more forward than on the nose as well. The finish rolls on with the oaky spices, adding a leathery character into the mix.

Jack Daniel's Gentleman Jack

This is the original premium expression of Jack Daniel's, introduced in 1990, and therefore part of the same era that gave us the Jim Beam Small Batch Collection, Elijah Craig 12-Year-Old, and Blanton's. To create it, the distillery decided to double down on filtration through sugar maple charcoal, giving the whiskey a round before and after barreling.

The nose tells you everything you need to know about this whiskey: there is a little barrel char and a hint of aniseed-style spiciness in there, but it's really a stack of banana pancakes with a light drizzle of maple syrup. Or maybe Nilla Wafers stuck into banana pudding with a vanilla drizzle.

The palate and short, light finish follow those lines to a tee.

Jack Daniel's No. 27 Gold Double Barreled Tennessee Whiskey

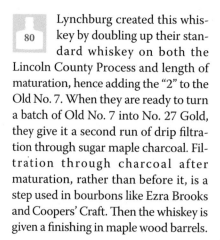

Lynchburg created this whiskey by doubling up their standard whiskey on both the Lincoln County Process and length of maturation, hence adding the "2" to the Old No. 7. When they are ready to turn a batch of Old No. 7 into No. 27 Gold, they give it a second run of drip filtration through sugar maple charcoal. Filtration through charcoal after maturation, rather than before it, is a step used in bourbons like Ezra Brooks and Coopers' Craft. Then the whiskey is given a finishing in maple wood barrels.

Jack Daniel's "Gold Label" was made specifically for the international market. You are much more likely to see it in Asia and Europe (though it is available in the United States).

Despite being filtered through charcoal twice (to say nothing of whatever filtering the distillery carries out prior to bottling), the nose remains quite creamy. It smells like a fruitcake, with dried dark fruits, sweet booziness, and spices.

A sip shows a velvety mouthfeel, the same boozy fruitcake quality layering up plus a honey glaze and some earthy cocoa, with a little wet tobacco rising up on the back end. It's supremely smooth, and I think the finish suffers a little because of that; it's sweet, but short and undistinguished.

CHRIS FLETCHER

I first met Chris Fletcher in 2012, when he was working as the lead chemist at Buffalo Trace. I left that sit-down thinking he was a fellow to watch. I was quite surprised a couple of years later when I discovered that, in a trade built to a large extent on family dynasties, Fletcher came from a family with whiskey ties, in Lynchburg, Tennessee! So, I was not surprised at all when Fletcher returned to his hometown in January 2014 to become assistant master distiller at the Jack Daniel's Distillery.

Fletcher's grandfather Frank Bobo was hired at Jack Daniel's in 1957, eventually rising to be master distiller there from 1966 to 1988. His granddad is the most illustrious family tie to the whiskey business, but hardly the only one. Lynchburg is a small town and Jack Daniel's is by far the biggest employer, so he has many other relations who have worked, or are working, at the distillery, including at one point his grandmother.

Despite practically growing up at the distillery, making whiskey was not what Fletcher was thinking about when he went to the Tennessee Technological University to study chemistry. "I chose chemistry because I enjoyed it," says Fletcher, "but didn't really have any idea that I'd eventually work in the distilling industry." That realization came only after college, when Fletcher returned to Lynchburg and worked as a part-time tour guide at the distillery. After about a year of showing folks around, he began thinking about a career in the whiskey business. He took a job in 2003 with Brown-Forman, the parent company for Jack Daniel's, in their Louisville research lab. In 2011, he moved over to work at Buffalo Trace Distillery as the lead chemist.

Then in December 2013, he took a call from Jeff Arnett, Jack Daniel's master distiller at the time, inviting him to come home and work as Arnett's number two. Fletcher started on January 2, 2014, 57 years to the day Frank Bobo began working there. Fletcher even works out of Bobo's old office and uses his old desk.

Having worked at Brown-Forman's headquarters, Buffalo Trace, and now Jack Daniel's means that Fletcher has had the opportunity to learn from a wider and deeper pool of whiskey lore than those who spend their entire careers working at a single distillery. But he naturally points to Bobo as a major source of advice that has helped him surmount challenges in the lab and the stillhouse. "I'm able to have conversations with my grandfather, who has over 30 years of distilling experience," says Fletcher. "He oversaw production at Jack Daniel's from 1966 when it was a very small brand, to 1989 when it had become a brand that was known and loved around the world. Being guided by him and by others has thankfully helped me to avoid any major problems."

As Fletcher is a rising figure in whiskey-making, when he went back to Lynchburg most observers recognized him as the heir apparent at Jack Daniel's. That observation was confirmed when Jeff Arnett retired, and Fletcher was promoted in October 2020 to become Jack Daniel's eighth master distiller. Even though he has only been at the helm for a brief time, many of the recent releases from Jack Daniel's are either already his creations or have his fingerprints all over them. Fletcher is still a young man, and he has plenty of time to widen and deepen his stamp on defining Jack Daniel's whiskey.

90 Going back to the days of the Rat Pack, if not before, Frank Sinatra was a big booster for Jack Daniel's. So, the company decided to pay tribute to Ol' Blue Eyes, but this is more than just a commemorative release. The Brown-Forman Cooperage in Louisville made a batch of barrels with deep, concentric grooves cut into the insides, both exposing virgin oak inside the charred staves and increasing the surface area inside the barrel. Whiskey aged in these specially made barrels is then blended with whiskey from other specially chosen, but otherwise normal barrels. It's then bottled at 90 proof, the original strength of modern Jack Daniel's.

The nose has a big vanilla-and-oak current running through the center, flanked by soft, sweet honey on one side and fresh stone fruits on the other.

A sip, however, is not like that at all. Instead, the flavor oozes caramel and butterscotch syrup, with orange zest sprinkled on the top and a whiff of slightly acrid smoke in the background. It's pungent, just enough to define everything else present on the palate, and that in no way detracts from it. The finish goes down vanilla sweet and with trademark Jack Daniel's smoothness.

JACK DANIEL'S SINGLE BARREL TENNESSEE RYE WHISKEY

94

When Jack Daniel's decided to do a rye, it meant they were introducing their first new mash bill in a century. They did not follow the Kentucky pattern or adapt their own high-corn style; instead, they went for 70% rye, 18% corn, and 12% malted barley. After making the initial batches, they gave the public a peek at their rye in stages. The first out was the unaged, white rye bottling in 2012, followed by the aged but youthful Rested Rye in 2014. Then in 2016, they released a four-year-old single-barrel rye.

This expression continues in regular release as the premium expression of JD rye whiskey, with the current version said to be at least five years old.

The scent here is brown sugar, pretty solid notes of caramel, and that trademark Jack Daniel's banana, as well as a quite modest current of spiciness.

The palate is fruit-forward, like a bowl of baked bananas and plantains, undergirded by a little oak and a little rye spice. The finish is where things finally turn spicier than fruit, with the sip going out on cinnamon.

Jack Daniel's Single Barrel Barrel Proof Tennessee Whiskey

Whenever I find myself having to persuade a bourbon enthusiast who looks askance at Jack Daniel's to give them another try, Single Barrel Barrel Proof is where I steer them. JD draws barrels from the upper floors of their rickhouses for their single-barrel expressions, and this one is no exception. As a cask-strength whiskey, and one that isn't batched with other barrels at that, the proof can vary wildly from bottle to bottle. Officially, the rule is 125 to 140 proof, and nothing I've seen on store shelves departs from that. Part of the reason why I recommend Single Barrel Barrel Proof so highly is that it exemplifies much of what is best with Jack Daniel's whiskeys.

This is high-octane stuff, and the strongest examples could power your car, but you would not pick that up from a sniff. Instead, what you get is full-bodied caramel-and-maple candy with notes of banana and barrel char.

The flavor leads with that same caramel-maple candy and banana sweetness, rounded out with leaf tobacco and earthy nuttiness. The high proof doesn't reveal itself until you get to the finish, which kicks off oaky, tannic, and a touch hot, but that subsides. As it does, one is left with traces of maple and barrel char.

Single Barrel Barrel Proof has become my new "sucker puncher" favorite; it's a whiskey that if you order a double of it at the bar, you'll have little idea how potent it is until you try to stand up.

The story of Jack Daniel's rye whiskeys reached its culmination with JD Tennessee Rye. The Single Barrel Rye became a premium expression, whereas this release (which came out in 2017) is intended to serve as the distillery's flagship rye.

It has a typical rye look in the glass, with its orange-tinted, light amber appearance. A coating of the glass streams legs.

A whiff reveals a fresh whiskey, fruity with orange zest, and mildly herbal with mint and fresh-cut grass.

The flavor goes over to being very cereals-forward, with a strong current of vanilla and peppery spices, a little orange zest, and a teaspoon of butterscotch. The finish is, strangely, a little nutty, but nothing that jumps out at you as it is light and fades fast. This is a mass-market creation, and in terms of rye content it sits in a zone between the MGP 95% rye and the Kentucky-made ryes. I think it's lacking in the finish, but otherwise it's a pleasant, flavorful sipper, and is as good as a slew of MGP-based ryes in its price range.

— NELSON'S GREEN BRIER DISTILLERY —

Located in Nashville, Tennessee, Nelson's Green Brier is the revival of what had been one of the biggest distilleries in the state prior to the enactment of statewide prohibition in 1909. It is very much a family business, started by brothers Andy and Charles Nelson, descendants of the original owners. They entered their 2015 initial production run of wheated Tennessee Whiskey into 30-gallon barrels and made that into a sneak-peek release in 2017, but everything since that first run has gone into standard 53-gallon barrels. While the Nelsons waited on that stock of whiskey to mature, they relied upon the sourced whiskeys going into their Belle Meade brand, and finally released their own regular edition, white-labeled Nelson's Green Brier Tennessee Whiskey in 2019.

BELLE MEADE STRAIGHT BOURBON WHISKEY

90.4 Belle Meade Bourbon is made in very small batches of just four barrels, drawing on two different stocks of MGP bourbons aged six to nine years to create a whiskey with an aggregate mash bill of 64% corn, 30% rye, and 6% malted barley. I've found Belle Meade quite smooth and balanced for what is effectively a high-rye bourbon. The dry spiciness that sometimes attends the high rye content just isn't there.

Instead, on the nose and the palate it comes across very much in the traditional bourbon sweet spot with candy corn, orange zest, vanilla, and just a little old leather and oak to round things out. It's on the finish that the high rye makes itself apparent, and that runs peppery and dry, but in a way that gives the whiskey a nice character.

Nelson's Green Brier Sour Mash Tennessee Whiskey

91 Beyond what I wrote above, there are two things to know about this bottle. First is that while there are some wheated Tennessee bourbons around, at the time I am writing this it is the only example of a wheated Tennessee Whiskey on the market (i.e., a whiskey made with a wheated, bourbon mash bill and that has received the Lincoln County Process). That makes this whiskey quite a novelty. Second, the batches are made drawing on stock between two and five years old.

A pour of this whiskey takes on a solid, middling amber look in the glass.

I found the nose to lead with Apple Jacks atop gingerbread, accented with a surprising current of nuttiness coupled to (unsurprising) green wood shavings and caramel.

The liquid sits lightly on the palate, and the core notes of apples, ginger, cloves, vanilla, and nuts are all there. The finish went down lightly spiced. Nelson's Green Brier is a good, easy drinking whiskey that challenges assumptions about Tennessee while punching well above its weight. Moreover, I strongly encourage all enthusiasts (who can line up all three of the following bottles) to try it in tandem with Jack Daniel's Old No. 7 and George Dickel No. 12 and see what you think about the Lincoln County Process after that.

Uncle Nearest 1884 Small Batch Whiskey

93

In 2016, the *New York Times* published a story that put the spotlight on a quasi-open secret: contrary to the popular story, the man who actually taught Jack Daniel how to make whiskey was not the preacher and grocer Dan Call, but a hired-out slave in Call's employ, Nathan "Nearest" Green. After emancipation in 1863, Green stayed on with Call, and his heritage is interwoven into that of Tennessee Whiskey. His descendants have been working at the distillery in Lynchburg since the beginning, and a few were employed there when the story broke.

Uncle Nearest, the brand named for Green, is the creation of best-selling author Fawn Weaver (daughter of Motown legend Frank Wilson), who was the person most responsible for publicizing the role Green played in laying the foundation for Jack Daniel's Tennessee Whiskey. The Nearest Green Distillery opened to visitors in 2019, nestled into what was a horse farm, and is part of a new, small, and growing class of distilleries owned and operated by African Americans.

The 1884 Small Batch is sourced, and is said to be 7 years old, despite not bearing an age statement.

This pour has a gold coloring in the glass, which in my mind is suggestive of used barrel aging (a la Early Times or Barrell Whiskey). That said, I didn't find much in the rest of the experience that yelled "not aged in new white oak," and frankly the color of a whiskey is the least indicative part of it. So, don't assume it's used barrel whiskey (and there would be nothing wrong with it if it were) just because it's named "whiskey," not bourbon or Tennessee Whiskey, and it has a gold coloring. Maybe it is, but it's hard to tell from sipping on it.

A sniff is reminiscent of a graham cracker with caramel drizzled over the top, plus shavings of candy corn.

The flavor follows in that vein, only now all of that is put on top of a cinnamon graham cracker. The finish starts sweet, then turns a little cinnamon spicy as it fades away. Uncle Nearest Small Batch is pretty nice stuff, and makes for fine, pleasant, but ultimately, simple sipping. It's the kind of whiskey you enjoy, rather than ponder.

— OLE SMOKY MOONSHINE —

Thanks to its locations in Gatlinburg and Pigeon Forge, collectively one of the biggest resort destinations in the United States, Ole Smoky Moonshine is the most visited moonshine distillery in America. It's also the most widely available moonshine. Many legal moonshines aren't whiskeys, due to the prevalence of mixing sugar into the grain mash. Such corn-and-sugar moonshines, for example, are quite common in the South.

OLE SMOKY BLUE FLAME MOONSHINE

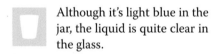

This moonshine qualifies as corn whiskey under the law; it's made from a mash bill of 84% corn, 8% rye, and 8% malted barley. When most people think of moonshine, they think of something with the potency of rocket fuel and this one doesn't disappoint.

Although it's light blue in the jar, the liquid is quite clear in the glass.

The nose is sweet, creamy corn, like corn pudding that is just a little undercooked. There is no corn husk grassiness to the scent whatsoever.

It's amazingly smooth when one considers that it's 64% ABV. Mind you, I tasted from a tumbler, but even so it gave me no burn whatsoever. The flavor is simple and full-bodied: thick, buttery sweet corn, but sweeter than any sweet corn I've had. It's not like sugar-added, but just more intense. The finish finally brings out the corn husk, but it's quite smooth and understated. It's warm, but not hot and with no bite at all. Once again, this is quite a surprise for such a strong and unaged liquor.

Simple, clear, big bodied, and not even remotely harsh, this high-octane other direction 'shine defies the rocket fuel stereotype.

Ole Smoky Apple Pie Moonshine

70 Drinking moonshine is an acquired taste for most, and for some no amount of trying can temper the issues of imbibing potent, unaged whiskey. One of the traditional means of making moonshine more palatable is called Apple Pie, where one adds apple juice, cinnamon, and other baking spices.

The nose on this iced tea–looking liquid smacks of baking spices (cinnamon first and foremost) and apple juice, but mostly the spices.

The apple comes forward on the palate to evenly share center stage, and the flavor really is like apple pie, and it's not at all a boozy apple pie taste either. In fact, the first hint of booze (and a hint is all it is) comes only with the sweetly spiced finish.

— PRICHARD'S DISTILLERY —

Prichard's Distillery is one of just a few outfits that, like Old Potrero, can claim to be craft whiskey before there was any concept of craft whiskey. When Phil Prichard opened his first distillery in Lincoln County in 1997 (a second plant was opened in 2014), there was just his shop, Jack Daniel's, and George Dickel in Tennessee. After making a deep dive into the life of a whiskey-making ancestor, Benjamin Prichard, Phil has decided to draw on a different part of the Tennessee whiskey legacy.

BENJAMIN PRICHARD'S TENNESSEE WHISKEY

Whiskey at Prichard's is not made with the Lincoln County Process, despite being in the county from which that process gets its name. Prichard also uses white corn instead of yellow corn in his mash, deep barrel charring, and copper pot stills. When the statehouse passed the Tennessee Whiskey Law of 2013, Prichard's Distillery was grandfathered in, and allowed to continue calling some of its existing products "Tennessee Whiskey," even though they did not comply with the law. That exemption points specifically to Benjamin Prichard's Tennessee Whiskey.

A pour is aromatic, despite its minimum proof. A current of sweet corn and vanilla runs through, accented by a generous helping of cinnamon and nutmeg and a little white pepper, and crowned by red berries.

The flavor takes a more earthy turn, going to malty honey, cocoa and coffee grounds, and cherries served up on a foundation of toasty oak. The finish makes a transition back to some of the spiciness present in the nose, and lingers on in that vein.

86

Whereas the mash bill for Prichard's Tennessee Whiskey is something of a secret (we know it is made with white corn, rye, and malted barley, but not how much of each), the details for their rye are clearer: 70% rye, 15% corn, and 15% malted barley. It's said to draw on stock aged for three to five years.

Despite the relatively high rye content, this whiskey is not endowed with big-bodied spiciness. Instead, it's an example of a fruity rye, where the spice is more subtle.

The nose comes across with sarsaparilla, apple, mint, and dried leaf tobacco, rounded out by notes of sweet apple cider and vanilla cream.

The taste is vanilla cream–stuffed caramel candy, dusted with cinnamon and cloves. As is so often the case with rye whiskeys, especially when they aren't Kentucky-style ryes, the finish turns dry. The spices run to mint and ginger, but the conclusion is predominately oaky and dry, and just a little tannic.

VIRGINIA

— A. SMITH BOWMAN DISTILLERY —

The greatest survivor of modern American whiskey history is Abraham Smith Bowman. Let's say you were sitting in a bar in the mid-1990s, talking whiskey and sipping on one of the new small-batch bourbons that had just come into vogue. The Depression that had hung over the whiskey industry since the bust of the 1970s looked to be finally over, but that bust had claimed every whiskey-making distillery in the United States outside of Kentucky, Indiana, and Tennessee. All except for one, that is: Abraham Smith Bowman, last remnant of Virginia's whiskey industry.

The A. Smith Bowman Distillery was founded after Prohibition, in the middle 1930s, by its namesake Abraham Bowman. Bowman had been a banker and got out of the liquor business with Prohibition; in 1927 he bought a 4,000-acre farm in what was then rural northern Virginia. With the repeal of Prohibition, he immediately set about establishing a distillery on the property. In the early days, grain from his farm and even oak from the parcel were used in making whiskey. In the 1940s, Bowman bought another tract of land, almost doubling the size of his property.

By the 1960s, however, the growth of the Washington, DC metropolitan area and rising real estate prices forced the sale of nearly all of the Bowman property, excepting the distillery's immediate surroundings. That land is now Reston, Virginia. The Bowman distillery went on to survive the industry's crash in the next decade, but the growth of the city finally compelled it to move to Fredericksburg, Virginia, in 1988. The distillery was acquired by Sazerac in 2003.

The move, however, cost the distillery its ability to mill, mash, and ferment grain in-house. Bowman switched to having bourbon spirit shipped to it for final distillation at their site, whereupon they would barrel it, age it, and bottle it as Virginia Gentleman Bourbon. It's only in recent years that Bowman has added the equipment necessary to ferment in-house.

It is the copper at Bowman that reinforces their status as a hard-bitten survivor of some dark times. They have a still, dubbed "Mary," of a design unlike any working still I've laid eyes on (although I've seen a couple of discarded wrecks that are similar). Mary was part of the original distillery (now a park in downtown Reston), and Master Distiller Brian Prewitt says it is the handiwork of a defunct Philadelphia copperworks; today, maintenance is done by Vendome.

Prewitt has added a second, smaller Vendome-made still, which he uses for some of the brand's experimental releases. He considers Bowman to be a micro-distillery, with some elements of the facility having more in common with the craft sector than the big distillers in Kentucky and Tennessee. To cite just one example of their way of doing things, Bowman makes both sour-mash and sweet-mash whiskey.

Bowman Brothers Small Batch Straight Bourbon Whiskey

The standard-bearer bourbon from A. Smith Bowman is triple-distilled from a traditional corn, rye, and malted barley recipe. The bourbon spends several years in barrels featuring a #3 char, and although the whiskey doesn't bear an age statement, batches are usually (though not always) aged for a minimum of seven years. For a bourbon at its price point, Bowman Brothers is remarkably complex, transitioning markedly from nose to palate to finish.

A whiff of this packs applesauce with plenty of cinnamon, along with a solid note of vanilla and a hint of nuts.

It turns sharply once it's on the palate, the profile becoming one of ginger cookies and toffee, with a nice current of toasty wood rising on the back side to provide a hint of barrel char. Corn syrup sweetness turns up on the short, simple finish.

John J. Bowman Single Barrel Straight Virginia Bourbon Whiskey

100

Bowman's single-barrel expression starts from the same place as Bowman Brothers Small Batch. The key differences are: (1) it's single barrel, not a small batch; (2) it's bottled at 100 proof, not 90; and (3) the barrels chosen are usually nine or 10 years old. Once again, there is no age statement on the bottle, and individual bottlings could very well be less than that, but that is what the press materials regarding this expression have claimed.

Having spent more time in the barrel, this is a much more wood-forward and traditionally flavored bourbon, and that comes at you right off the bat on the nose. Compared to its small-batch sibling, its scent is like a caramel apple, with emphasis on the caramel. There is a strong current of leathery old oak running right through it too, like you cannot smell the apple without also smelling the stick it's stuck on, and that stick has some old leather wrapped around the handle.

This single-barrel bourbon doesn't travel all over the map the way the younger small-batch version did, with the flavor staying very much in the same traditional bourbon territory as revealed by the nose. It is corn syrup and brown sugar sweet, seasoned with plentiful helpings of vanilla, and served up on an oaken platter. The finish runs much longer here too, starting earthy and leathery before turning oaky and dry.

Isaac Bowman Port Barrel Finished Bourbon Whiskey

92

Following the enthusiastic reception of their limited-edition Port-finished bourbon, A. Smith Bowman made this a permanent addition to their lineup in 2016. Initially, Bowman used a mix of Portuguese and Virginia Port wine casks to give their bourbon a finish of several months. However, on a 2018 visit to the distillery, I was told they were unable to secure a steady supply of Virginia Port casks to continue with that practice, and now rely entirely on Portuguese casks.

A pour reveals light amber coloring, lighter than I expected given the overall maturation. A swish and coat of the glass gave a thick coat that dropped just a few legs.

A sniff gave me thick vanilla, cherry jam, nuttiness, toasted graham crackers, and aged wine.

The flavor is wood-driven in the main, and quite spicy, but rounded out by light caramel and tawny wine. The finish ran on a nutty note that lingered for quite a while.

BRIAN PREWITT

If things always went as expected, Brian Prewitt shouldn't be at the helm of A. Smith Bowman. Prewitt, a Colorado native, got his start working at New Belgium Brewing Company while working on his bachelor's in food science at Colorado State University. After building on his brewing knowledge at the Master Brewers program at the University of California, Davis, he went back to Colorado to work at Great Divide Brewing Company, eventually becoming brewer there.

He moved to distilling by taking a post making brandy at E&J Distilleries in Modesto, California. There he learned under two seasoned master distillers with a combined experience of more than 70 years, and gained knowledge that later proved quite transferrable to making Virginia bourbon. This is true even of his stint making tequila, which Prewitt frankly admits he didn't particularly care for when he began working with it, and even now regards as an acquired taste.

"You can't make a good whiskey with a bad beer, you can't make a good brandy with a bad wine," says Prewitt. "The goal of a good distiller is to maximize those characters and bring out the essence of the base material, to really let it shine, and then if a spirit is undergoing a maturation process to build upon the flavors that the spirit has, you can mold it into something that accentuates the process and tells the story of how that spirit came to be."

Bowman has grown since Prewitt took over, expanding both its profile among whiskey enthusiasts and its production capacity, including adding a second, small still partly devoted to experimental whiskeys.

Prewitt has been on the job long enough now to have stamped his style on Bowman's identity, and the expression he is most pleased with is the Isaac Bowman Port Barrel Finished Bourbon. "It is not a single one time and done experiment, although it was based off of one of our experiments," he explains. "I love the complexity and the flavor profile. It breaks out of the mold of a traditional bourbon and incorporates wonderful fruit and jam notes on top of vanilla and toasty oak. It is a bourbon that I feel can be appreciated by someone new to bourbon and someone who considers bourbon their main drink of choice. So approachable, yet still sophisticated."

— CATOCTIN CREEK DISTILLING COMPANY —

Founded in 2009 in Loudon County, Catoctin Creek was an early entrant into the craft whiskey explosion and among the first micro-distilleries to start up in the Old Dominion in modern times. They were also a forerunner in the ever-expanding role women have come to occupy in the whiskey-making sphere, as Becky Harris has been master distiller there from the beginning. They have become quite popular in the Washington, DC area, with a reputation built on various iterations of their 100% organic rye whiskey distillate.

CATOCTIN CREEK RABBLE ROUSER BOTTLED IN BOND RYE WHISKY

Rabble Rouser has been around since 2015. Although it has been a four-year-old expression from the beginning, it was not initially labeled a bottled in bond and therefore cannot be considered as the forerunner of the craft bottled in bond whiskeys that started coming out in 2017. Even so, it was quite novel to have a four-year age statement on a craft rye back in 2015.

Catoctin Creek used their house 100% rye mash to make Rabble Rouser, but the distillate isn't the same as what goes into Roundstone Rye. Instead, they chose to distill it to a lower proof, a choice that puts more of just about everything but alcohol in the new make. Past that, it's a bottled in bond: distilled at Catoctin Creek in a single season; four years old, the minimum for the category; and aged under government supervision.

In the glass, it has the look of brightly polished copper. A coating of the glass forms a beady crown and drops skinny legs.

The scent comes on with dill and cookie spices first, followed by a spoonful of brown sugar, then some musty old wood and pine needles underneath.

A sip reveals a whiskey that is deeply spicy, albeit mildly and pleasantly so. A moderate dollop of ginger and pepper is rounded out with cinnamon and cardamom, and sweetened just a touch with vanilla. The finish is briefly spicy, but this fades fast and leaves behind that musty wood from the nose. With this wonderful complexity at work, it's easy to see how distilling at a lower proof yields dividends in the flavor.

The flagship Roundstone Rye is aged for two or three years in new white oak barrels sourced from Minnesota (Catoctin Creek isn't the only distillery sourcing barrels from Minnesota coopers, and oak from that region is noted for its tighter wood grain, which restricts the access the whiskey has to the wood).

It has a golden look in the glass.

The nose carries a pleasant scent of spring wildflowers in the main, with sweet, wet leather and oak coming on with more air and more nosing.

The flavor is fruity, with a banana note giving that fruitiness a tropical vein, and a spoonful of baking spice serving the full notice that this is indeed a 100% rye mash bill whisky. Throw in a touch of almonds, and you've got the character of this light rye, mainly because the finish is so short as to hardly be there.

Catoctin Creek Braddock Oak Single Barrel Rye Whisky

This is essentially the single-barrel version of the distillery's Roundstone Rye.

Like most rye whiskeys, it has a lighter coloring than a similarly aged bourbon would have, more golden and coppered than amber. After coating the glass, the legs are hesitant to make their appearance, and when they do come out, they are skinny and slow.

The nose is light on the spice, with hints of sweetness, wet leather, and oak.

It has a light mouthfeel, starting out on the palate in a way that belies that it's a rye. At first it follows in that sweet, wet leather and oaky vein from the nose, with the first hint of its rye character being a sweet tobacco leaf note. On the back end, the flavor starts to turn peppery. That rolls into a long, dry, and spicy finish.

— COPPER FOX DISTILLERY —

Modeling itself on Bowmore, one of the famed Islay distilleries of Scotland where founder Rick Wasmund interned, Copper Fox opened in 2005 in Sperryville with its own malt floor and kiln. Wasmund is even more particular about his grain than that, however; on top of malting all the barley he uses himself, he sources it all from a single Virginia farmer. To fire the kiln, Copper Fox uses fruit tree wood instead of peat.

COPPER FOX ORIGINAL RYE WHISKEY

90 This noted rye whiskey is made with a mash bill of two-thirds rye and one-third barley, and it's been aged in a mix of new and used barrels before bottling.

It's definitely a young whiskey, showing a strong current of green wood on the nose, but also some applewood smoke.

The flavor is spicy and sweet, the latter being a mix of honey and berry fruit, but it's also more than a little hot. The finish starts on a plain cookie note before running into green wood astringency, ending up bitter and hot.

COPPER FOX WASMUND'S SINGLE MALT WHISKEY

96 This whiskey is made with 100% malted barley, all of it malted at Copper Fox.

The dark, coppery look in the glass points to a woody whiskey, and it is certainly that.

The nose is herbal and vegetal, like someone just cleared a patch of honeysuckle, with a hint of smoke in the background, like the lingering embers of the burn pile from yesterday's clearing work.

The palate holds on to that scene while turning to astringent green oak, balanced against strong notes of apple and cherry, with a hovering smoky note. The finish is oaky before fading to astringency.

Copper Fox Original Rye may be the distillery's best-known whiskey, but their single malt is probably the thing people should pay the most attention to.

— VIRGINIA DISTILLERY COMPANY —

One can be forgiven for thinking the "Highland" reference on the label of a Virginia Distillery Company whisky refers to its location between Charlottesville and Lynchburg, in the foothills of the Blue Ridge Mountains. But, in fact, that term points straight to Virginia Distillery Company being one of the most Scottish-influenced whisky makers in America. "Virginia-Highland" indicates that part of the whisky is imported Highland single malt from Scotland. The other part is made in Virginia, but even this has a Scots element to it, because Virginia Distillery Company's stills are Scottish-made. These two elements are blended together under the guidance of Nancy Fraley, and then given several months of finishing in cider casks from Potter's Craft Cider in Charlottesville.

Virginia Distillery Co. Cider Cask Virginia–Highland Whisky

92 The look of this globalized malt is like that of white wine. It's a viscous liquid, one that forms a thick crown and drops some heavy, ponderously slow-moving tears.

It comes across with the scent of musty old wood on top, and crisp, youthful, and somewhat acidic apples and pears underneath, rounded out with a pinch of pie spice.

The flavor starts with a light, fruity note that is soon swamped by rising, peppery spices. The short finish runs on with that peppery note.

Virginia Distillery Co. Port Cask Finished Virginia–Highland Malt Whisky

92 One distinguishing feature of Virginia Distillery Company is their reliance upon locally sourced casks from other Virginia liquor makers for finishing stock. The Port casks for the fifth batch of this, the most recent release as of 2018, came from King Family Vineyards and Veritas Vineyard. This edition received a 10-month finish.

In the glass, the whisky is so coppery in color that it looks like flashing metal. A swish reveals a viscous liquid, one that forms a solid crown and leaves a scattering of slow-moving tears.

Nosing took in raisins and dried currants, with a handful of straw, a dollop of vanilla, and a pinch of baking spices.

A sip showed the whisky to have a soft, silken texture, and yielded the sweet stuff of ruby, fruity Port along with toffee and vanilla at first. Then straw and baking spice was thrown on top of this, which was in turn subsumed by a toasty, almost smoky flavor. This last part disappeared briefly on the finish, turning to tobacco leaf, before once again running to toasted oak.

Courage & Conviction American Single Malt

92 Starting in 2019, Virginia Distillery began showing their in-house malt in its own right, no imported Scotch added. It draws on three cask stocks of whiskey: approximately 50% ex-bourbon barrels, 25% sherry casks, and 25% Cuvee casks. Each of these casks has an expression all its own in the series. Courage & Conviction is aged for a minimum of three years.

A pour of this whiskey has the coloring of a blonde lager; if you let it sit in the glass, it looks like Miller High Life without the fizz.

The scent of that pour has a foundation of toasted cereals, layered with bundles of dried clover, fresh cut lavender, and a single overripe apricot.

A sip reveals a rich, malty whiskey, with honeyed cereals leading the way. A boozy fruit cake that went heavy on raisins follows, only to be subsumed in turn by a wave of dry, peppery wood. The finish follows in that vein, but is a light short one, so I think of it as being more of a sliver of that dry, peppery oak.

WEST VIRGINIA

— SMOOTH AMBLER SPIRITS —

Founded in 2009, Smooth Ambler followed the path of introducing sourced whiskeys to build their brand while they built their distillery and developed in-house spirits. They quickly became a fan favorite with their original iteration of Old Scout Bourbon, which back in those days was wholly sourced from middle-aged MGP whiskey.

Compared to most outfits that start sourcing and bottling prior to distilling their own spirits, Smooth Ambler began making the transition to making their own whiskeys early. Their distillery went operational in February 2010, and the next year they introduced Yearling, a wheated bourbon expression that started out as a one-year-old and saw its age statement increase with each passing year. Yearling has since been discontinued, but the sourced and in-house blend Contradiction was introduced in 2015, and the wheated bourbon stock from Yearling is now going into Big Level. French drinks giant Pernod Ricard acquired Smooth Ambler in 2017.

In designing their distillery, Smooth Ambler chose Vendome to build its still, but acquired their fermenters from Spokane Industries and have generally shopped around for other equipment. Smooth Ambler runs a sour-mash operation, with their new make coming off the still at about 140 proof.

In their early years, Smooth Ambler tinkered quite a bit with their production process, ultimately settling on yeast as the thing they needed to perfect to get the most out of their distillate. As a result, they are now using a proprietary blend of yeast strains for fermentation, and won't discuss what's in it.

Smooth Ambler's popularity means they are working pretty much around the clock, with a production target of filling 300 barrels a month. At the time of writing, they ran two day and two night shifts, mashing and distilling seven days a week, and pushing their equipment to its limits.

This move to produce at maximum capacity in 2017 meant their demand for grain quickly outstripped what the local farms in the Greenbrier Valley could provide. The distillery was then forced to make up the difference by importing grain from the Midwest and Canada.

The distillery purchases its barrels from Independent Stave Company and Speyside Cooperage, which are ordered with either #3 or #4 char. Smooth Ambler barrels their newmake spirit at about 120 proof.

Smooth Ambler Contradiction
Blended Straight Bourbon Whiskey

92 Introduced in 2015, Contradiction was Smooth Ambler's first step in the move from a bottler of sourced whiskeys to becoming an independent distillery, reliant on its own production. Contradiction is a blend of in-house and sourced whiskeys. The former comprises slightly more than a quarter of the blend, and is a two-year-old wheated bourbon, made from a mash bill of 60% wheat, 20% corn, and 20% malted barley. The latter is from MGP, a nine-year-old from their 75% corn, 21% rye, and 4% malted barley stock.

Since Contradiction was introduced, two things of note have happened to it and around it. First, in August 2018, the strength was cut to 92 proof. Also, Smooth Ambler's first entirely in-house whiskey, Big Level (see next page), came out that same summer. Interestingly, Big Level is also a wheated bourbon, but one made from a different mash bill than Contradiction.

It has a light copper appearance in the glass, and swishing it left long, beady legs.

The nose was full of graham crackers and caramel, backed by roasted nuts. Taking a sip showed a liquid with a light texture, one that shows both the mature and the young whiskeys in the blend.

The flavor is candy corn and an earthy green oak in the main, with spices and vanilla coming up alongside and behind. The finish is nutty, but also a touch astringent.

Smooth Ambler Big Level Wheated Bourbon

100 Big Level, released in the summer of 2018, isn't a mix of in-house and sourced whiskeys, but an entirely in-house product. It is a wheated bourbon made from a mash of 71% corn, 21% wheat, and 8% malted barley, distilled using a mix of column and pot stills, and aged for at least five years in 53-gallon barrels charred to level #4. The whiskey is bottled unfiltered.

Once in the glass, it looks like the polished copper it was distilled in. Swishing the glass yields a lightly oiled coat and scattered tears.

The nose reminded me of plums and tangerines, seasoned with cookie spices and mint. A little vanilla cream is daubed on top, and a hint of cedarwood in the background ties up the scent.

In strong contrast to the scent, and quite the opposite of what I was expecting for a wheated bourbon, a sip revealed a dry whiskey. Pleasant, as soft as a wheated bourbon should be, but dry all the same. The flavor has vanilla and cedar, plus a modest current of citrus zest, with spiciness coming up on the back end. The finish follows from there, running moderately spicy and dry.

96

This is one of those clever blends that certain independent bottlers and blenders (Smooth Ambler, Barrell Craft Spirits, High West, and so on) are so noted for. They started with a stock of high-rye (36% rye content) bourbon that is over nine years old and sourced from MGP. To this they have added some five-year-old whiskey made in Tennessee. The latter was distilled from a bourbonesque mash, but aged in used barrels that received a fresh charring. Because bourbon calls for aging in new oak, the use of even a re-charred barrel makes it something else. Blending the two stocks together makes it American whiskey.

It has a look that straddles the line between copper and gold. A pour forms a beady crown in the glass, one so sticky that it refuses to drop tears in any reasonable period of time.

The nose is simple, straightforward, and full of character: roasted nuts take the lead, and are quickly joined by butterscotch and wood.

A sip shows a light, creamy texture and a sweet flavor at first. This turns spicy, before allowing the roasted notes and wood to come back up. The finish runs short, showing a pinch of mint before disappearing.

The blending brings together some lovely elements, and the palate even shows a little sophistication. The finish was a bit disappointing, but I found myself genuinely surprised by just how much I liked it overall.

ND

SD

NE

KS

MIDWEST
REGION

MN

WI

IA

MI

IL

IN

OH

MO

ILLINOIS

FEW Spirits wasn't among the first crop of small distilleries, not even in its home area around Chicago, but that hasn't stopped the distillery from achieving a high profile. Their whiskeys are written about often, while their bourbon frequently appears on the shelves of whiskey bars, upscale liquor stores, and big liquor retailers. The distillery is also one of the "Four Kings," participating in the original craft whiskey collaboration bottling.

FEW's founder, Paul Hletko, has an archetypal backstory: going from a corporate job to blue-collar distilling. He was a burned-out patent lawyer—he once described it as spending his life fighting with people—looking for a change. He also came from a Czech brewing family, and pursued home brewing as a hobby. He began studying and organizing, developed a business plan, raised money, and then made the leap. FEW Spirits was born, and production began in June 2011.

The distillery has expanded steadily since its founding, experiencing explosive growth within a couple years of getting started. They have now assembled a set of equipment from Vendome, Sprinkman, Kothe, and elsewhere. As head distiller, Hletko runs his heterogeneous distillery two shifts a day, seven days a week. On his equipment, that turns out about five barrels worth of spirits per day.

Those barrels come from a Minnesota cooperage, and that choice, coupled with FEW's growth and popularity, is what brought the issue of the sourcing of oak for barrels more widespread attention. FEW uses small barrels and has pointed to the Minnesota oak as having tempered some of the downsides of using smaller barrels. Minnesota has a shorter growing season, so the grain of the wood is tighter, which in turn restricts the whiskey's access to the wood. By comparison, most of the wood used by the major cooperages feeding the big distillers comes from a band of states running from Missouri and Arkansas to Appalachia. FEW's barrels receive a #3 char.

Hletko runs a sweet-mash distillery. As a Midwestern distiller, he hasn't needed to go far to find his grain, with suppliers in Illinois, Indiana, and Wisconsin. He uses saison beer yeast for his bourbon and Loire Valley wine yeast for his rye. They distill up to 135 proof and enter the new make into the barrel at 118 proof.

Like many craft distilleries, FEW Spirits had a white whiskey as part of its lineup when they got started, back when they had to get a product on the market. However, white whiskey has become less important since the early 2010s, and that product was withdrawn. Its only unaged spirit these days is the gin. In addition to the bourbon and rye whiskey FEW produces, late in 2018 the distillery introduced a single malt.

Drawing on its location in Evanston, outside of Chicago, FEW bills its bourbon as "Southern tradition meets northern rye." It could just as well say northern oak too, because FEW sources their barrels from Minnesota. That matters because the white oak used to make barrels for the big distillers typically comes from more southerly locales, like Missouri, Alabama, and Tennessee.

93

The traditional mash bill (70% corn, 20% rye, and 10% malted barley) combines with the peppery yeast and "less than four years" in those Minnesota oak barrels to bring out each element of the whiskey in a straightforward, but balanced manner.

The nose is kind of like a Cracker Jack sprinkled with a bit of sweet, hot paprika.

This transitions into a flavor where vanilla, crushed red pepper, baking spices, and corn syrup all share the stage. The finish runs long, carrying a bit of rye spice and a bit of oak.

FEW Spirits went operational in 2011, and its bourbon has since become a craft whiskey fixture. Bloggers have been murmuring about how much they would like to see a version that is a couple years older since at least 2014, but there really isn't the need. FEW Bourbon is fine as is.

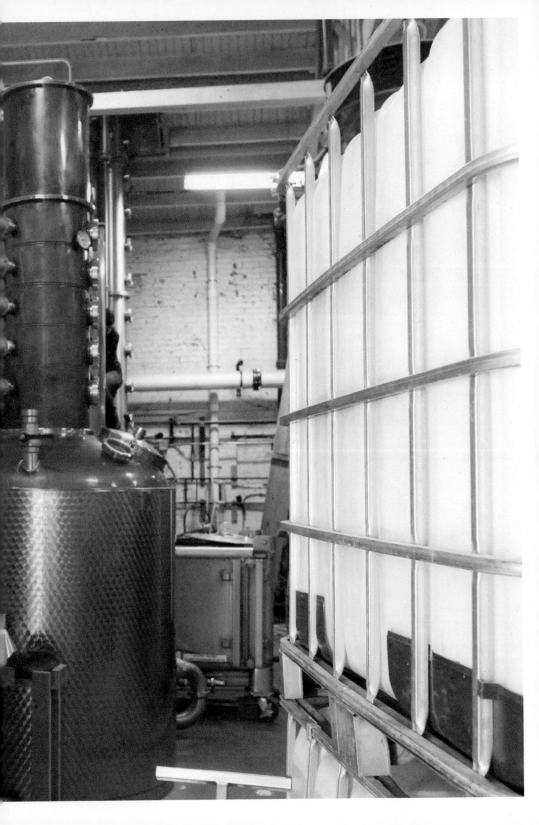

FEW RYE WHISKEY

93 One of the things FEW's product line allows a whiskey enthusiast to do is see what happens when a distiller decides to invert a mash bill, as FEW Rye takes the distillery's bourbon recipe and flips it.

The mash bill here is 70% rye, 20% corn, and 10% malted barley. Otherwise, it is made with the same equipment, in the same style, aged in the same kind of barrels, and bottled at the same strength as FEW Bourbon.

A sniff brings out allspice and pepper at first, followed by a rising tide of mango.

That fruity note is what predominates on the palate, really bringing out the fruity character rye whiskey sometimes has, and in some ways it's like someone spread a thick cherry jam onto a sweet corn muffin. The whiskey also shows its rye-ness through its crisp, dry texture. The fruitiness turns tart on the finish, runs dry, and ultimately fades to a faint, spicy note.

— KOVAL DISTILLERY —

Being the "first distillery to open in X since Prohibition" is a common boast in the craft spirits sphere. In the early days a new distillery could claim to be the first in a state, then later first in a city, but these claims are almost invariably tied to Prohibition and the death of what had heretofore been a nationwide industry.

Chicago's KOVAL Distillery, opened in 2008, is part of the initial wave of small distilleries and can fairly trumpet being "first since," but in KOVAL's case it isn't just since Prohibition. In a peculiar twist on Chicago history, KOVAL is the first (legal) distillery to open there since the mid-19th century. In an early example of small distillers lobbying at the state-house to get outdated laws changed, KOVAL founders Sonat and Robert Birnecker were in Springfield getting Prohibition legacy laws blocking new distilleries revised. In terms of getting there first, it helps if you're also the one clearing the legal hurdles!

KOVAL set up shop in Ravenswood, a Chicago district along some railroad tracks that now hosts several breweries and has become known as "Malt Row." Its distilling equipment is imported from Germany's Kothe Distilling Technologies, and as a result, KOVAL has also become a showcase in America for Kothe's handiwork.

Even though KOVAL has only been around for a decade, that decade has been in the midst of the Bourbon

Boom, and it has outgrown two facilities. For KOVAL's first expansion in 2011, it set up a second production plant in Ravenswood. This was necessary at that time because Illinois law capped production for craft distillers at 35,000 gallons a year, but allowed the holding of multiple licenses at different locations. In 2016, the law was amended so as to raise the limit for a craft distillery to 100,000 gallons, while at the same time eliminat-

ing the multiple licenses provision. So, in early 2017, KOVAL bought the building housing its second distillery. Once the leases of the other tenants in the building expired in mid-2018, KOVAL was free to occupy the entire 45,000-square-foot building, consolidating all operations under one roof.

KOVAL now produces between 60,000 and 70,000 gallons of spirit a year, making it a medium-size operation in craft terms. It sources all its

grain through an organic Midwest grain co-op, and its products have always been certified organic and kosher. While not extraordinary now, it was exotic when KOVAL started in 2008. The yeast comes from the Canadian company Lallemand, and the distillery's 30-gallon barrels come from The Barrel Mill in Minnesota, all made with #3 char. Even the barrels contribute to the company's organic emphasis: KOVAL uses beeswax instead of the more common paraffin to seal the barrel heads.

Being a trailblazer in organic spirits isn't KOVAL's only odd duck quality. All of its whiskeys are single-barrel expressions, and KOVAL is one of just a handful of distillers using the sweet-mash method. Even though KOVAL was a pioneer in craft whiskey, creating an example that many have since followed, in at least a couple of respects it is still an outlier in American whiskey.

KOVAL Single Barrel Bourbon Whiskey

94

KOVAL's bourbon is one of those uncommon two-grain whiskeys, made from a mash of 51% corn and 49% millet. The millet alone would make it a serious oddball whiskey, but the high proportion makes it unique. Insofar as I know, there are no other examples of a "high-millet" bourbon out there, even in an experimental version, and this one has been around for a decade. The whiskey is aged for two to four years in Minnesota oak casks (much like KOVAL's neighbor, FEW Spirits).

This whiskey was bottled unfiltered and has a very high content of an unorthodox grain; these factors show in the glass, right from the start. It's a viscous, dirty golden liquid, and a coating of the glass drops chunky, slow-moving tears off a respectable crown.

A sniff gives a toffee aroma, accented with a dash of vanilla and a hint of oak.

The flavor is surprisingly spicy, featuring currents of cinnamon, cardamom, and pepper in the main, with a solid hunk of oak and a hint of caramel. The finish goes down woody and spicy, but not hot.

KOVAL Single Barrel Four Grain Whiskey

94

This whiskey has no lead grain (i.e., no grain at 51% or higher in the mash bill). Moreover, the exact grain recipe is unknown, except to say it's malted barley, oats, rye, and wheat, and the proportions go unstated. However, like everything KOVAL does, it's a single barrel and aged in 30-gallon barrels.

Once in the glass, the whiskey's coloring straddles the line between gold and copper. Swishing and coating the glass prompted a few thick tears.

The nose was quite rich, surprisingly so, in fact. If I had to guess, I would attribute the weight of the scent to the oats and the barley. It's sweet with berries and molasses, spiced up with cinnamon.

The flavor profile, however, is quite different from that. It's still rich and full-bodied, but more like a caramel candy seasoned with cake spices. The berries are gone, and the molasses clings on as a mere trace note. The finish is crisply spicy, but fades fast.

KOVAL Single Barrel Rye Whiskey

80

As a rule, small and medium-size distillers do not follow the lower-rye pattern of the Kentucky style, and KOVAL is no exception. Instead, it went in the opposite direction and made a 100% rye whiskey. This rye is aged for 1½ to two years in 30-gallon barrels and bottled unfiltered.

In the glass, the color bridges the gap between copper and amber. Coating the inside of the glass leaves behind a spread of thin, slow-moving legs.

Taking a sniff got me acquainted with a sharp, clear scent, with the aroma of green apples sitting in the middle. Supplementing that slightly sour, mostly sweet fruitiness is a dollop of holiday spices and tinge of green wood.

On the palate, the liquid is silky smooth. That slightly sour apple fruitiness is joined by vanilla and honey, making the flavor sweeter than the scent, with cracked pepper sprinkled on top and a hint of green wood rising on the back end. The finish lingers for a lengthy time, with equal but light measures of pepper and green oak.

INDIANA

Most of the sourced whiskeys described before and after the Indiana section are placed there because even if those distilleries partly or entirely source their liquor from a second party; they have a distillery and call it home. However, some whiskeys, like those made by Redemption Whiskey and This Is Stolen, are sourced from MGP in Indiana, aren't attached to a working distillery, and in my opinion are worth knowing about. Rather than place these in the state where a company office or bottling plant might be, I list them where they were made: Indiana.

— BEAR WALLOW DISTILLERY —

Some readers may be surprised to learn that MGP is not the only distillery in Indiana. Micro-distilling has put down roots among the Hoosiers too, with Brown County's Bear Wallow Distillery in operation since 2011.

BEAR WALLOW GNAW BONE STRAIGHT BOURBON WHISKEY

Gnaw Bone Bourbon is a "wheater," made from a mash bill of 65% corn, 25% wheat, and 10% malted barley. It's aged in charred, new oak barrels coming from the Kelvin Cooperage and bottled without chill filtration.

The scent strikes a balance between the grassy and corn-sweet graininess of a young bourbon and the vanilla flavors of one that has sat in the barrel for a decent length of time.

The flavor has an apple and pear sweetness, seasoned with caramel, vanilla, and oak. All in all, it's a pretty fair example of what a wheated bourbon is supposed to be: soft, floral, and sweet.

— MIDWEST GRAIN PRODUCTS (MGP) —

Although MGP Ingredients Distillery in Lawrenceburg has been getting some press in the last decade, it remains the most obscure of America's major distilleries. Its in-house whiskey brands, George Remus Bourbon and Rossville Union Rye, are not very big; the distillery isn't open to the public, and even visits by journalists are rare, and few have visited it. In contrast to the prevailing trend of the American whiskey industry, master distiller David Whitmer isn't in the spotlight. Yet if the sales of all the sourced brands based, in part or in whole, were tallied, MGP would surely place in the top five of all American whiskey makers.

The distillery now called MGP started in 1847 as the Rossville Distillery, and was acquired by Seagram in 1933, following the end of Prohibition. It was renamed the Jos. E. Seagram Lawrenceburg Plant and would be known by that name for decades. Seagram was a Canadian conglomerate and drinks industry behemoth during those years, but poor business choices in the modern era led to the breakup of the company. In 2000, the liquor assets went to the industry's two goliaths: Britain's Diageo and France's Pernod Ricard.

The Lawrenceburg plant went to Pernod Ricard, and in April 2006, the decision to close the plant was announced. But then Pernod Ricard changed course and sold the distillery to a Caribbean holding firm, whereupon it became Lawrenceburg Distillers Indiana, or LDI. In 2011, the distillery was sold on to MGP Ingredients, a Kansas-based distiller and producer of specialty wheat proteins and starches for the food and beverage industry. This is how what is by far the largest distillery in Indiana acquired its current name.

Pernod Ricard's sale of the distillery in 2006 coincided with the start of the craft distilling movement and the takeoff of the Bourbon Boom. As the popularity of American whiskey soared, the other big distilleries in Kentucky and Tennessee would find they needed to retain their production capacity to meet demand for their own products. One by one, they retreated trading aged whiskey stock, leaving LDI/MGP as the only major supplier of ready-to-go, aged whiskey in the country.

It fit that role so well because the distillery had several mash bills in production, coming out of their Seagram days, and even expanded upon its offerings in 2013. Most major distilleries produce one formulation of rye whiskey, if even that, but MGP has three. Beyond the ubiquitous 95% rye, 5% malted barley rye whiskey, it also has a 51% rye, 49% malted barley whiskey, and a 51% rye, 45% corn, and 4% malted barley whiskey. Add to those five separate bourbons, a wheat whiskey, a single malt whiskey, a corn whiskey, and a light whiskey.

The only distillery in America with a wider diversity of whiskeys is Bardstown Bourbon Company (BBCo), who are producing over thirty different whiskeys. But all of that is contract production and meeting the specific requirements of their clients. A large chunk of MGP's production is intended for sale as aged stock whiskey to Non-Distiller Producers (NDPs). If you walk into a liquor store and go to the whiskey section, you will be surrounded by bottles containing MGP whiskey.

In terms of how MGP does things, it is very much in line with other big distillers. It makes sour mash whiskeys, with most of the equipment coming from Vendome, and MGP's demand for barrels is so great that they maintain multiple suppliers. MGP typically enters the whiskey into the barrel at 120 proof, and those barrels are usually charred to level 4 ("alligator char").

MGP has struggled to raise its profile and develop its own brands but took what could be a leap forward in addressing that problem by purchasing one of its largest and most consistent customers: Luxco. The April 2021, $475 million acquisition brought with it both the Limestone Branch and Luxrow distilleries in Kentucky, and with them the Blood Oath, David Nicholson Reserve, Daviess County, Ezra Brooks, Luxrow, Minor Case, Rebel Yell, and Yellowstone brands.

Accompanying this push by MGP has been the partial renaming of the distillery itself. In September, the company announced that the Remus and Rossville brands are now made at what they called the Ross & Squibb Distillery, the same building but with a name reflecting their pre-Civil War origins. However, the aged spirits sold to third parties continues to come from the MGP Distillery. Luxco now formally manages the sale and marketing of the Remus and Rossville brands.

GREG METZE

Billed in the press as "America's Unknown Master Distiller" and as the "Unsung Hero of Whiskey," only the keenest of bourbon enthusiasts knew of Greg Metze prior to MGP developing brands of its own. Master distillers at the Lawrenceburg plant weren't strictly anonymous, but they weren't promoted as larger-than-life rock stars either, as the master distillers of the other major distilleries typically are.

That began to change in 2015, when MGP introduced Metze's Select Bourbon, the same year Metze was named Distiller of the Year by *Whisky Advocate*. He'd started working at Lawrenceburg in 1978, shortly after receiving his degree in chemical engineering from the University of Cincinnati. He worked in every aspect of maintenance and production before he started training under then Master Distiller Larry Ebersold. "Ebersold taught me the art of making world-class whiskey and spirits," says Metze. "I became highly skilled in the production of whiskeys, batch light whiskey, gin, and neutral grain spirits." He succeeded Ebersold as master distiller in 2002.

It was during his tenure at MGP that Metze faced what he considers his sternest challenge: the routine of making that distillery's near-ubiquitous 95% rye, 5% malted barley rye whiskey. According to Metze, "this is by far the most difficult mash bill to produce and create [as a] world-class quality spirit, day in and day out."

Metze was also in charge in 2013, when MGP introduced six new whiskeys, the first created at the distillery since its Seagram days. These included a Kentucky-style rye, a high-malt rye, a wheat whiskey, a single malt, and a pair of two-grain bourbons, one with 45% wheat and the other with 49% malted barley.

Despite having MGP's first step into its own brands named after him, Metze left the distillery in May 2016, after 38 years of working there. He started a consulting firm, Master Distiller Methods, but he also started work on the Old Elk Distillery in Colorado that same year. Being master distiller at Old Elk is now Metze's principal job, although he still dabbles a little in consulting. He considers Old Elk a first in his career, because he has never been in the pioneer's role of creating a new spirit for a new brand.

That spirit is an unusual, high-malt bourbon, made with 51% corn, 34% malted barley, and 15% rye, which Metze helped develop while still working at MGP. The current Old Elk Bourbon is a blend, drawing on sourced (MGP) whiskeys and Old Elk's own product, but all of it can be said to have been made by Metze himself.

George Remus Straight Bourbon Whiskey

After releasing a couple of one-shot Metze's Select bottlings, named for former Master Distiller Greg Metze, MGP decided to get into owning their own brands in late 2016. Their first move was to acquire a brand that was already established and also sourcing its whiskey from MGP, George Remus, named for the infamous Cincinnati-based bootlegger. Thus, MGP could seamlessly pick up and continue operating the brand, which it revamped in mid-2017.

This flagship expression is billed as a blend of MGP high-rye bourbons (the distillery has a 36% rye bourbon as part of its repertoire), aged for approximately four years.

The reddish amber liquid declares this bourbon's high-rye bona fides straight away.

The nose smacks you with some full-bodied pepper up front, supplemented by notes of floral fruitiness, vanilla, and candy corn.

The liquid sits more lightly on the tongue than the aromas did in the nostrils, but once again it leads with rye spiciness. The fruity and candy corn notes from the nose merge into lemon drops, with a hint of vanilla lurking in the background. The finish runs spicy and sweet, and quite warm to boot.

George Remus Repeal Reserve Series II
Straight Bourbon Whiskey

100

The premium end of the George Remus line is represented by their Repeal Reserve releases. These bourbons are blends of middle-aged MGP bourbons, and Series II was about two-thirds from their 75% corn, 21% rye bourbon stock and one-third from their high-rye, 60% corn, 36% rye bourbon stock (both are 4% malted barley), all of it distilled in 2007 and 2008. Series II was released in fall 2018.

94

MGP is best known for its 95% rye whiskey, which supplies dozens of sourced expressions. Rossville Union, started in May 2018, is the company's effort to get some of their whiskey out under their own name.

The interesting part is that this isn't just another MGP 95% rye bottling. Instead, it's a blend of their famous stock whiskey and their newer 51% rye, 49% malted barley whiskey. The latter is a peculiar mash bill, where the malted barley has scarcely less presence in the new-make spirit than the rye. MGP used five- and six-year-old whiskeys in the blend.

The nose is crisp, with spiciness showing itself with hot cinnamon and mint, and the malted barley on display in the whiskey's sweet butter cream character.

The spicy side is subdued in the flavor, with the whiskey coming on as a honey, brown sugar, and mint syrup. The finish turns peppery and a touch woody, and winds down fast.

— REDEMPTION WHISKEY —

Something that continues to make Redemption worth paying attention to, at a time when store shelves are crowded with MGP-sourced brands, are its releases of middle-aged, cask-strength versions of those MGP whiskeys. Once upon a time, the middling age statement and the cask strength would have been rare enough to see separately and were never seen together; seeing both designations on the same label continues to be rare today.

REDEMPTION 9–YEAR–OLD BARREL PROOF BOURBON WHISKEY

116+ This nine-year-old is drawn from MGP's "normal" bourbon stock, made from 75% corn, 21% rye, and 4% malted barley. As a cask-strength release, proof varies from year to year, but it's reliably around 116.

For a whiskey pushing 120 proof, I found it to be surprisingly un-hot. The scent was that of thick crème brûlée with vanilla bean, a hint of cedar, and dashes of mint and dill.

Once on my palate, it switched to a more nondescript, but still robust bourbon profile: corn sweet with vanilla, seasoned with peppermint.

This is drawn from the 95% rye stock, and while individual bottlings vary in terms of strength, one can expect it to have a proof of around 110.

It has a deep red amber appearance in the glass.

 The spiciness of the nose presents itself as pumpkin pie spice with double the ginger in the mix, stirred into a caramel candy with molasses, and vanilla drizzled on top.

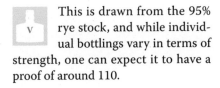 That candy turns to dark chocolate and caramel on the palate, imparting an earthy note to the whiskey, while the spiciness takes on a drier quality: licorice and anise on one hand, with pepper and cardamom on the other. The finish runs long and spicy.

IOWA

— CEDAR RIDGE WINERY & DISTILLERY —

Swisher, Iowa is a little place with fewer than a thousand inhabitants, located south of Cedar Rapids. It is also home to a winery (their website is still "crwine.com"), and that winery would come to grow into Cedar Ridge Distillery. They later added food service and live entertainments in a 3,500 square foot events space and see 100,000 visitors a year. They even host an annual Bourbon and Blues Festival. Cedar Ridge has become one of those places that seems to do a little bit of everything, except make beer.

That jack of all trades mentality extends into their whiskey making, so much so that I often find it simpler when speaking about Cedar Ridge to briefly describe what they aren't doing. Their tanks and mashing equipment are made by Letina and Aegir, and they let the mash ferment for five days. Their stills come from the German firm CARL. In a typical working day, they produce enough spirit to fill ten standard barrels.

Independent Stave Company furnishes those barrels, with a standard char of level 3. The distillery sends filled barrels to what they call "barrel sheds," where they are racked wide and low, never rising higher than five rows. Their newest shed stores 2,000 barrels, and there are several smaller sheds on the property. None of those buildings has even a nod to climate mitigation, and the average daily temperature can fluctuate by as much as 30 degrees Fahrenheit. Cedar Ridge plans to add three more sheds on the 2,000-barrel line by 2027.

CEDAR RIDGE IOWA BOURBON WHISKEY

80

Being in a state renowned as the best place in the world to grow yellow corn, it's not surprising that the Cedar Ridge line includes a bourbon made with a mash bill of 75% corn, 15% malted barley, and 10% rye.

In the glass, the bourbon has a look that isn't the expected amber at all, but instead like the yellow of a richly endowed white wine. It's almost golden raisin color, really.

With its nose of sweet candy corn, ripe grain, and caramel apples, the whiskey has a carnival-like atmosphere about it.

The flavor follows from there, with caramel apple in the main, accented by oak and corn. The finish is on the short side, leading with a light and rapidly fading presence of woodiness and pepper.

Basically, Cedar Ridge's Bourbon is nice. It's a little bit intriguing while remaining direct and uncomplicated.

CEDAR RIDGE MALTED RYE WHISKEY

Leaving aside the bit about making bourbon in the heart of corn country if you are aware of Iowa whiskey at all, you probably associate it with rye whiskey. This is thanks to an entirely different company that I address on page 394, but Cedar Ridge came out with a rye of their own in 2014.

Cedar Ridge followed an unorthodox course for this whiskey, making it a four-grain malted rye, with a mash bill of 51% malted rye, 34% rye, 12% corn, and 3% malted barley. It would almost be in the style of a Pennsylvania rye but for the modest amount of corn and barley.

It is golden with just a hint of red in there, not enough to make it anything like copper, but sufficient to make it off-gold. The swish reveals a fairly viscous liquid, because it leaves only a few slow-moving tears on the glass.

The nose here has the spicy and bready quality of a marbled rye. Throw in some notes of vanilla, honey, and a little hoppy citric acid.

The liquid has a good bit of substance on the palate. It's not really creamy or oily, but it certainly has some heft to it. That strong marbled rye current from the nose is still there, once again accented by honey and vanilla sweetness. It is also a touch astringent. The finish is a little spicy and a little toasty, and quite understated.

Cedar Ridge does a lot of things at once, and with their single malt whiskey they cannot seem to settle on a single expression. Starting in 2014, they've released a cluster of them, even going so far as to adopt the solera system in 2015. The single malt whiskey I got to try was the Batch 7, aged in a 15-gallon former bourbon barrel and finished in a Madeira cask.

The look of this American malt is golden, with a coat of the glass dropping a spread of middling legs.

The nose is straightforward, smacking of cereals and oak (this is the 15-gallon barrel showing itself), and accented with honey and clove.

A silky middleweight of a whiskey on the tongue, the flavor is surprisingly forward with caramel, given that the aging was in an former bourbon barrel, with notes of pine, mint, and cocoa. It's in the finish that the (no pun intended here) finishing barrel shows up best, because it turns decidedly nutty early on in a long and warm wind-down.

Cedar Ridge Wheat Whiskey

80 Following their pattern of not actually having a pattern, Cedar Ridge chose to make their wheat whiskey from 100% malted wheat, a whiskey of which there are only a few examples out there.

The color in the glass is light and in the vein of white wine. A swish yields a strikingly viscous coat, one that drops very few tears that were hesitant in the extreme.

The nose is rather grainy and grassy, with notes of honey and spice.

The flavor is also grainy and grassy, but softer, with the same hint of honey and spice but also a bit of caramel. From there, finish is light and fades fast.

Cedar Ridge The QuintEssential Single Malt

92 Cedar Ridge started making malt whiskey in 2014 and has been steadily perfecting it ever since. Each successive batch released has shown one tweak or another, with no two batches coming from the same cask and finishing cask stock. At one point, they were using a solera system as well.

With the release of QuintEssential, the distillery looks very much like it has settled on a format and profile for its malt whiskey; the tinkering phase is over. The bottle, labeling, and canister it all comes in are exactly like what one would expect from a Scottish single malt. Also, the production process draws on pretty much everything Cedar Ridge has done with their malts heretofore: it receives primary maturation in ex-bourbon barrels, gets a finish in a variety of secondary casks (brandy, rum, wine, port, or sherry), and then all of this is married in a solera vat.

The look of the QuintEssential is light gold.

The scent is effervescent. I set it down, left the room for several minutes, and returned to find the nose meeting me from a distance of a couple of yards. That nose led with red pears and honey, followed by notes of peppermint and lavender, this atop a foundation of toasted cereals.

The flavor keeps those elements but swaps their precedence and prominence. On the palate, the toasted cereals and honeyed syrup lead, while the red pears and herbs bring up the rear. The finish is sweet with honey and spice. If the packaging does state an intention to mirror Scotch, then The QuintEssential fits nicely into the broad Speyside flavor profile.

— MISSISSIPPI RIVER DISTILLING COMPANY —

Mississippi River Distilling Company (MRDC) stands along its namesake river in LeClaire, a town known for two things, beyond being MRDC's home: (1) it's the hometown of "Buffalo Bill" Cody, for whom the distillery's whiskeys are named; and (2) it's also where Antique Archaeology, the company from *American Pickers*, hangs its hat.

CODY ROAD SINGLE BARREL BOURBON WHISKEY

105 The statement I see most often on blogs about craft whiskeys is along the lines of "I hope to see a more mature version of this whiskey in the future." I've written words to that effect myself. In 2016, MRDC marked the fifth anniversary of Cody Road Bourbon by releasing a four-year-old, single-barrel expression of their bourbon. It's the same stuff as the standard Cody Road, just older and stronger.

In the glass, it has a clear, lustrous, and rich orange-copper appearance. A swish leaves a thin but sticky coat around the glass, one that drops only a few thick, long legs, and reluctantly at that.

The nose is red berries sweet, seasoned with an herbal, spearmint edge and just a touch of vanilla.

The liquid itself sits light but nutty on the palate, and the flavors come across on the light side as well. Predominant is a certain field-like aspect, where grassiness and that spearmint spiciness are just slightly more present than the vanilla. In contrast to the nose, the flavor isn't particularly sweet. The finish leaves very little warmth while showing the most sophistication, leaving an aftertaste of spearmint, barrel char, and nuttiness that gradually winds down to just the nuttiness.

Despite being bottled at 105 proof, this bourbon is surprisingly light, but not lacking in substance. What it doesn't do is sit cozily inside what I would call the traditional flavor profile for a bourbon. Aspects of that profile are there, but overall it's not what one might expect, which is why I describe it here. This outside-the-box version shows that a few extra years can achieve surprising results.

CODY ROAD BOURBON WHISKEY

Cody Road Bourbon started being produced in 2010, using a mash bill of 70% corn, 20% wheat, and 10% barley, with the corn coming from around LeClaire and the other grains from across the river in Illinois. They age the whiskey for one year in 30-gallon barrels.

It has a deep amber coloring in the glass.

The airy nose carries notes of vanilla and raspberry, coupled to a light touch of grassiness.

The experience on the palate is straightforward from there: the raspberry leads, followed by cereals, and then corn syrup and vanilla. It's exactly what I would expect from a young, wheated bourbon.

Cody Road Rye Whiskey

 MRDC released its rye the year after its bourbon, in 2012. It's a 100% rye made with grain sourced from across the river in Illinois.

Two main aspects define rye whiskey, especially one with a high-rye content: spiciness and fruitiness. This one comes across as mild, sweet, and fruity.

 The look of the liquid in the glass is of gold-speckled copper.

 The nose is clementines, berries, and apricots coated with salty caramel and sprinkled with a pinch of pepper.

 A sip reveals the fruitiness evolving to apricots, citrus, and blackberries, with a hint of butterscotch and pepper coming on at the end. From there, the finish dives into spiciness and oak. Like the bourbon, this is a young whiskey, but surprisingly sophisticated despite that youth.

— TEMPLETON RYE —

Templeton Rye is a brand still at least partly under a cloud, as it was once the poster figure for the "deceptive whiskey" controversy that raged among bloggers and enthusiasts in the early part of the 2010s. They earned that reputation as arguably the clearest example of a company that bottled sourced whiskey while pretending to be a working, commercial distillery, selling their sourced product with a smoke screen of folksy tales. The tales were largely true—there were bootleggers making a rye-based moonshine in the Templeton area—but the whiskey the brand used was a version of MGP's prevalent 95% rye, 5% malted barley whiskey. Templeton has opened its own distillery since that controversy, but its in-house products are still two or three years from being bottled.

TEMPLETON RYE WHISKEY

This 80-proof whiskey has a deep orange appearance in the glass, typical of a reasonably aged rye (averaging four years, in fact).

The nose has a sweet character, where vanilla mingles with the strong cinnamon flavor of Red Hots over a base of banana, and a current of cedarwood that runs throughout.

The flavor follows from there. It's balanced on its sweet and spicy sides, and the woody current that is more cedar than oak runs throughout, now with a minty tinge that nicely complements the spiciness.

91.5 The company came clean about its marketing, sourcing, and production in 2014, and finally opened a $35 million distillery in 2018. But years before those events, in 2010, the company started holding back stocks of whiskey for further aging. In 2017, they released their first regular brand extension in the form of this six-year-old. Usually an MGP-based rye whiskey with an age statement is a limited edition, so this one is the only example you'll find regularly on store shelves and at a reasonable price.

The higher proof compared to Templeton Rye and extra couple years in the barrel show in the glass. The look is one of bright copper, and a swish and coat of the glass positively run with legs.

The nose comes out with butterscotch up front, then combines floral sweetness with pumpernickel rye spice.

The palate is fruity and brown sugar sweet, seasoned with cinnamon and apple mint, coming across as something like a candied bomb. Or it would be a candied bomb, were it not for the hint of toasty oak that comes up at the end. The finish continues that vein of sweet cinnamon before fading to an almost dill-like note.

The extra time and higher proof are a huge improvement on what was already a decent whiskey, making for a bolder and more sophisticated expression.

oppercraft is in the midst of making the transition from sourced spirits to in-house whiskeys, and the distillery has chosen to start that transition by blending their youngish in-house spirits with more-aged, sourced spirits. Seeing as how Coppercraft has been around since 2012, it certainly has some young but mature stock to work with.

COPPERCRAFT BLEND OF STRAIGHT BOURBON WHISKIES

100 This blend incorporates four-year-old Coppercraft bourbon with sourced four- and 10-year-old bourbons. The company certainly made a good choice when selecting an individual to help it craft that diverse stock into something pleasant in Nancy Fraley, a whiskey-and-rum blender noted for her nosing prowess, and who also serves as director of research at the American Distilling Institute.

It has an orange-amber appearance, so it's a good guess the four-year-old whiskeys predominate in the blend. Even so, it's a viscous liquid, easily forming a beaded crown inside the glass while dropping just a few skinny legs.

A nosing gives a faint and light whiskey. There is some rye spice, herbs, and oak there, but it takes some doing to find all three of those notes.

The flavor has more body to it, sitting well inside the normal bourbon profile of caramel, a little rye spice, and a little oak. But it is neither as woody nor as spicy as the nose suggested. The finish, however, turned oaky. It's not overpoweringly oaky in the end, but decisively so nonetheless.

COPPERCRAFT STRAIGHT BOURBON WHISKEY

Unlike the other Coppercraft whiskeys, this one is entirely sourced. Although it doesn't bear an age statement, this expression is described as a small batch drawn from barrels over 10 years old.

A pour has a copper coloring in the glass, not especially dark for something this age at almost 100 proof. Swishing the glass left behind a coat of thick legs.

The scent is corn syrup sweet with citrus zest, accented by light notes of nuts and vanilla.

The flavor takes a turn from there, becoming much spicier, although the corn syrup sweetness and spooned helpings of citrus, vanilla, and nuts remain. These are joined by a hint of oak. The finish starts with the vanilla, which is subsumed by a spiciness that lingers on the tongue.

Coppercraft Straight Rye Whiskey

90 Some folks will look at Coppercraft Rye's mash bill statement of 95% rye and 5% malted barley and make the common and mistaken assumption that it is sourced from MGP. In fact, that is only partly correct, because Coppercraft is part of a growing crop of distilleries that have also adopted that mash bill as their own, and this rye is a blend of in-house and sourced ryes.

The look is golden, between white wine and apple juice. Coating the glass leaves a sprinkle of decent legs all around.

A sniff gives gingerbread, root beer, and cedar, so it's a rye that is as spicy as it is sweet, and the woody side has some character to it.

The flavor is pumpernickel rye bread, giving way to a toasted and more general cereals character. The finish pushes on into a toasty quality.

— JOURNEYMAN DISTILLERY —

Michigan's Journeyman Distillery is part of what I sometimes call the middle wave of the craft whiskey movement. It wasn't part of the initial group from the mid-2000s, but instead got started in 2010, just as craft distilling picked up momentum and swelled from dozens of distilleries into hundreds, seemingly overnight.

Journeyman is also part of a class of small distillers that places the interesting part of its backstory not in some whiskey-making ancestor or tales of Prohibition bootlegging, but in the historic building it calls home. The distillery occupies what was a late 19th-century leather goods factory where items like buggy whips and corsets were made, which often inspire the names of their whiskeys.

Like several Midwestern distilleries, Journeyman bought its still and much of its other equipment from Kothe, the German fabricator, and currently has three pot/column hybrid Kothe stills in operation: a 150-liter, a 1,000-liter, and a 5,000-liter. There are also three cookers and 16 fermenters of varying sizes in the facility.

Journeyman is a sweet-mash operation, and it uses only organically grown grains. As with other Midwestern distilleries, sourcing that grain isn't a problem: if Michigan doesn't happen to have what Journeyman needs, neighboring states can always provide it. For yeast, it relies on dry distiller's strains provided by Lalle-mand in Canada and Ferm Solutions in Kentucky, among others.

Journeyman's production is centered on whiskey, with nine different expressions in its regular lineup, including rye, bourbon, wheat whiskey, American malt, and a four-grain whiskey. However, it has followed the path of being a distillery that does a little bit of everything. Thus, Journeyman also makes vodka, gin, rum, and brandy. Distillation, even for the whiskey, isn't done to a set proof, but nothing is distilled lower than 120 proof.

Proofs for whiskey when it is entered into the barrel also varies, ranging between 110 and 120 proof. Journeyman's barrels are made by The Barrel Mill in Minnesota and Independent Stave Company, with all barrels done with a #3 char. In terms of sizes, the new barrels range from the tiny to the full-size American Standard Barrel: the distillery has 5-, 15-, 30-, and 53-gallon new oak barrels currently in use. For the finished whiskeys, the company draws from sources as needed, such as wineries in Berrien County, Michigan.

Like most successful small distillers, Journeyman is looking to expand, and in 2018, it announced plans to do just that. However, they won't be at the existing location in Three Oaks, Michigan. Instead, founder Bill Welter intends to open a brewery, restaurant, and hotel in the old ANCO plant in his hometown of Valparaiso, Indiana.

Journeyman Buggy Whip Wheat Whiskey

90

This whiskey is made from 100% organic wheat.

It has the soft profile one expects from a wheat whis- key, and that takes some of the sharpness off the youth and green oak, allowing the citrus zest and caramel notes to come forward and shine a little more.

Journeyman Corsets, Whips & Whiskey

115– 120

Like its stablemate above, the saucy-sounding name of this whiskey is actually derived from the Featherbone Factory's time making leather goods. The similarity to Buggy Whip is intentional, because it's the cask-strength version of Buggy Whip. As a cask-strength whiskey, the proof varies with the batch.

This expression is much bolder than its cousin, and consequently the green oak current is stronger in the nose. Yet the citrus and berry notes are stronger also, as is the caramel.

On the palate, however, it's the caramel that is predominant, accompanied by the green oak and pepper. The fruity aspect is almost overpowered, while the finish turns increasingly peppery as it runs.

JOURNEYMAN LAST FEATHER RYE WHISKEY

90

Journeyman considers Last Feather its flagship product, and it's an odd duck among ryes. There are some ryes using wheat and malted barley as the secondary grain, but Last Feather is heavily wheated: the mash bill here is 60% rye and 40% wheat. It is named thus because Journeyman got into legal tussles over the names of its preceding three rye whiskey brands, so finally the distillery reached its "last feather."

Journeyman was shooting for something that was almost as spicy as it was soft and fruity, and I think the company succeeded to a large extent. It's smooth and smacks of berries and bananas, but has a solid current of peppermint running right through the middle of it, accented by a dollop of vanilla from the barrel aging.

JOURNEYMAN
Distillery™

HANDMADE · RYE

NOT A KING™
Whiskey

DISTILLED AND BOTTLED
BY JOURNEYMAN DISTILLERY
IN THREE OAKS, MI.

750ml
45% Alcohol By Volume (90 Proof)

Journeyman Featherbone Bourbon Whiskey

 90 The distillery's bourbon is made from 70% corn, 25% wheat, and 5% rye.

The nose shows the corn coming on strong, and presenting itself more as a cereal than as a sweetener, with notes of citrus zest and a pinch of mint.

A sip, however, brings it straight around to what I might expect from a youthful wheated bourbon: a soft mouthfeel with vanilla and green oak in the main, plus modest notes of citrusy fruit and pepper. The finish is a surprise, changing over to sweet tobacco leaf, but it's over quickly.

Journeyman Not a King Rye Whiskey

90 A nod to George Washington, one of America's first big whiskey distillers, Not a King takes the 60:40 mash bill ratio of Last Feather, but turns to corn instead of wheat, so it's mostly rye with a big helping of corn.

The result comes across as surprisingly sweet on the nose, redolent with honey, plus notes of caramel and green oak from the barrel aging.

With a sip, the profile turns to candy corn with that caramel and green wood again, before turning peppery. The finish follows off that pepper, running quite spicy, if not a bit hot.

— TRAVERSE CITY WHISKEY COMPANY —

TRAVERSE CITY STRAIGHT BOURBON WHISKEY

A pour of this 86-proof bourbon has a light amber, quite coppery look. A coating of the glass proved surprisingly thick, and dropped a curtain of legs.

I believe that thick coating of the glass causes a lot of evaporation, because while I would not call it a hot whiskey based on what comes later, that initial sniff had some serious burn to it. After letting it settle down a bit, the scent was one of molasses and baking spices, with a little honey and a little oak.

It sits lightly on the tongue, with a flavor that is corn sweet with vanilla in the main, plus a dash of cinnamon. The finish follows from that cinnamon spice.

It's clearly a youngish bourbon, but nice enough that I'm curious as to what an extra couple of years in the barrel might yield.

— TWO JAMES SPIRITS —

W hen Two James Distillery opened in Detroit in 2013, they became the first legal distillery in the Motor City since Prohibition.

TWO JAMES CATCHER'S RYE WHISKEY

98.8 This rye is made from a 100% rye mash bill, matured in 53-gallon charred new oak barrels for at least two years.

The nose shows the youth of the whiskey, but has some interesting characteristics nonetheless. It is fruitier rather than spicier, as the scent carries some ruby Port and citrus zest.

A sip reveals a thin liquid, and the flavor is akin to a caramel apple at first, with a wave of nutmeg, cinnamon, and cardamom coming on later. That spiciness doesn't carry very far into the finish, however, which wound down with brown sugar and vanilla.

I never would have guessed that this is a 100% rye, had I not known from the outset. Instead, it's reminiscent of the sweeter, almost bourbonized Kentucky-style rye whiskeys.

NEBRASKA

— CUT SPIKE DISTILLERY —

CUT SPIKE SINGLE MALT WHISKEY

86 Cut Spike is a "brewstillery," or a distillery that is paired in some way with a brewery. In this case, La Vista's Lucky Bucket Brewing set up some distilling equipment in 2008, and Cut Spike Single Malt followed in 2012. As a single malt, this is made from 100% malted barley, and aged for two years in charred, new oak barrels.

A pour of Cut Spike has a look that is lighter than a bourbon or even a rye, but darker than anyone accustomed to Scotch would expect. That is the barrel showing itself, since new oak always adds more color, and Scotch is predominately aged in used oak. The swish and coat of the glass show it to be a thin liquid, leaving plenty of skinny legs and a coat prone to forming droplets.

The nose, however, is pleasant, clear, and smooth, redolent of fruit generously sprinkled on top of butterscotch.

A sip follows in kind. It's sweet with fruitiness, honey, and vanilla, and in my imagination Cut Spike has turned out like an Irish malt that was aged in new oak (albeit for less than the minimum three years required in Ireland).

OHIO

— CLEVELAND WHISKEY —

CLEVELAND BLACK RESERVE AMERICAN BOURBON WHISKEY

In Cleveland, Tom Lix invented a hack that manages to get around the traditional maturation of whiskey and complies with the law while also pursuing a radically different aging process.

Cleveland Whiskey puts its new make into charred, new oak barrels for six months, thereby complying with federal law. From there, he transfers the whiskey to stainless steel vats, which is where his real aging process begins. Bits of charred new oak are in the vats along with the whiskey, and the contents are placed under pressure, basically applying muscle and speed to the absorption of flavors and colors from the wood. After putting the contents under pressure for just a week, the company claims to have produced a bourbon with the same flavors as a mature whiskey.

Alas, I disagree with the conclusion that it's the same as a traditionally matured whiskey. The results are very similar to what a typical "Craft Whiskey 1.0" small-barrel bourbon yielded after several months of aging: a hot, raw spirit that was vanilla and wood spice–forward, with a short finish distinguished mostly by its heat.

Cleveland Whiskey also has a line called "Underground," which puts various wood finishes (apple, maple, honey locust, and so on) on this unorthodox bourbon.

— WATERSHED DISTILLERY —

A little family anecdote about Watershed describes how many Southerners, to say nothing of Kentuckians in particular, feel about bourbon coming from other parts of the country. My grandfather used to live in Columbus, where Watershed makes its liquor. When I first came across Watershed Bourbon in 2014, I thought my mom would find the connection interesting.

So, I told her I was working on a bourbon from Columbus.

She gave me a disapproving look and said, with no shortage of finality, "Yankees can't make bourbon."

"Ohioans aren't Yankees. They're Buckeyes," I replied.

"It's the same thing, and they can't make bourbon."

A lot of folks share that opinion, despite the fact that plenty of bourbon used to be made across the Ohio River. What is more, bourbon whiskey's most infamous bootlegger, George Remus, was a Cincinnati lawyer.

WATERSHED BOURBON WHISKEY

94

Watershed is a four-grain, spelted bourbon. Spelt, also known as hulled wheat or dinkel wheat, fell out of favor with farmers and food processors decades ago because it is harder to thresh. However, spelt has different qualities from common red winter wheat, which has brought it into favor with craft bakers in recent years. So why not craft distillers as well?

The distillery started out aging in 10- and 30-gallon barrels, but has since transitioned to 53-gallon barrels, and now all Watershed Bourbon bottlings come from full-size barrels.

The color is surprisingly light. Even young small-barrel bourbons can come out quite dark, but this has a bright, coppery, middle amber appearance.

The nose is fragrant with cedar and pine, giving it a crisp quality that balances against the corn sweetness and dollop of vanilla.

The flavor is light, offering up a subdued caramel sweetness and a hint of toasty wood. A tiny rye spice note is in there, too, one that grows on the tongue to the point of elbowing the other flavors off center stage. The finish leaves a light, lingering spicy afterglow.

WISCONSIN

DEATH'S DOOR WHITE WHISKY

80

In the early days of micro-distilling, white whiskeys were commonplace, as start-ups were anxious to get products on the market and build their brands. Most of these unaged or very briefly aged whiskeys were simply the watered-down versions of that distillery's white dog, and these were replaced or downplayed as aged whiskeys became (more) available.

Death's Door, on the other hand, was introduced as a stand-alone white whisky, with no aged counterpart ever intended. The folks at Death's Door Spirits decided their 80% wheat, 20% malted barley whiskey was good as is, and since 2008 they have left it alone. The whisky receives a three-day resting in uncharred Minnesota-grown white oak barrels. Neighboring Minnesota has a short growing season, producing a tighter-grained oak that is noted for restricting absorption of flavors from the wood. Not charring the barrels restricts that absorption even more, so it's safe to say Death's Door gets almost nothing from the wood.

The whisky itself is creamy and malty, with notes of vanilla and white chocolate.

— GREAT LAKES DISTILLERY —

GREAT LAKES KINNICKINNIC WHISKEY

86

Great Lakes was a little ahead of the micro-distilling curve, having started in 2006, and KinnicKinnic was their first whiskey. It's also the distillery's most familiar whiskey, at least outside of Wisconsin.

It is an American blend, mixing different types of whiskeys (these are sometimes called "hybrids"). Great Lakes sourced some four-year-old Kentucky bourbon and blended it with its in-house rye and malt whiskeys.

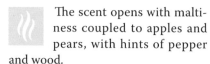
It has a golden, just-touching-on-amber look in the glass.

The scent opens with maltiness coupled to apples and pears, with hints of pepper and wood.

A sip reveals a liquid with a quite buttery texture, and a flavor that runs cereals and grassiness in the main, plus a dollop of caramel and a hint of hot cinnamon. The finish runs from that cinnamon off into pepperiness.

GREAT LAKES STILL & OAK STRAIGHT BOURBON WHISKEY

86

Whereas KinnicKinnic is a craft trailblazer, indeed one of the earliest examples of blending sourced and in-house whiskeys there is, the Still & Oak Bourbon and Rye are newcomers, first released in spring 2018.

Great Lakes chose to go with a "malted bourbon," i.e., a bourbon with malted barley as the secondary grain: 67% corn, 22% malt, and 11% rye. As a straight bourbon, it's aged at least two years, and in full-size, 53-gallon barrels to boot; it's not chill-filtered.

Alongside the expected brown sugar and vanilla aromas on the nose is a telltale nuttiness.

The flavor has the expected caramel sweetness, but also some dried apricot, more nuts, and a hint of clove. It's youthful, so a trace of green wood is there as well. Despite its youthful nature, Great Lakes's decision to go with a malted bourbon makes Still & Oak a tasty, interesting pour.

Like its stablemate, this rye is a straight whiskey (at least two years old), aged in 53-gallon, charred new oak barrels, and is not chill-filtered. The mash bill is 78% rye and 22% malted rye.

 The scent carries vanilla, molasses, and spearmint.

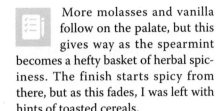 More molasses and vanilla follow on the palate, but this gives way as the spearmint becomes a hefty basket of herbal spiciness. The finish starts spicy from there, but as this fades, I was left with hints of toasted cereals.

— YAHARA BAY DISTILLERS —

This family-run distillery was also a bit ahead of the micro-distilling curve, opening in 2007, which is after Great Lakes Distillery but still before most of the outfits that are thought of as founders of American craft whiskey.

Yahara Bay is one of those companies that has its fingers and toes in dozens of spirits, producing a slew of liqueurs, gin, vodka, schnapps, rum, and more, plus a few whiskeys.

YAHARA BAY SINGLE BARREL WHISKEY

80 This expression was the distillery's first whiskey and is billed as the first whiskey released in Wisconsin since Prohibition. Yahara Bay also says this whiskey is its best seller. It's a four-grain whiskey with no dominant grain, so the corn, rye, wheat, and malted barley content are all below 51%. Aged for two years in former bourbon barrels, it's a single-barrel expression.

It's grilled sweet corn in the main on the nose, with notes of maple syrup and vanilla, underscored by a distinct, albeit faint, trace of pine.

The palate experience is simple and short, having a sugar cookies-meet-cereals quality. The finish is nondescript and dissipates quickly.

SMALL BATCH 90 PROOF
BOURBON WHISKEY

45% ALC/VOL/750ML

YAHARA BAY V SMALL BATCH BOURBON WHISKEY

90 The distillery began making bourbon in the fifth year, hence the Roman numeral *V*. Like Yahara Bay's staple whiskey, this is made with a four-grain mash bill. The company doesn't reveal what the proportions are, but as a bourbon we know the corn must be at least 51%, and Yahara Bay says the rye is at 20%. Ergo, the malted barley and wheat must be modest parts of the recipe.

It's sweet with the expected brown sugar and barrel-driven vanilla on the nose, with a hint of woodiness.

The palate brings that same basic bourbon flavor profile along, but the sweet vanilla current is joined by hints of cinnamon and cranberry, and the oaky aspect is larger and more tannic.

AZ

NM

O

TX

SOUTHWEST
REGION

— HAMILTON DISTILLERS —

When Stephen Paul, founder of Tucson's Hamilton Distillers, got started in 2006, he brought together a couple of elements that were just developing at the time but would become staples of the American craft whiskey movement. One was a love for Scotch, so he went where the big distillers weren't and into American Malts. Second was exploring the regional character of Arizona. Those two factors led him to build his own floor-malting facility, burning mesquite instead of peat to dry the malt. Paul also followed the Scottish model by using a 100% malted barley mash and double-distilling in copper pots. Aside from the mesquite smoking, the only concession to the American style is to age in new oak barrels. The result is Del Bac Dorado, a mesquite-smoked single malt. In tandem with Dorado is the Del Bac Classic, an unsmoked version of Hamilton's malt whiskey.

DEL BAC CLASSIC WHISKEY

90 When Stephen Paul, founder of Tuscon's Hamilton Distillers, got started in 2006, he brought together a couple elements that were just developing at the time but would become staples of the American craft whiskey movement. One was a love for Scotch, so he went where the big distillers weren't and into American malts. Second was exploring the *terroir* of Arizona. Those two factors led him to build his own floor-malting facility, burning mesquite instead of peat to dry the malt. The result is Del Bac Dorado, a mesquite-smoked single malt.

The coloring is a bright, middle amber.

My nosing gave me a spread of toasty cereals on a bed of dry straw and oak chips, accented by a hint of cookie spices.

The texture was silky, with a flavor inhabiting a place where American and Scottish malts meet. Caramel and butterscotch come together, and despite the lack of mesquite smoking, they do so with just a touch of barrel char-style ash. The finish takes a smooth vein, smacking of Cracker Jacks with its toasted corn and caramel. This Arizona whiskey is a fine and well-rounded, if simple and youthful, drinker.

NEW MEXICO

— SANTA FE SPIRITS —

Santa Fe Spirits was founded in 2010 by an English architect migrating from the Virgin Islands, who joined together with John Jeffery to produce Scottish-style malts in New Mexico.

That Englishman is none other than Colin Keegan, so you can see where the name of the single malt below comes from.

SANTA FE SPIRITS COLKEGAN SINGLE MALT WHISKEY

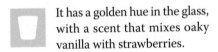

This American single malt was distilled from a 100% malted barley mash, with some of that malt smoked with mesquite. It was then aged for a minimum of two years in a mix of new white oak and former bourbon barrels.

It has a golden hue in the glass, with a scent that mixes oaky vanilla with strawberries.

It tastes sweet initially, with that same berry fruit and woody vanilla character as on the nose, but then it morphs into something more earthy and grassy, akin to sod. The smokiness finally rears its head in the finish, which has a modest combination of vanilla and leathery tobacco that is eventually covered by wood smoke.

SANTA FE SPIRITS SILVER COYOTE PURE MALT WHISKEY

The white dog version of the distillery's Colkegan Single Malt, Silver Coyote is almost a look at what new-make Scottish malt whisky is like. Silver Coyote was made with a combination of European and American malts and fermented with Scottish yeast.

The nose is a little different from the lion's share of unaged whiskeys, in that white dogs in America are typically made mostly from corn, with the resultant corn husk grassiness. Although the scent here is quite grainy, it's softer and not grassy at all.

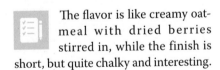

The flavor is like creamy oatmeal with dried berries stirred in, while the finish is short, but quite chalky and interesting.

Craft whiskey did not come as early to the Lone Star State as it came to some other places, but it still came pretty early on, and with two of the most renowned names in the industry: Balcones and Garrison Brothers. This pair released their inaugural whiskeys in 2008, but some say Garrison Brothers should be considered an earlier entrant than that.

Garrison Brothers makes traditional bourbon, albeit traditional bourbon adapted to the sweltering Texas climate, and that takes time. The distillery was founded in 2005, and thus part of the same class as Stranahan's and Tuthilltown. However, that commitment to traditional methods meant also being committed to about a five-year wait until they had something properly matured for market. Then Balcones came along, poised to release their pioneering blue corn whiskey, Baby Blue, in 2008 after several months of aging in small barrels. The two launched in the same year and have gone on to become beloved by enthusiasts—Garrison Brothers for their bold, barrel-forward bourbon, and Balcones for their highly innovative approach to whiskey making.

The two distilleries have blazed a substantial path. While the annual release of Garrison Brothers Cowboy Bourbon came to see at least a few folks camped outside the distillery, awaiting their chance at a bottle, in 2016, Balcones became one of the first craft distillers to graduate from a start-up to a $14.5 million, midsize operation. Firestone & Robertson released a well-done blend of sourced whiskeys and a well-regarded in-house bourbon; Kooper Family Whiskey Company did such a respectable job in sourcing and crafting their blended rye whiskey that it has become one of those hard-to-get items. Among the newest arrivals on the Texas whiskey scene is Milam & Greene, which boasts one of the most talented and experienced teams of any small distillery project in America. Small whiskey makers in Texas have at least a big toe planted in everything going on with American whiskey: American malts, wheat whiskey, artful sourcing and blending, wide-ranging barrel finishes, brewstilleries. You name it and someone in Texas has tried it or is doing it.

The Texas whiskey scene has kept on going from strength to strength in the years since I penned the first edition of this book. By 2020, I could no longer see any other state in the Union as its peer, and Texas had clearly come to occupy third place behind Tennessee and Kentucky in the pecking order.

— BALCONES DISTILLING —

BALCONES BABY BLUE CORN WHISKY

92

This expression was a trailblazer, both for Texas and craft whiskey in general. Released in 2008, it was the state's first post-Prohibition whiskey, beating the competition to the punch in terms of "getting there first." Even considering its early entrant status, Baby Blue was and remains novel in that it's made with 100% Hopi blue corn. Using varietals other than distiller's yellow corn has caught on, but the use of blue corn remains relatively uncommon. It was unheard of when Baby Blue came out.

Aged in used five-gallon barrels for about six months, a production practice that hasn't changed since it was initially released, Baby Blue is an excellent example of "Craft Whiskey 1.0," as barrels that small have fallen out of favor as the industry has grown.

The appearance is golden, like a pilsner without the carbonated fizz. Swishing the glass puts a thick coat on the inside, which drops a few thick, fast-moving tears.

The nose is rich, as oily as it is buttery. It's like someone smeared butter on the top of freshly baked, creamy, sweet corn bread while it was still sitting in a well-oiled pan. Hints of vanilla, baking spice, and banana lurk underneath that hefty corn bread goodness.

A sip gives more sweet corn across a rich, creamy mouthfeel. It's very corny, but in a surprisingly sophisticated way. First, candy corn sweetness meets a note of fire-roasted sweet corn. Past that, the corn husk that is present in very nearly all corn whiskeys is there, and that is off-putting for some, but in Baby Blue it is quite muted. The banana, baking spice, and vanilla from the nose are there, too. After that quite flavorful experience, the finish was a generic spicy and sweet conclusion and something of a letdown.

On the one hand, Baby Blue shows its youth. Yet for a whisky that reveals its lack of years, it is quite sophisticated. The use of blue corn takes the corn whiskey flavor profile in a direction that few have pursued, and given the results, one has to wonder why.

Balcones chose to mark their tenth anniversary in 2018 by launching this rye whiskey, their first ever. It's a 100% rye, but one drawing on four different varietals: locally sourced Elbon rye, grown in the northern part of Texas, as well as crystal, chocolate, and roasted ryes. The latter three are more often found in a brewery than a distillery.

The look here is a mid-amber coloring in the glass, while the swish and coat left behind a sheet of thick legs.

The scent carries caramel and a current of tropical fruits, pineapple in the main, plus a light dusting of peppers and dry oak shavings.

A sip showed me a liquid that was light, but with an oily texture. Once again, it was tropical, fruity, and sweet, accented strongly with vanilla. The peppery spices came along to make their presence felt only on the back end of the palate. This spiciness ran into a substantially more complex finish, which continued the tropical fruit salad, seasoned with an ample helping of ginger, and rounded out with a touch of barrel char.

BALCONES POT STILL BOURBON

When Balcones opened their new distillery in 2016, at the heart of the operation was a set of copper pot stills made by Forsyths of Scotland. To help inaugurate the fancy new kit, they produced a four-grain (blue corn, Texas-grown wheat, rye, and malted barley), pot-distilled bourbon.

A pour of this bourbon has a light amber coloring in the glass, with a sticky, oily look to it.

The nose opens on oily butterscotch and dry straw and toasty oak, with a little Granny Smith apple to round it out. This start marks the peculiar theme of the bourbon, in that it's more like many a Speyside malt I've imbibed, and far from the standard bourbon flavor profile.

A taste is mellower than the scent, however, because that dry straw and toasty oak combination give the nose a pungent side. Butterscotch and vanilla are a much larger presence on the tongue than the straw and oak, and even when a dash of pepper rises on the back end the whiskey remains more sweet than spicy or dry. The finish trails off on a light sprinkle of cinnamon. It's definitely an odd duck of a bourbon, but one with loads of character.

Jared Himstedt

Jared Himstedt helped build Balcones with hand-made equipment in an old welding shop under a bridge in Waco; his fingerprints are on those first production choices that have since become staples of the craft scene, such as the use of exotic grains and going where the big distillers weren't. He saw the potential for explosive growth and rode the challenges of expansion; and he kept his cool during the dramatic departure of company cofounder Chip Tate in 2014, when the heat was in the courtroom rather than the stillhouse.

Himstedt studied social work and studio ceramics at school, neither of which sounds like training for a future as a master distiller, but Himstedt believes both gave him valuable skills to draw on. "Some of the macro social work training definitely feeds into management and big-picture planning," he says. "The craft of ceramic art has been super valuable, [like] when we bricked in and insulated our first gas-fired stills."

As the head distiller at Balcones these past few years, Himstedt has come fully into the spotlight, but without actually taking on that rock star-like persona that some master distillers have. When it comes to dealing with enthusiasts, he enjoys simply being a fellow whiskey geek. "Ten years ago someone may have asked what the difference is between rum and single malt. Today they're going to ask about fermentation parameters, or wash pH," says Himstedt. "Those are way more fun rabbit holes to go down than a simple Whisky101."

As head distiller, Himstedt remains very process-focused: "I decided long ago that, as we grew, I would be unhappy if I moved away from certain parts of the process. If spreadsheets and meeting with people took me away from the sensory evaluation and blending side of things, I would have lost my way."

Even with Balcones's transition from a garage-style start-up to a $14.5 million, state-of-the-art distillery, to hear Himstedt tell it, his approach to distilling has changed only in its trappings. He remains much invested in his Texas terroir, pointing to how factors like the "ridiculous climate of central Texas" and the local bacteria and yeast in the air influence their whiskey making. He is just as devoted to tinkering and experimenting as ever, and sees the bigger, more industrial facilities he works with now as a help, not a hindrance, because the equipment gives him more control over the process.

Balcones "1" Texas Single Malt Whisky

106 The American Single Malt Whiskey Commission formed in 2016 to give the category more definition than federal law offered for American malts. In another example of just how ahead of the curve Balcones has been, it had a whisky that met that firmer definition several years before anyone was talking about applying it.

Texas Single Malt is made entirely with Golden Promise barley, the varietal that was commonly grown in Scotland before it was supplanted with a cheaper, higher-yielding but less flavorful variety (a practice common in industrial agriculture). The new-make whisky is aged in barrels of differing sizes and types before blending and receiving a second round of maturation in a full-size barrel.

It has a solid amber coloring. Coating the glass leaves a thin film behind, but a sticky one that drops only a few tears.

The nose told me that it needed water from the outset, not because it was too hot (at 106 proof, that would be a bad sign), but because it was too crowded and needed a little "opening up." So, in went a few drops. That done, the scent was grassy, with overtones of molasses sweetness and butterscotch, with a note of solid oak hovering in the background and a prevailing, light brushing of pepper throughout. It is a very rich, very thick nose, even with the water added. What is more, after my pour absorbed some air, an additional note of berries came out.

Compared to that quite complex, yet also quite heavy aroma, the palate experience was more straightforward: a mix of toasty cereals, straw, and pepper. While flavorful, it was a bit of a letdown after what the nose promised. The finish started peppery, before rolling over to the toasted cereals.

— BANNER DISTILLING COMPANY —

BANNER WHEAT WHISKEY

92

Many of the story elements in this East Austin–made whiskey are staples of the micro-distilling scene. First, it's a wheat whiskey, so Banner Distilling Company staked out some territory where the big distillers aren't taking up most of the space. Second, one of the founders claims to have a family background in bootlegging, while the other has a more practical grounding in chemistry. An added, outside-the-box touch was reviving the name of Banner Distilling, which had belonged to a Cincinnati-based company that operated before World War I.

Banner's Wheat Whiskey is turned out in small batches of approximately 175 bottles per batch, and those are half-size, 375-milliliter bottles. The mash bill is 95% wheat and 5% malted barley, and the water used to cut the whiskey between dumping barrels and bottling is collected rainwater.

The liquid has a burnt orange look in the glass.

The nose is caramel candy apple, dried fruits, and hints of marzipan and wood. It's said that wheat produces a softer profile in wheated bourbon, and that character is very much on display here.

A sip reveals a light but buttery liquid. It's a little peppery up front, then hoppy, and finally nutty with almonds. Consequently, the character is somewhat bitter and a little on the dry side. It's not like most other wheat whiskeys, but is still smooth and easy drinking.

— FIRESTONE & ROBERTSON —
DISTILLING COMPANY

Firestone & Robertson TX Blended Whiskey

82

In America, the words "blended whiskey" have a bad reputation, being associated with cheap rotgut. To cite a well-known example, Four Roses went from a popular, quality bourbon to a not-as-popular American blended whiskey before being revived into what is a popular bourbon once again. Yet there is nothing intrinsically cheap about blending different types of whiskey, as the many fine blended whiskeys made in Ireland and Scotland attest.

Firestone & Robertson set out to introduce a good blend prior to opening their distillery, and they made it from straight bourbon and other whiskeys matured in former bourbon barrels, as well as neutral grain spirits. The latter point might provoke a grimace from purists, but the company largely succeeded in their ambition.

It has a light but richly coppered coloring in the glass.

The nose is predominately and thickly sweet with honey and caramel, mixed with baked apples, but there is also a tiny toasted note to it as well. I would be tempted to describe the latter as giving the scent a Cracker Jack aspect, were it not more nutty than corny.

On the palate, this creamy liquid presents a more buttery, baked apple set of flavors, a set that is also thick with butterscotch and honey. I found the finish to run lighter, being a little warm and with a speck of that toastiness there at the start. That rapidly drops out, however, leaving only a butterscotch-style sweetness. TX Whiskey is a pretty good sipper.

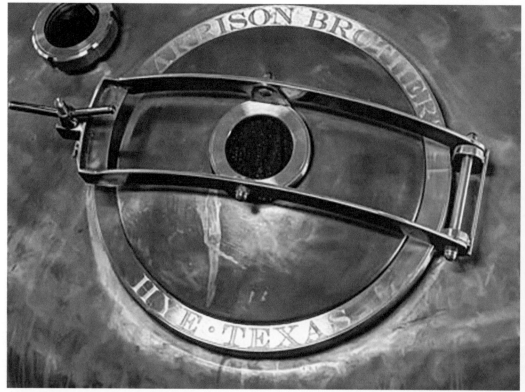

— GARRISON BROTHERS DISTILLERY —

Garrison Brothers was so early to the craft whiskey movement that when I first read about them in the mid-2000s, I remember thinking how remarkable and strange it was that anyone would start a whiskey distillery (this when some of the big Kentucky distillers still had production time to contract out), let alone in Texas. What is more, in iconoclastic, Lone Star style, Garrison Brothers didn't hesitate to go where the big distillers already were. The distillery staked its future on making bourbon, and only bourbon, made by harnessing the fierce Texas climate.

Dan Garrison began the preliminaries on his distillery as far back as 2001, founded it in 2004, and got his federal permit in 2007. As Garrison tells it, only 24 such permits had been issued at the time, and Bill Samuels Sr. over at Maker's Mark (who Garrison sees as a mentor) was congratulating him on starting the first new bourbon distillery since Prohibition. At the time, the only other small whiskey distillers he knew of were Ralph Erenzo at Tuthilltown and Jess Graber at Strahanan's. It was that small of a community. Erenzo and Graber have since sold their distilleries to larger liquor companies; Garrison Brothers is still owned by its founder.

Following in the tried-and-true bourbon tradition, Garrison Brothers picked up their still and some other equipment from Vendome. They run a sweet-mash operation, and they are producing more or less around the clock, 365 days a year. Going all day

means they are filling about 40 or 41 barrels a day.

A key aspect of Garrison Brothers bourbon making is their maturation, specifically harnessing the Texas climate of the Piney Woods region, where it is about 10 degrees warmer than Kentucky at any given time of year. Although the Angel's Share in Kentucky could be as high as 10% during the first year in the rickhouse, the average comes to about 4% per year. Garrison Brothers reports 13% per year, which says two things about maturing whiskey in Texas: the barrels are being cooked in the warehouse, and you need to get aging over with sooner rather than later, otherwise you will have no whiskey left when you open the barrel.

"What primarily evaporates from the barrel during maturation is the water," says Garrison. "The whiskey remains in the barrel and the caramelized sugar-to-whiskey ratio becomes more concentrated. There's a reason Garrison Brothers is so dark, has no burn, and has such a long gentle finish. That's thanks to the angels."

Garrison Brothers uses a variety of barrel stock. On the small barrel side, they have tiny casks and 10- to 20-gallon barrels in storage. However, the distillery also utilizes standard 53-gallon barrels and 59-gallon barrels bought from wine cooperages. Between its renowned ability to navigate the harsh Texas climate and the variety of barrel stock, Garrison Brothers (unsurprisingly) considers their entry proof a secret.

Garrison Brothers Small Batch Straight Bourbon Whiskey

94

The distillery's flagship is unlike most entry-level expressions in that it's released in vintages and each one is essentially a limited edition. So, one would speak of it not as Garrison Brothers Small Batch, but as Small Batch 2018. Even in its most basic bourbon, Garrison Brothers doesn't really shoot for a consistent flavor profile, so each vintage is a little different.

What is consistent is that Garrison Brothers has made some good whiskey. What is in the bottle always has a deep, flavorful character far out of proportion to either its proof or its length of aging of "at least four years."

On top of the brown sugar and vanilla customary to bourbon, the nose of this is often floral, fruity, and a bit grassy.

The barrel char aspect usually expresses itself in a toasty note. Throw in some spice and some oak, and you've got Garrison Brothers pretty much nailed down. The emphasis tends to shift from batch to batch, but this is what is usually present in this appropriately big-bodied Lone Star State whiskey.

GARRISON BROTHERS SINGLE BARREL STRAIGHT BOURBON WHISKEY

94

The single-barrel version of Garrison Brothers bourbon was introduced as soon as Texas legalized the sale of liquor straight from the distillery, and this expression started as a distillery-only release. From there it expanded into a private barrel program, whereby retailers, restaurants, and bars could choose a barrel for their own individualized bottling. Otherwise, Single Barrel is very much like Small Batch, and should be seen as an especially nice version of Small Batch. It is also aged for at least four years.

That said, if you have experienced the difference between a normal expression and that expression's private barrel version, you know the latter is often a very real step up. Garrison Brothers Single Barrel is no exception.

GARRISON BROTHERS COWBOY STRAIGHT BOURBON WHISKEY

135+ Cowboy Bourbon has developed a cult following since its inception in 2012. The overwhelming majority of the approximately 4,800 bottles from Cowboy Bourbon 2018 went into distribution, both in Texas and outside the state. But the distillery kept back 400 bottles for a launch event and sale at the distillery: news of that sale caused a massive traffic jam, with cars backed up for miles trying to get in, and the whiskey sold out in a few hours.

The premise of Cowboy Bourbon is straightforward: Master Distiller Dennis Todd identifies promising barrels and holds these back for extra aging. When he judges those barrels to have reached their peak, they go into a batch of Cowboy Bourbon, which is bottled at cask strength. The result is a Texas-size bold and flavorful bourbon with an oily texture that clocks in at 135 proof or greater. Each batch of Cowboy Bourbon, like most limited editions, is unique, and varies somewhat in its flavor profile from batch to batch.

Cowboy Bourbon is not just the best Garrison Brothers has to offer, but it's also one of craft whiskey's most brilliant stars. In Cowboy Bourbon, craft whiskey has an expression that can contend with most of the limited-edition offerings coming out of Kentucky and Tennessee.

— RANGER CREEK BREWING & DISTILLING —

RANGER CREEK .36 STRAIGHT BOURBON WHISKEY

96 Ranger Creek .36 Straight Bourbon is this San Antonio brewstillery's standard-bearer. It's an evolution of their earlier .36 Bourbon from their Small Caliber Series, so named because it used small barrels, and became a regular release in 2017. The latter was a typical example of early craft bourbon, but the Straight Bourbon uses standard 53-gallon barrels. Whereas Ranger Creek's small-barrel bourbon took nine to 18 months to mature, .36 Straight Bourbon is aged for two to four years.

The flavor profile reflects that it is a youthful bourbon, albeit one aged in Texas, not the Mid-South. The whiskey has picked up more from the barrel than one would expect from a comparably aged Kentucky whiskey. The taste smacks of brown sugar and caramel with a dab of spice and butterscotch, plus a solid note of green oak.

RANGER CREEK .44 TEXAS RYE WHISKEY

This is a small-barrel whiskey, and the barrels used were former bourbon barrels, left over from earlier iterations of .36 Straight Bourbon, and it comes in half-size bottles.

94

It is made from a 100% rye mash bill, and because it's a small-barrel whiskey made in old bourbon barrels it's quite spirit-forward. Whereas whiskey aged in new oak has a strong barrel-aging influence, even when small barrels are used, here you are getting an all-rye spirit with just a little barrel polish.

The scent is full of spiciness, in this case cinnamon, pepper, and cloves, plus a dollop of vanilla and toffee.

The palate follows along those lines, and even the finish doesn't deviate from the pattern. It's flavorful, albeit simple, straightforward, and constant.

96

Ranger Creek produced an early example of what has become a signature style for whiskey making in the Southwest: an American malt made using malted barley smoked in mesquite. As a brewstillery, Ranger Creek's beer- and whiskey-making operations share certain articles of equipment, and often whiskey is made from the same wort as beer. In the case of .36 Bourbon and .44 Rye, the mash bills are ill-suited to making beer. Rimfire, however, is made from the same wort as their Mesquite Smoked Porter, sans the hops. Like .44 Rye, it's aged in small former bourbon barrels from the .36 Straight Bourbon.

Think of this as a whiskey inspired by Scotland but made in Texas. It's 100% malted barley (albeit five different beer-making malts) and aged in used barrels, just like Scotch. Yet instead of smoking that malt with peat, Ranger Creek used mesquite.

The nose is one of tropical fruits drizzled with vanilla.

On the palate the whiskey turns to malty sweetness. The finish is a long one, and from start to finish Rimfire has a moderate, but sharp current of smoke running through it.

— TREATY OAK DISTILLING —

Treaty Oak Ghost Hill Texas Bourbon Whiskey

95 Some of Treaty Oak's expressions are sourced, but this one is in-house, named for the ranch where the distillery is located. It's made from a mash bill of 57% yellow Texas corn, 32% Texas wheat, and 11% malted barley sourced outside of Texas, and aged for four years in new American oak barrels that have received a #3 char level. The recipe for this bourbon is therefore quite noteworthy, because although one sees a lot of wheated bourbons, and sometimes sees high-rye bourbons, one rarely sees a high-wheat bourbon!

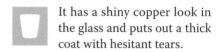 It has a shiny copper look in the glass and puts out a thick coat with hesitant tears.

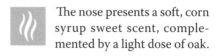 The nose presents a soft, corn syrup sweet scent, complemented by a light dose of oak.

A sip puts a creamy coating on the mouth, one that points back to the whiskey's appearance, and the flavor surprisingly starts off a bit spicy. The Red Hots cinnamon opening is quickly tamed by a softer profile of candy corn and dried apricots. The finish turns spicy again, running from cinnamon to pepper.

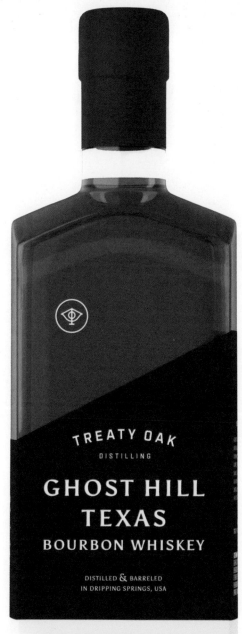

TREATY OAK

DISTILLING

GHOST HILL
TEXAS
BOURBON WHISKEY

DISTILLED & BARRELED
IN DRIPPING SPRINGS, USA

750ML   ALC. 47.5% BY VOL. (95 PROOF)

— WITHERSPOON DISTILLERY —

WITHERSPOON TEXAS STRAIGHT BOURBON WHISKEY

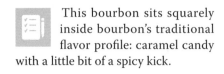

100 This craft distillery is located north of Dallas in Lewisville, and for their bourbon they chose to go with a 75% corn mash bill, with the rest malted barley and rye. The distillery describes that as "high corn," but in reality that level of corn is about as normal as a normal bourbon mash bill gets (Jim Beam's standard mash bill is 77% corn).

This bourbon sits squarely inside bourbon's traditional flavor profile: caramel candy with a little bit of a spicy kick.

— YELLOW ROSE DISTILLING —

If one were to open a spirits company in Texas, and Houston in particular, Yellow Rose is without a doubt the most appropriate name to give it. Like many craft operators, when Yellow Rose got started in 2010, it was with a line of sourced whiskeys. They have since opened a distillery of their own, while at the same time the sourced whiskey market has changed, so both their lineup and the brands within it have undergone some changes.

Yellow Rose Premium American Whiskey

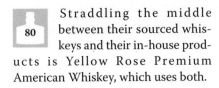 Straddling the middle between their sourced whiskeys and their in-house products is Yellow Rose Premium American Whiskey, which uses both.

 The nose is fruity with apples and citrus, like a fruit juice blend aged in an oak barrel.

The body is neither light nor heavy. Yet the finish is absolutely light, as in not carrying much warmth, and goes down almost clear. The fruity character and light body make it an easy sipper in warm weather, and thus ideally suited for drinking most of the year where it's made. Put it on ice, take it out on the porch in June, and sip away. The usual warmth that comes with whiskey shouldn't bother you.

Yellow Rose Single Malt Whiskey

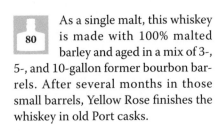 As a single malt, this whiskey is made with 100% malted barley and aged in a mix of 3-, 5-, and 10-gallon former bourbon barrels. After several months in those small barrels, Yellow Rose finishes the whiskey in old Port casks.

 The scent is of berries, nuts, and vanilla with a touch of spiciness and oak.

 The flavor follows along similar lines, but the finish turns spicy and to an earthy coffee note in equal measure.

WA

MT

OR

ID

WY

NV

CA

UT

CO

WEST
REGION

CALIFORNIA

— CHARBAY DISTILLERY —

Charbay's distilling grew out of its winemaking, and thus saw the company distilling aperitifs, liqueurs, brandy, and Port wine in Northern California. When it got into whiskey distilling in 1999, several years before the craft whiskey movement took off, Charbay broke ground on what is still a unique track: it distills whiskey from finished, ready-to-bottle beer. Even among the class of craft "brewstilleries," the norm is to make a beer and a whiskey from a common wort, not to literally turn beer into whiskey.

CHARBAY DOUBLED & TWISTED WHISKEY

90 Doubled & Twisted is a recent example of where Charbay's unique path has taken the company some 20 years later. It's made from a blend of different double-distilled, alembic-pot whiskeys, two of them distilled from beer: 50% aged single malt (three years); 30% aged stout whiskey (seven years); and 20% aged pilsner whiskey (three years). With a pedigree like that, it's best to expect something different in the glass.

Doubled & Twisted is oily, carrying musty, toasted cereals and baking spices.

That spiciness turns a bit pungent on the palate, reminiscent of green, unprocessed spices. If you've ever had fresh green peppercorns, you understand that is a quite different experience from dried pepper, although I'm not suggesting the flavor is actually peppery. Quite the opposite: those pungent, green spices lend punch to what is otherwise a honeyed, malty whiskey. The musty note from the nose persists on the back end. It's with the finish that the pungency finally turns peppery.

— OLD POTRERO DISTILLERY —
HOTALING & CO.

In 1989, the Bomberger Distillery in Pennsylvania went into bankruptcy and the whiskey crash that started in the 1970s finally reached its low point. Although the physical contraction of the whiskey industry can be said to have stopped at the end of the 1980s, the start of the modern craft distilling boom wouldn't arrive until the mid-2000s. In between, just a few distilleries would open, some of them becoming craft whiskey before craft whiskey became a thing. Among them was a true pioneer for small distillers, Old Potrero.

Old Potrero was started in 1993 by Fritz Maytag, who was already known as a forerunner of craft brewing for buying and revamping Anchor Brewing in the 1960s. A few years later, the distillery introduced a pot-distilled malted rye whiskey called Old Potrero 18th Century Rye. The choice to make a malted rye whiskey, something no one was doing at the time and thereby going where the big distillers weren't, would become a hallmark of the craft whiskey movement.

The distillery was also a predecessor of "brewstilleries" in some respects. Although Old Potrero and Anchor Brewing weren't in the same building, they were parts of the same company until 2010, and shared certain resources. For example, Old Potrero whiskeys have been fermented for decades using the Anchor Brewing house ale yeast. Its malted rye comes from a Wisconsin malt master who had been supplying Anchor Brewing with specialty malts since the 1970s.

Despite having been around for a quarter century, Old Potrero remains a small operation. It normally fills 10 53-gallon barrels with whiskey per week, and the distillery has evolved rather than expanded over the years. Take the stills: its has two pot stills, one made by CARL and the other by Holstein. The tops were made by a Bay Area coppersmith. Old Potrero's first condenser was made in-house, but eventually was replaced with a Vendome. The distillery recently brought in a wash still and condenser from Forsyths. Most of the other distillery equipment was acquired secondhand from breweries and wineries. The Hotaling & Co. (Old Potrero's parent company) Instagram feed has not heralded the installation of a brand-new, multimillion-dollar, four-story column still, and it's doubtful it ever will.

Most of what Old Potrero does today remains the same as it was in the mid-1990s when the distillery released its first whiskey. Old Potrero is a sweet-mash distillery and typically distills to 144 proof. Its barrels have come from Independent Stave Company in Missouri from the beginning, and Old Potrero has put a major emphasis on working with that company to ensure barrel quality. Theirs are made with 24-month air-dried staves, toasted by hand before charring to either #3 or #4.

Lately, Old Potrero has been tinkering with its entry proof. Historically it was pegged to around 124 proof, but the last few years the distillery has entered whiskey into the barrels at between 112 and 125 proof. Thus, even one of the forerunners of craft whiskey is still doing a little tuning, trying to dial in its production process to get it just right.

OLD POTRERO SINGLE MALT STRAIGHT RYE WHISKEY

The distillery's flagship expression is a no-age-statement whiskey.

It has a dark gold appearance in the glass.

The nose is candy sweet and seasoned with spiciness.

A sip dresses the palate with a light but noticeable coating, and tastes of Red Hots cinnamon; tart, fruity candy; and a hint of nuts. It's a notably smooth whiskey, and very much so on the finish.

ESSAY
10-RW-ARM-3-L

SINGLE MALT   EST'D. 1993

OLD POTRERO

ANCHOR DISTILLING CO.

TRADITIONAL   (A)   POT DISTILLED
                TRADEMARK
              SAN FRANCISCO

18TH CENTURY STYLE
WHISKEY

Pot distilled from 100%
rye malt mash & aged 2 years 6 months
in uncharred oak barrels

750 ml   ANCHOR DISTILLING COMPANY   51.2% Alc/vol
                          SAN FRANCISCO, CALIFORNIA   (102.4 Proof)

Old Potrero 18th Century Style Whiskey

102.4 This expression is the distillery's attempt to take its malted rye and use it to create a whiskey more authentic to Colonial and Revolutionary times, or "America's original whiskey." What that means in practice is that this is a young whiskey, aged for just two years, but aged in new and used oak barrels that have not been charred, but merely toasted.

Once in the glass, the 18th Century Style Whiskey has the look of a richly endowed white wine, and coating the glass puts down some big, heavy legs.

The nose is thick with that molasses scent I've come to expect from malted rye whiskeys (to say nothing of 100% malted rye), plus a pumpernickel bread note and a certain vague fruitiness.

On the palate, that mix of undefined fruitiness, molasses, and pumpernickel (quite like an earthy, boozy fruitcake really) comes forward, followed by a spicy note of cinnamon. After it sat on my tongue for a bit, green wood and a pinch of astringency came up, too. The finish ran with spicy heat over to a layer of that indistinct fruit.

100

Craft whiskeys that are truly well-aged remain a rarity. Outside of the major distillers, only Old Potrero has put out repeated releases of whiskeys with age statements in the teens. Even though the distillery was doing craft whiskey years before craft whiskey became a thing, it decided early on to set aside some stock for long-term aging, which has resulted in the existence of the Hotaling's line.

The first batch was an 11-year-old, released in 2006. Batches at different ages have been released since, the oldest being an 18-year-old from 2013. As I write this, the most recent release was 2017's 11-year-old.

Like all Old Potrero whiskey, this is a 100% malted rye whiskey, both a "single malt" insofar as Americans are concerned, and a rye whiskey. It was aged in barrels previously used to mature the basic Old Potrero whiskey, and this batch was released as a single-barrel expression.

In the glass, the 2017 Hotaling's has a golden, white wine appearance. Coating the glass yields a curtain of tears.

Taking a sniff, I found dried fruits, that fresh-baked pumpernickel scent so common to malted ryes, a dollop of vanilla, and a hint of leather.

The latter aspect really came forward on the palate; this middle-aged Hotaling's takes that fruity, dark rye bread character and puts a wonderful earthy twist on it. From there the finish reverts to something more typical of malted ryes: a trickling current of molasses and pumpernickel.

— SONOMA DISTILLING COMPANY —

Sonoma Distilling Company's bourbon has evolved a bit since the distillery started. Initially there was a series of releases called "West of Kentucky." In 2018, the distillery revamped its whiskey line, with West of Kentucky No. 1 becoming Cherrywood Smoked Bourbon and West of Kentucky No. 2 becoming the standard Sonoma Bourbon.

SONOMA BOURBON WHISKEY

92 Sonoma chose to go with a wheated mash bill for its regular bourbon. It's a young whiskey, aged a minimum of 15 months with more than half the barrels in a given batch being two years or older. It's sometimes said Stitzel-Weller and Maker's Mark chose to go with wheated bourbon upon starting because the softer profile tastes better at younger ages, but then again it's also said that wheated bourbon withstands longer aging periods better, too. Sonoma chose to go with a 70% corn, 25% wheat, and 5% malted barley mash bill.

A pour of Sonoma Bourbon has a light copper coloring in the glass, and coating the glass leaves an array of tears behind.

The nose has a current of marzipan that has been glazed with vanilla.

The mouthfeel is light, but it's still a flavorful bourbon. It is a simple but tasty one, with an earthy caramel base and a layer of candy corn on top, plus a very modest woody tinge. The finish, however, runs quite short.

Sonoma Cherrywood Smoked Bourbon Whiskey

As mentioned on page 467, West of Kentucky No. 1 became the Cherrywood Smoked Bourbon. It's made with 67% corn, 20% rye, and 13% smoked malted barley. Like the standard bourbon from Sonoma, the minimum age is 15 months, but more than half of a given batch is two years or older.

This whiskey has a bright copper look in the glass, and coating the inside drops plenty of legs.

The nose comes across with caramel, cocktail cherries, and a spot of leathery wood.

The flavor sits squarely in traditional bourbon territory, but with a slight twist. It tastes of vanilla and brown sugar, with a touch of that cocktail cherry (much less than on the nose). That spot of leathery wood from the nose takes on an ashy, marginally astringent character once on your tongue, like a charred bit of green oak. The finish is short and a touch smoky.

Sonoma Rye Whiskey

An earlier version of Sonoma's rye, which featured a different label, was bottled at a slightly stronger 96 proof. So don't confuse this iteration with the prior version.

This is made with 100% rye, a mix of malted and unmalted rye, and double-distilled in alembic pots. The new-make spirit is then aged in small barrels and finished in used bourbon barrels. It is unfiltered.

A pour of Sonoma's Rye Whiskey has the look of polished copper in the glass, and giving the glass a swish leaves behind lazy, beady tears.

The scent comes forward with a mix of berries and banana, backed by that malty rye pumpernickel and molasses aroma.

The balance of notes on the nose is slightly in favor of the bread and molasses, but this flips on the palate. The same elements are there, but inverted. The profile is that straightforward. From there, the finish runs in a lightly spiced vein and lingers for a decent, warm spell.

Sonoma Cherrywood Smoked Rye Whiskey

95.6 You might expect Sonoma's Cherrywood Smoked Rye to be a variant on its house rye whiskey, but that is actually a different animal. The flagship rye is a 100% rye that gets a finish in former bourbon barrels. This is a wheated and smoked rye whiskey; the mash bill is 80% rye, 10% cherrywood smoked and malted barley, and 10% wheat. The whiskey is then aged in barrels partly sourced from Missouri and partly from that tight-grained, northern Minnesota oak.

This copper-colored whiskey leaves behind a few chunky tears after a swish and coat of the glass.

A sniff reveals an alcoholic tinge, but not so much that I would describe the whiskey as hot. It's just there, and brashly announces the whiskey's youth. The nose has that dark rye bread spiciness, a note of molasses and vanilla, and a current of cedar.

A sip of the whiskey leads with cherry and vanilla sweetness, followed by cinnamon spice and pinewood. The spices turn peppery in the end, leaving a peppery and piney finish. Most curious of all, there isn't so much as a whiff of smoke or char through the entire experience.

PREMIUM CALIFORNIA WHISKEYS

SONOMA
DISTILLING CO.

CHERRYWOOD RYE WHISKEY

80% RYE (CALIFORNIA & CANADA), 10% WHEAT (CALIFORNIA) &
10% CHERRYWOOD SMOKED MALTED BARLEY
RADICALLY DOUBLE POT DISTILLED IN SONOMA COUNTY, CALIFORNIA

TASTES LIKE: DRIED FIGS · TOASTED ALMONDS · BAKED CHERRIES

— SPIRIT WORKS DISTILLERY —

SPIRIT WORKS STRAIGHT RYE WHISKEY

90

Spirit Works Distillery was founded by a husband-and-wife team, Timo and Ashby Marshall, in Sebastopol, a town nestled in the midst of the Sonoma wine country. As a straight rye, it's aged a minimum of two years. Indicative of where the craft movement has been heading, Spirit Works' whiskey is aged in 53-gallon American Standard Barrels, not the smaller barrels that once were near universal among small distillers. It's also not chill-filtered.

A pour shows a golden brown look in the glass.

The youthful scent carries undistinguished sweetness and oak and cedar woodiness.

Taking a sip gives one an oily mouthfeel, with a sweetness that is a bit like honey and apples, seasoned with vanilla and baking spices. It still tastes like a young whiskey, until the finish comes in with a richly honeyed, spicy note.

SPIRIT WORKS STRAIGHT WHEAT WHISKEY

90

In making a wheat whiskey, Spirit Works decided to turn sharply into the category, electing for a 100% red winter wheat mash bill. Like its stablemate, this straight whiskey is aged for at least two years in 53-gallon barrels and bottled without chill filtration.

This wheat whiskey has an orange color in the glass.

A sniff reveals another youthful spirit while giving off a note of butterscotch candy and oak.

The flavor is more along the lines of Cracker Jack caramel and sweet peach tea. Once again, the finish is the best part of sipping on a Spirit Works whiskey. In this instance, it delivers successive waves of ginger and earthy cocoa before departing on a trace of vanilla.

— ST. GEORGE'S DISTILLERY —

Alameda's St. George's Distillery is one of those distilleries that was in craft spirits long before craft spirits became a thing, but they weren't making whiskey that whole time. When Jörg Rupf started the distillery in 1982, it was part of a small class of California brandy makers in the midst of a very vine-and-fruit-oriented state. The turn to whiskey came in 1996, when one-time brewer and former nuclear scientist Lance Winters turned up, with a bottle of his homemade whiskey in hand as a resume. As it happened, the mid-1990s coincided with the emergence of the other distillers I like to refer to as "craft whiskey before there was craft whiskey." Lot 1 of St. George's Single Malt followed in 2000, and they have released a new batch every year since.

St. George's Single Malt Whiskey, Lot 21

86

Dave Smith, the head distiller and blender, chose twenty-six barrels from the inventory for Lot 21. The mash is very much a brewer's creation, utilizing two-row barley sourced from Wisconsin (pale malt, crystal malt, chocolate malt, black patent malt) and German Bamberg malt (unroasted barley smoked over beech and alder wood). Those twenty-six casks range in age from 4 ½ to 10 years, plus some cask blends older than the distillery. The chosen cask stock includes used Kentucky bourbon barrels, used Tennessee whiskey barrels, American and French oak apple brandy casks, Agricole rum casks, and California Sauternes-style casks.

A glass of Lot 21 has a golden cast to it, which isn't surprising when you consider how much used wood was used to age it. The amber color of so many American whiskeys is down to the new oak its aged in; used wood imparts less color.

The scent was like a hunk of freshly baked barley bread, smeared with a rich marmalade and served under the shade of a pine tree.

A sip reveals a whiskey that is strongly malt driven, full of honey sweetness, but also notes of charred wood. These aspects are gently subsumed in a lapping wave of earthy-but-sweet chocolate and ash. The finish went down light, herbaceous, and honey sweet.

— STARK SPIRITS DISTILLERY —

STARK SPIRITS PEATED SINGLE MALT WHISKEY

92 California distilleries tend to either be historic or have a wine country connection, so Pasadena might seem like an unlikely place to find one. Yet that is where Greg and Karen Stark run their nano-distillery, and to be even more offbeat, they are making a peated single malt whiskey.

In the suburbs of Los Angeles, Stark ages its whiskey in small new oak barrels, and, in keeping with that practice, the nose is packed with caramel and oak, which dominate the notes of peat smoke, leather, and pastry.

The whiskey has a silken texture, with a flavor that is oaky and leathery on the one hand and cinnamon and clove spicy on the other, with modest hints of caramel and smoke.

⊰ COLORADO ⊱

The Centennial State's claim to being a top whiskey-making region begins with Stranahan's, part of the initial crop of craft whiskey distilleries, and the first one to get into American malts. Recall that when Stranahan's began selling its Colorado single malt whiskey in 2006, no one in America had an American malt in regular production. Others soon followed Stranahan's, and Colorado is now home to over two dozen small whiskey-making distilleries.

Some of them have added interesting features to their production process, such as Distillery 291's use of aspen wood inserts to finish its whiskeys, or contributed to the revival of lost whiskey styles that hadn't come back even in their native states yet, as when Leopold Bros. launched a Maryland-style rye whiskey. Colorado whiskeys have made considerable contributions to the growing maturity of the national craft whiskey scene, both with Stranahan's older expressions and with the bonded releases from Laws Whiskey House. At the same time, Old Elk Distillery has brought some major industry know-how to the state in the form of MGP legend Greg Metze.

Colorado already has a certain status for crafty things, due in no small part to its host of small breweries, the envy of beer lovers around the country. People also tend to associate its rugged reputation with whiskey drinking. With so much substance to go with that style, it's easy to see why Colorado's stature as a whiskey state is continually growing.

— DISTILLERY 291 —

Founded in 2011 in Colorado Springs by Michael Meyers, 291 Distillery brings three twists to its production process. Going where other distillers aren't is the name of the game for craft whiskey, but it would be fair to say 291 Distillery's approaches are, at present, either unique or nearly so: first is the so-called "El Paso County Process," (Meyers grew up on a farm near George Dickel's Cascade Hollow, hence the nod to the Lincoln County Process), which is to add stillage from an IPA to the whiskey mash; second is to use stave inserts made from aspen

for finishing the whiskey; third is their reliance on malted rye—the distillery uses malted rye not only for their rye whiskey (where, while not typical, would still be unremarkable nowadays), but also in their bourbon (where it is remarkable indeed).

In late 2020, Distillery 291 moved into the building that had previously housed Colorado Gold Distillery. The new space is almost twice the size of their old facility, and they announced plans to use the expansion to increase production and barrel storage.

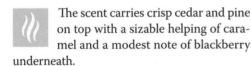

DISTILLERY 291 COLORADO BOURBON WHISKEY

100

The mash bill is high-corn (another Tennessee inspiration) at 80%, with 19% malted rye and 1% malted barley.

This bright amber bourbon leaves a thin coat on the glass, and a curtain of skinny, short legs along with it.

The scent carries crisp cedar and pine on top with a sizable helping of caramel and a modest note of blackberry underneath.

A sip reveals a light mouthfeel, as well as a lighter flavor than the nose suggests. It's a little peppery and a little fruity, with just a hint of vanilla. The peppery spice continues into the finish, which turns a touch hot in the end.

101.7 This 291 rye is made from 61% malted rye and 39% corn before being aged for less than two years in 10-gallon barrels. This whiskey also uses the distillery's "El Paso County Process."

In the glass, it has the look of polished brass. Swishing the glass leaves behind a coat with scattered but quite thick tears.

The nose on 291 Rye is quite musty, a feature that often attends the use of malted rye, and here we have plenty of it. The scent is molasses and peppery spices in the main, underscored by spruce.

On the palate, overtones of spruce and cedar run over molasses and pumpernickel, and once again the whole thing has a pronounced, musty character. The whiskey goes down like a big flavorful pumpernickel that is about to turn.

Putting 291's bourbon and rye together into a common experience, I cannot put my finger on what their El Paso County Process does exactly, but the influence of the aspen staves is quite clear.

10TH MOUNTAIN WHISKEY & SPIRIT CO.

With their World War II military branding, one might be surprised to learn that 10th Mountain is located in Vail, home of the famed ski resort. But it's also in the middle of White River National Forest, where the 10th Mountain Division was created in 1943. Vail itself is named for a 10th Mountain veteran. So, if you're going to set up a distillery in Vail, nodding to a particular outfit and group of veterans makes sense.

10TH MOUNTAIN BOURBON WHISKEY

10th Mountain Bourbon is almost a high-corn bourbon, being 75% corn and the rest traditional rye and malted barley. It's also young, reportedly just six months old.

The scent is corn syrup with a slight hint of vanilla, herbs, and green wood.

The flavor profile comes across as young, but not hot, instead being quite sweet and smooth.

It stays sweet, but turns a little minty and nutty. The finish is all oaky vanilla. It's not complex or subtle, but it is easygoing, enjoyable stuff.

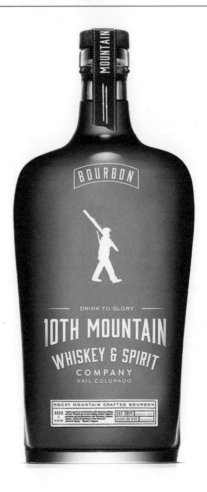

— LAWS WHISKEY HOUSE —

Colorado's craft whiskey scene is one of the oldest in America, dating back to 2004, but some of their most interesting small distilleries are more recent creations. Laws Whiskey House, founded by Alan and Marianne Laws in 2011 with some help from Jake Norris, is one such example. When the craft sector began releasing its first crop of bottled in bond whiskeys in 2017, Laws Whiskey House was the only distillery in Colorado that was part of that pack. At the time of writing, the distillery has released four separate bottled in bond expressions.

Laws Whiskey House lives up to its name, covering all the major categories of American whiskey with at least one distillate. The main bourbon at Laws is a four-grain whiskey, but they also have a two-grain bourbon. Other whiskeys made there include a 95% rye and 5% malted barley rye whiskey; an 86% corn and 14% malted barley corn whiskey; a 100% wheat whiskey; and 100% malted barley American single malts. All the distillates have been released as at least straight whiskeys, and some as cask-strength, single-barrel, or bottled in bond expressions.

The hardware at Laws comes from some familiar vendors. The copper was crafted at Vendome, along with the stainless steel cooker, while the distillery's other various stainless steel tanks and vats were fabricated by Custom Metalcraft in Missouri.

That equipment is being used to near capacity to make sour-mash whiskey, and Laws is probably ripe for an expansion. It has five full-time distillers on staff, working two 10-hour shifts a day, seven days a week. The schedule on its current set of equipment fills approximately 70 53-gallon barrels a month.

Those new oak barrels are charred to level 3, and are made at Independent Stave in Missouri. Most of the seasoned barrels used for special finishes come from Rocky Mountain Barrel Company, a Colorado purveyor of used wine and spirits barrels.

The standard barrel entry proof at Laws is 110 proof, the same as Maker's Mark. What makes that entry proof interesting is that 110 proof used to be the maximum, but this was raised to the current limit of 125 in 1962. As a rule, lower-entry proof is a more expensive choice (because cutting the new make down further means putting slightly less of it and more water in each barrel), but that additional water improves the breakdown of certain compounds and sugars that makes a whiskey tastier. So, Laws is spending a little extra money on barrel stock to get a better whiskey.

LAWS 6–YEAR–OLD FOUR GRAIN BONDED BOURBON

 Laws Whiskey House made its commitment to producing bottled in bond whiskeys from the outset, and since those bonded whiskeys were introduced, they have been getting steadily older. Currently, their bottled in bond bourbon is 6 years old. The distillery has two versions of their Four Grain bourbon, one straight and one bonded, so the bonded should be seen as the step up. Still, they both come from the same new make, one made from 50% corn, 20% Colorado-grown wheat, 10% Colorado-grown rye, 10% Colorado-grown barley.

In the glass, this bourbon has a light and red-tinted amber look.

 The scent is markedly unusual, with the sweet aroma of freshly cut grass just under soft notes of cotton candy and light caramel.

 The nose is a sweet one, like someone stirred crushed candy corn into a dish of vanilla pudding, with a sprinkle of finely chopped ginger and mint on the top.

LAWS SAN LUIS VALLEY 6–YEAR–OLD BONDED RYE WHISKEY

Although the mash bill on this whiskey is 95% rye and 5% malted barley, it is part of a class using that mash not sourced from MGP. It's a lovely rye, and one that points to how whiskey is so much more than the sum of a mash bill, because it is so unlike any of the aforementioned MGP-derived ryes I've had over the years.

The look in the glass is a reddened amber to be sure, but it is darker than one usually gets from rye whiskeys.

The nose combines that malty-style pumpernickel with freshly cut grass, plus notes of musty wood and molasses.

The flavor turns much spicier. Instead of pumpernickel, it's herbaceous with peppermint, anise, and fennel. The sweet aspect turns from molasses to caramel, and the woody end goes from mustiness to charred. The finish jinks away from the spiciness, however, running to sweet leaf tobacco instead.

LAWS CENTENNIAL 5-YEAR-OLD BONDED WHEAT WHISKEY

100 Whereas a wheat whiskey need only be 51% wheat, and often is pretty close to that mark, Laws went all the way to 100% wheat. They also chose the namesake Centennial varietal, a white spring wheat. Most wheat whiskeys use red winter wheat, which is hardier and also harder, an odd thing to say when one considers wheated bourbons and wheat whiskeys are supposed to be floral and soft. Moving hard in that softer direction paid real dividends with this wheat whiskey, making it one of the best in its class.

This whiskey has a coppered look in the glass.

The nose is fragrant and airy, leading with the smell of a prairie in bloom. It's a dry day on the prairie though. Accenting this is a smear of sharp marmalade and rich honeyed sweetness.

That honey is much more prevalent on the palate, coming to share center stage. The citrus current continues but turns more herbal. It is now more akin to a tea seasoned with orange zest and garden herbs than jam. The finish takes the biggest twist of all, turning to pine and pepper.

— LEOPOLD BROS. DISTILLERY —

Leopold Bros. was started by two brothers, one with a solid grounding in brewing and the other in economics and manufacturing. They started out as micro-brewers in Michigan, but eventually moved to Colorado. From a whiskey point of view, the most noteworthy thing the brothers did was revive Maryland-style rye whiskey before anyone in Maryland got the chance to.

LEOPOLD BROS. MARYLAND—STYLE RYE WHISKEY

86

This is made with a 65% rye mash bill, the rest being corn and malted barley. Although this is a no-age-statement whiskey, it is known to be aged for about four years before bottling. It's also a single barrel, although it isn't specifically declared as such, but every bottle declares what barrel it came from. When I got to try it, the whiskey came from Barrel 158.

In the glass, the whiskey has a dull gold color. A swish leaves a coating with a thick crown and a curtain of weighty tears.

The nose opens with blackberry jam smeared on dark rye bread, with a touch of molasses added for good measure. The scent is a bit musty at first, but that fades with some time in the open air.

The flavor isn't far removed from those aromas: dark berry fruit with a daub of molasses and a dash of hot cinnamon. From there, the Maryland-style rye concludes as expected, with lingering blackberries and currant on the tongue, and plenty of warmth.

— OLD ELK DISTILLERY —

OLD ELK BLENDED STRAIGHT BOURBON WHISKEY

88 Old Elk Distillery is the current project of Greg Metze, formerly of MGP fame. This is a sourced whiskey, something created to start the brand. Old Elk speaks of three partners, so presumably it's a blend of whiskeys from three separate distilleries.

It has a dull copper look in the glass. Making a swish leaves behind a thick coat, but one that lets plentiful tears fall through it.

A sniff gives caramel with a current of cloves, tinged with dry cedar.

The mouthfeel of the whiskey is fairly light, with a flavor that is predominately spicy and dry. The sweetness and vanilla take a backseat for a whiskey that is actually quite reminiscent of high-rye bourbons, like those based on MGP's high-rye mash bill stock or Basil Hayden. From there, the finish is short and runs drier and spicier, due to the sweetness having faded away altogether.

— STRANAHAN'S DISTILLERY —

A pretty good argument can be made for Stranahan's having been the first modern craft whiskey distillery. In the 1990s, there were a few that heralded what was coming, like Prichard's in Tennessee and Old Potrero in California. But when Stranahan's got its license in March 2004, making it the first legal distillery in the Centennial State since Prohibition, it was part of a small group of micro-distilleries that would be followed by dozens, then hundreds more. The distillery's first bottling of American Single Malt followed not long after in 2006.

Stranahan's soon outgrew their original space and in 2009 moved to its present digs, a former brewery. Initially, the distillery occupied just the back part of the building, but as it happens Stranahan's was also one of the first craft distilleries to be acquired by a big drinks company; the Mexican liquor giant Proximo Spirits bought Stranahan's in 2010, setting the stage for a 2011 expansion that tripled its production capacity.

When it first got started in 2004, Stranahan's was only capable of filling a few 53-gallon barrels a week. That doubled to six a week by 2006, and by 2012 it was reportedly up to about 30 barrels a week.

In its earliest incarnation, Stranahan's shared equipment with a craft brewery, and some of its production process continues to be firmly rooted in brewing, something reflected in both equipment and terminology. The distillery has a mash tun rather than a cooker; refers to its mash/wort as beer wash; it lauters, or clarifies, that wash; and it uses a boil kettle. Fermentation lasts for six days at Stranahan's, and the distillery refers to what they have at the end of that as "distiller's wash."

Vendome built the copper that Stranahan's currently employs: one set of three 800-liter stills and one set of two 160-liter stills. Both sets are of the hybrid pot/column design. The whiskey comes off the still at around 140 proof, which Stranahan's cuts with Eldorado Springs water down to about 110 proof for barrel entry.

Stranahan's takes a lot of pride in its Colorado roots, so it sources most of its barley from Colorado and has it malted locally. Roughly 10% of the distillery's malted barley is more specialized, and is from the wider Rocky Mountains region. Stranahan's yeast is a proprietary strain, produced locally, and the distillery has an unusual propagation vessel on-site for that yeast, which bears a striking resemblance to a Star Wars astromech (R2-D2 or one of the R4s).

The distillery buys its 53-gallon new oak barrels from Independent Stave Company, and those come with a #3 char. The Diamond Peak expression adds to the mix a set of 620-gallon Foeders, which are used for vatting, and a little extra solera-style aging before bottling.

STRANAHAN'S COLORADO WHISKEY

Stranahan's basic single malt has evolved over the last decade or so, and the present version is a blend of up to 20 barrels of stock ranging from two to five years in age. Given that the expression started as a two-year-old, give or take, it's come a long way.

The whiskey still shows its relative youth in its light, dull coppery amber coloring, and it streams hefty legs in the glass.

The scent is very Scotch-like in one respect, in that it's packed with cereals and cut and dried grass. However, there is also a sweet side to it, a certain marshmallow quality that comes from the malt, but also a dollop of vanilla from the white oak barrel aging.

The flavor delivers many of the staple elements I have come to expect from an American malt whiskey: a malty, honeyed sweetness, seasoned with light touches of peppermint and anise, a trickle of nuttiness, plus the overlay of vanilla coming from the barrel. The finish starts with a little pepper on the tip of the tongue, but as that fades with the declining warmth, a certain earthiness remains.

As the American malt sector has grown, I have come to think of Stranahan's Colorado Whiskey as the most uncomplicated. It's not fancy, but it is nonetheless a tasty, easy-drinking, and sturdy example of what malt whiskey aged in virgin white oak is supposed to be.

STRANAHAN'S SNOWFLAKE COLORADO SINGLE MALT WHISKEY

94 Only a few limited editions from small distillers have risen to the levels of hype that greet the titans of Kentucky's annual autumn release season, that time when most of the hot-ticket whiskeys come out. Although born of far more humble origins than the big distillers' stuff, Stranahan's Snowflake has come to match them in some respects.

Snowflake was born several years ago, initially featuring one or more separate barrel finishes each year. When Rob Dietrich took over as master distiller in 2011, Snowflake grew into a tour de force blend of multiple finished whiskeys. For the 2018 installment, dubbed "Mt. Elbert," nine different casks were used: Syrah; Muscat; Port; chocolate stout (first used to age Stranahan's, then stout, and finally to finish Stranahan's); Merlot; Zinfandel; two Madeira casks; and rum.

In the glass, Snowflake 2018 has a mid-amber appearance, balancing its red and its brown. The liquid is viscous in the glass, laying down a solid coating with a clear, thick crown. That crown stubbornly refuses to drop tears, taking so long I gave up watching for them.

The nose is rich and comes on almost entirely at once, but manages that crowd of scents without overwhelming the senses. The aroma is like a bowl of red fruits and berries with a crumble of graham crackers and ginger cookies layered on the top, plus a note of dry, toasty wood hovering in the background.

A sip of the whiskey is just as richly endowed as the nose. The liquid has a silken texture, with a foundation of very wine-driven red and dark fruits (red apples, plums, raisins, dried apricots) and fruitcake spices. It turns a bit tart on the back end, as if someone had put raspberries in at the last minute. The finish changes course, unwinding with cinnamon and turning a little peppery as it fades away.

This Snowflake is a flavorful, deep whiskey, with enough complexity to showcase how to make the most out of a wide stock of whiskeys that have received a variety of barrel finishes.

STRANAHAN'S SHERRY CASK SINGLE MALT WHISKEY

94 Introduced in 2017, this single malt takes Stranahan's four-year-old whiskey and gives it a finish in Oloroso Sherry butts that have been properly seasoned over four decades of use. The demand for Sherry casks in the world whiskey industry is such that many casks are created especially for it, receiving a minimum of use in aging Sherry, but not the ones acquired by Stranahan's.

Rob Dietrich felt it necessary to go with genuinely aged Sherry casks. Having received enough of a new oak aging to qualify as mature, the single malt coming out of Stranahan's has a much hardier flavor profile than Scotch single malt of comparable maturity (not age, maturity) coming out of what is usually either a former bourbon barrel or a hogshead made of former bourbon barrel staves. In Dietrich's view, he needed the deeper, richer flavor of Sherry-soaked wood to draw on if he was going to achieve a properly Sherried whiskey.

It has a shiny and scintillating orange look in the glass. The swish and coat leaves a beady crown and scattered, skinny legs around the glass.

The nose is thoroughly Sherried, with dried and dark stone fruits atop malty honey, rounded out by an oaky note and a pinch of wood-driven spiciness.

The palate is much the same, only a bit more refined and running a little deeper. It tastes of raisins and dried currants over the same malty honey base, with the spices coming out more distinctly as hot cinnamon and once again rounded out by a nice hint of oak. A quite modest note of tobacco leaf comes up on the back end, which carries over into the finish. That lingers for quite some time, with the tobacco fading under a hot cinnamon current that sits lightly on the tongue for longer than I want to go without taking another sip.

JAKE NORRIS

Like a lot of people in craft distilling, Jake Norris didn't set out to work in distillation or even the liquor business. He went to art school. However, he had a background of sorts in distillation, having gleaned something about it from studying homesteading as a teenager. He was interested in applying that to alternative fuel production when he met Jess Graber and started working at Stranahan's in 2004.

Being involved in a start-up distillery years before anyone was talking about "craft whiskey" was an exercise in on-the-job training. "There was no blueprint to follow, no school to go to," says Norris. "We just had to sort it out. Jess had developed a set of skills as a contractor that was invaluable in fighting bureaucracy and powering through obstacles, and he trusted me to figure stuff out and empowered me to make mistakes."

When liquor giant Proximo Spirits bought Stranahan's in December 2010, Norris decided he wasn't interested in being an employee in a shop in which he was once a stakeholder. After several months of transition time with his lieutenant, Rob Dietrich (see page 497), Norris left Stranahan's and took some time for himself, "basically a yearlong summer camp, with a little consulting here and there." Eventually, Al Laws offered him the job of head distiller at a new start-up, Laws Whiskey House.

"I put in five years with Al," says Norris, "and we built an incredible team and made some of the best whiskey of my career. I am very proud to have been a part of the Laws team."

Beyond Stranahan's and Laws Whiskey House, Norris has worked with many other small distillers. Unfortunately, nondisclosure agreements are as common in whiskey consulting as they are in sourcing stock whiskey, but Norris is known to have worked with St. Augustine in Florida and Woody Creek Distillers in Colorado.

Having worked with at least three Colorado distilleries, including two of the best known, it's not an exaggeration to say Norris's fingerprints are all over Colorado whiskey. Just for starters, he is the creator of Stranahan's Snowflake: "[It] was something I came up with and had to really talk Jess into letting me do, and it really took off. It was a great experience creating those additional cask-maturation gems."

Norris is also proud of his work with Laws Whiskey House in creating bottled in bond (BIB) versions of their four-grain bourbon and rye whiskeys. "At the time we released those whiskeys," says Norris, "I don't think there were 20 BIB whiskeys on the market, let alone a craft BIB. To make a bottled in bond requires a commitment to take no shortcuts and really do things right. It was like a big badge saying that we were not amateurs f*cking around in a warehouse."

After a decade and a half in craft distilling, Norris is astounded by the explosive growth the sector has seen in recent years. "I was as surprised as anyone that craft distilleries became a trend," he says, pointing to the constant, rotating, and evolving difficulties of running a small distillery.

— WOOD'S HIGH MOUNTAIN DISTILLERY —

WOOD'S TENDERFOOT WHISKEY

90 Made in Salida, this whiskey is an example of how open-minded Americans are with the term "malt whiskey." In Europe, if you call something a malt, it's 100% malted barley. In the States, craft distillers are malting almost every grain that can possibly be malted and turning it into whiskey. So, Wood's Tenderfoot Whiskey is made from five malted grains: two-row barley malt, smoked barley malt, chocolate barley malt, malted rye, and malted wheat.

The distillery is named after its founders, the Wood brothers, but it's not a bad reference for the prominence of the barrel aging in the whiskey. Tenderfoot fits, too, because like a novice on the hiking trail, this is a young whiskey.

It has a dark orange coloring in the glass.

The nose is very heavy on the oak. It's like stepping into a room where someone is sanding down furniture and preparing to stain it.

A sip gives a creamy mouthfeel and a dollop of spice on the tongue, and then the wood piles up, runs on through, along with some notes of a bourbonesque barrel char and a little citrus zest. But it's the oak that is there to the end in a dry finish.

OREGON

MANY IDEAS HAVE EMERGED OVER A PINT OR TWO OF BEER. SOME GREAT AND OTHERS NOT SO MUCH.

BLACK BUTTE WHISKEY

94 PROOF 47% ALC/VOL

MALT WHISKEY

DISTILLED FROM GRAIN

750 MILLILITERS

CRAFTED IN COLLABORATION

 BREWED BY DESCHUTES BREWERY DISTILLED & BOTTLED BY BENDISTILLERY

BOTTLE NO 1192 /1192

— DESCHUTES BENDISTILLERY —

Given Oregon's heavyweight reputation in craft brewing, it follows that it also has a strong presence in the growing category of "brewstilling," or outfits that put a foot in both brewing beer and distilling whiskey by making dual use of certain articles of equipment and, often, applying the same wort used in the beer to the whiskey-making processes. Deschutes Brewery didn't turn brewstillery, but instead collaborated with a craft distiller. Bendistillery is one of those outfits that was doing craft spirits before micro-distilling became a "thing," having opened their doors in 1996. Their wares go under the brand Crater Lake Spirits, and include a 100% rye.

DESCHUTES BLACK BUTTE MALT WHISKEY

94 The wort for this whiskey comes from Deschutes Black Butte Porter. It's double-distilled by Bendistillery and aged for three years in new oak barrels charred to level 4.

Its nose has a current of vanilla running through it, but in the main it's spicy, musty, and oaky.

The flavor evolves to toffee and hazelnut, with the musty note in the nose turning to earthy cocoa on the palate. The vanilla from the barrel aging is there too, noticeable but off to one side. The finish runs down on toffee and wood.

— HOOD RIVER DISTILLERS —
CLEAR CREEK DISTILLERY

Hood River Distillers, established in 1934 as Oregon's first distiller after Prohibition, has owned Clear Creek Distillery since 2014.

McCARTHY'S OREGON SINGLE MALT WHISKEY

85 Similar to Bendistillery, Clear Creek is one of those handful of companies that has been a couple of decades ahead of the curve in terms doing craft whiskey. It started in the mid-1990s with the intent of making a Pacific Northwest spin on peated single malt Scotch.

Clear Creek imports peated malt from Scotland, which is then mashed and fermented at Widmer Brothers Brewery, before finally being hauled over to Clear Creek for distilling. Making the wash recently moved to Double Mountain Brewery, but at the time of writing, any bottle of McCarthy's Single Malt started life at Widmer. The new-make spirit is then aged for three years in barrels made from air-dried oak harvested from Oregon forests.

The scent of McCarthy's achieves its stated target: the peat smoke shares center stage with the expected vanilla from the new white oak aging, joined by traces of coconut and toffee.

The flavor gets more crowded. It's about half peat smoke, with the other half being a mix of malty honey, Granny Smith apples, and vanilla. The smoke fades off in the finish, turning first to toasted cereals before finally departing on just plain sweet cereals.

— HOUSE SPIRITS DISTILLERY —

Westward Oregon Straight Malt Whiskey

 90 This is a 100% malted barley whiskey, with the grain sourced from farms in the Pacific Northwest. It's fermented with ale yeast and double-distilled in copper pots. It's a straight whiskey, so we know it is aged for at least two years, and House Spirits chose to go light on the charring, using predominately #2 char and some #3 char for its barrels. Lighter char basically means less sugar and more tannin in the oak.

It has a light nose, carrying aromas of cereals, clay, and oak in the main.

The flavor is fruity sweet, accented by lemon zest, before cereals and hot, peppery spices rise up and take over. The finish goes over to a pipe tobacco note, before fading off clean and clear into a light, lingering touch of that now familiar lemon zest.

ROGUE
Spirits
DEAD GUY WHISKEY
Distilled in small batches from the same malts as award winning Dead Guy Ale.
Ocean aged in Oak Barrels for at least two years
40% ALC/VOL (80 Proof) - 750ML
Spirits

— ROGUE SPIRITS —

ROGUE DEAD GUY WHISKEY

80 This is a granddaddy in the category of whiskeys made from beer. Rogue took the wort for its Dead Guy Ale, fermented it with distiller's yeast, and distilled it instead of brewing it. From there it is aged in new white oak.

The scent is a light one, and fairly straightforward: grassy cereals mingled with a dab of honey and a pinch of orange zest.

The flavor is a bit of a surprise from there, because the malty honey and vanilla note are joined by a nuttiness that reminds me of smoked almonds. The finish delivers more of the same, but sweeter and less nutty and smoky, and you get a real handle on that because it takes its time fading away.

All in all, Rogue's Dead Guy Whiskey makes for some simple, flavorful, easy drinking.

ROGUE OREGON RYE MALT WHISKEY

This whiskey doesn't share a wort in common with one of Rogue's beers, but instead draws on its beer-making expertise by using its Dream Rye and Dare & Risk Malted Barley. The rye is also malted, and the mash is fermented with Pacman yeast, a rather neutral brewing yeast that is quite popular with home brewers.

A pour comes out golden in the glass, while giving that glass a swish leaves a coat that just streams with tears.

Taking in the aroma reminds me of toasted light rye bread, with fruity and light spice notes.

A sip shows the liquid to have a soft, silky texture. It's a smooth whiskey, but also light on flavor as well. It follows the profile of the nose, being something like a light rye toast with a nondescript fruit jam spread thinly across the top. That profile is more there in the nose than on the palate, though. The finish goes down with a modest bit of pumpernickel. But after that light start, it comes on more assertively with toasted cereals, and then runs on strong for a few moments before fading off.

Like the Oregon Rye Malt, this is made using some of Rogue's proprietary malt and yeast. Moreover, the recipe here is just one type of malted barley, instead of the handful of types common in not only whiskeys made from beer, but also in American malts in general. It's been aged for five years, a year beyond even the bottled in bond requirement that is a benchmark for mature craft whiskey nowadays.

After a pour, the whiskey has a bright, shining yellow appearance that isn't quite dull enough to be gold.

The nose is malty honey, a hint of straw, and some wet, green oak. In other words, it has a simple, easy, and straightforward smell incorporating all the elements I expect from an American malt aged in new oak with no wingding finishes.

The flavor is more honey, toasty cereals, a pinch of pepper, and crushed dry straw. The finish unfolds with honey and a slightly larger hint of pepper.

UTAH

— HIGH WEST DISTILLERY —

High West's best-known brands are sourced whiskeys, released back when it was building the distillery or had only white whiskey coming from their in-house production. These early offerings gained the distillery a reputation for transparency at a time when most sourced whiskeys strove to be as opaque as possible about their origins.

High West American Prairie Bourbon Whiskey

92 American Prairie is a perfect example of the High West model. They describe it as being made from a combination of MGP's 75% corn bourbon stock; an 84% corn, 4% rye, and 8% malted barley bourbon from an unknown source; and other bourbons that they cannot name because of contractual obligations. These bourbons range in age from 2 to 13 years, and the proportions therein are unstated.

The nose has the expected vanilla and caramel notes, but with a touch of astringency, suggesting that the aforementioned ages in the blend lean hard on the two-year-old end of that spectrum.

A sip shows some candy corn sweetness and nougat, which is met by a rising tide of spiciness, verging on becoming hot without ever becoming hot. That spicy current turns peppery for the finish.

HIGH WEST DOUBLE RYE! WHISKEY

92 As the name implies, this is a blend of two ryes, and the recipe behind Double Rye! changed in 2018. Originally it was made from two-year-old MGP 95% rye and a 16-year-old Barton 1792 rye whiskey. Nowadays, such an old rye can fetch several hundred dollars a bottle and is in short supply, so the whiskey has moved to a new recipe. The MGP rye is still there, now joined by High West's in-house 80% rye, 20% malted barley whiskey. The age on these two whiskeys ranges from two to seven years old.

In the glass this has a golden copper look.

The scent on the new iteration of Double Rye! has an herbal-spicy character. Clove and eucalyptus meet spearmint and sarsaparilla, with a daub of wet clay sitting in the background.

A sip takes that herbal, sweetly spiced blend in a peculiar direction. The herbal character adds a heavy note of juniper, so much so that it's almost as if someone put a splash of gin into the whiskey, while that wet clay grows into a slap of old leather. Compared to what has been a pretty exotic experience so far, the finish is humdrum, running spicy, but with just cinnamon.

HIGH WEST RENDEZVOUS RYE WHISKEY

92 The flagship expression and inaugural release for High West, Rendezvous is similar to Double Rye!, but made using older whiskeys and presumably blended in different proportions. Also like Double Rye!, the choice of whiskey stock used to make it has changed as ultra-aged rye whiskey made at Barton 1792 has become dear (perhaps even unavailable). So, instead of being made from mature MGP 95% rye and some very old Barton rye, it is now made with MGP rye and High West's very own rye whiskey, with the pair ranging from four to seven years of age.

This blended rye has a coppery color in the glass.

A sniff shows it to be a rye with herbal and sweet spiciness. The nose is balanced between a dollop of brown sugar and vanilla, a helping of cinnamon and cloves, and finally a pinch of dried mint flakes.

The balance is thrown off on the palate, though, as the whiskey veers away from its sweetness and goes quite spicy. The flavor has two strong currents of cinnamon and peppermint, with the sweet side taking a backseat. The vanilla is still there, but the sugary note is more like molasses. The finish goes down spicy, long, and slow.

WASHINGTON

— DRY FLY DISTILLING —

Spokane's Dry Fly takes a lot of pride in sourcing most of its grain from a handful of farms in eastern Washington, and it combines this with the crafty ethos of going where the big distillers aren't.

DRY FLY STRAIGHT TRITICALE WHISKEY

This 100% triticale whiskey made from locally farmed grain is a particularly good choice for a Washington craft distiller, since the state is the national leader in the production of this hybrid of wheat and rye. Triticale was never used in whiskey prior to the craft distilling movement, and even today there are only a few examples of it on the market, of which Dry Fly's is the best known.

It is aged for at least three years in 53-gallon barrels.

The scent is of cinnamon toast on whole grain bread, if one added some powdered ginger to the mix of sugar and cinnamon sprinkled on the top.

Add notes of vanilla and oak to that mix and you've got the flavor.

Using triticale is supposed to bring a soft, wheated whiskey polish to a flavorful rye, and Dry Fly's whiskey delivers in this respect.

SMALL
BATCH
DISTILLED

DRYFLY®

Straight Wheat
WHISKEY

AGED **3** YEARS

45% ALC/VOL | 90 PROOF | 750ML

Dry Fly Straight Wheat Whiskey

Dry Fly's flagship is its wheat whiskey. Whereas most of the wheat used in making whiskey is red winter wheat, Dry Fly chose to go with a local white wheat varietal in its 100% wheat whiskey. It is aged for three years in full-size barrels with a #3 char.

This whiskey has some aspects in common with the Triticale Whiskey, which isn't surprising given that triticale and wheat are closely related.

It smells like a hot, freshly toasted slice of whole grain bread with a thick layer of crafty fruit jam spread across the top.

A sip reveals a daub of honey and peanut butter smeared under that fruit jam, and some hot cinnamon sprinkled on the top. The finish runs with that spicy note, turning hot in the end.

— OOLA DISTILLERY —

OOLA was part of what I like to think of as the middle of the craft whiskey movement: the micro-distilleries that opened just as the sector exploded from dozens to hundreds of such establishments. They went operational at the start of 2010, making them one of the first distilleries to open in Seattle after Prohibition.

Founder Kirby Kallas-Lewis is an artist and was an art dealer, and his interest in connecting food and drink led him to study distilling for three years before he opened OOLA. His facility is an urban distillery, sporting a stylish sense of design, and located in Seattle's Capitol Hill neighborhood. Right next door is an events space and dance studio that serves as home to Lingo Productions, a dance company; neighbors on the block include a locavore diner, two gay-oriented bars, and an upscale gym. It's a far cry from most small distilleries, which even today are often found in quasi-suburban, light industrial sites, small satellite towns, and rural areas.

OOLA started out with a set of five 55-gallon stills made by the Seattle fabricator Amphora Society. It outgrew this set by 2016, though two of the five continue to be used in finishing OOLA's gin. For whiskey, the distillery now relies on a pair of larger stills, an alembic still from Global Stainless Systems, and a column still from Vendome.

Back in 2017, OOLA started work on what will initially be a tasting room and events space in the Georgetown neighborhood. That facility is ultimately intended to become a second distillery as well, once the licensing is in place.

The distillery runs as a sour-mash operation, and sources most of its grain from an organic farm in eastern Washington. What doesn't come from there is the malted barley, which is bought from Cargill at present. In the not-too-distant future, OOLA expects to partially transition to a Skagit Valley Malting. OOLA's yeast is a locally derived strain, which it considers proprietary.

Despite acquiring bigger equipment in 2016, OOLA is still a fairly small operation. It runs production during a normal, 40-hour workweek and manages to produce about 100 53-gallon barrels of whiskey a year. With their existing equipment, OOLA could double that output, and is nudging that number up with each passing year.

OOLA's new make comes off the still at somewhere between 136 and 144 proof. That new make is usually cut down to 116 for barrel entry, but OOLA has some experiments tucked away that were cut to 110 and 120 proof. Its standard new white oak barrels come from Independent Stave Company, and OOLA prefers to go for a very heavy char indeed. Some barrels are #4 char, but others are torched to what Independent Stave calls "Craft Distiller's Char," a higher level that would approximate #5 or #6.

OOLA Discourse C American Whiskey

Discourse C is paradoxically the first release in the Discourse series. When I first saw it, I assumed it was the third; the name is "C," after all. The purpose of the series is to start a dialogue, as much between drinkers as between the distillery and the public, about nontraditional whiskey making. Discourse C is a four-grain whiskey, made from a mash bill of 65% corn, 25% rye, 13% malted barley, and 12% white winter wheat. The first round of four years of aging is in the standard 53-gallon alligator-charred new oak barrels. Technically, it could be called a bourbon, although the distillery has chosen not to label it as such. Following primary maturation, the whiskey receives a finish in French oak barrels that were used to age Cabernet wine.

In the glass Discourse C has an oily look with a murky gold coloring. Coating the inside of the glass leaves a crown and just a few slow, skinny, beady legs slinking to the bottom.

The nose gives off the scent of apples and wine, girded with butterscotch and honey. Hovering in the background is the smell of dried straw, so the whole thing comes across as an odd bit of refreshment taken in a farmer's field.

A current of fruit drizzled with honey runs through the flavor. That sweet core is accented by a touch of vanilla on the front and a touch of pepper on the back. The finish opens sugary and peppery, but the sugar soon fades and leaves the pepper to drift away slowly.

I'm not sure if Discourse C was the right place to start with the intent of starting conversations about nontraditional whiskey-making methods. It is essentially a bourbon whiskey finished in Cabernet barrels. Although not exactly traditional, in an era when there are nearly 600 craft distillers making and exploring the boundaries of whiskey, what went into Discourse C can't really be described as the stuff that fosters discussion.

OOLA Discourse Three Shores Whiskey

94 This third installment in the Discourse series is a blend of their own high-rye American whiskey with imported Canadian whisky and Highland Scotch whisky. The imported whiskys are aged for an extra year in American white oak before blending, an interesting and perhaps unique choice. Although there are a handful of examples of world blends of this type around, I'm unaware of anyone giving their imported stock extra aging in a new cask prior to blending.

In the glass, the golden color of Three Shores looks a lot like a rich Scotch or Canadian whisky aged in used barrels. Coating the glass yields a few tears.

A sniff reveals a decidedly foreign nose, one that smacks of butterscotch, fresh-cut grass, and traces of woodiness.

The whiskey has a silky texture on the palate, and it's there that all three constituent whiskeys come into play, with a lightly honeyed sweetness balanced nicely against rye spices, and a vegetal, grassiness in the background. On the finish, the whiskey turns a bit peppery.

OOLA WAITSBURG BOURBON WHISKEY

94 This started out as a blend of sourced and in-house whiskeys, but nowadays it's an all in-house wheated bourbon, aged for five years in 53-gallon barrels. Unlike the Discourse whiskeys, this item has been and will continue in regular production.

Checking out a pour shows it to be a golden whiskey, and a viscous one. This bourbon lays a thick coating on the glass, one that lets out only a few strong, heavy tears.

The nose is a pleasant if simple one, smacking of apples, roasted nuts, and caramel. So, it's like an artisanal caramel apple rolled in nuts.

The flavor isn't so fruity but retains its charms: butterscotch and caramel candy supplemented by spices and pine. The latter aspects continue to rise up on the back end and carry over until they fade away during the finish. At the end, one is left with just a hint of butterscotch.

— WESTLAND DISTILLERY —

Although its size is firmly within the bounds of a "craft distillery," the folks at Westland eschew that term and prefer to be called a "single malt whiskey distillery." This is partly because Westland doesn't identify with what most craft distilleries do: it is part of a small class of distilleries making just one type of whiskey; and although small compared to the big distillers of Kentucky and Tennessee, Westland is quite large relative to others in the craft sphere.

It's not hard to see another source of the aversion to the term. Cofounder and Master Distiller Matt Hofmann was trained in Scotland, where there is no such thing as a craft distillery, and what Westland does would be almost normal. Westland doesn't even seem to like the American term "sweet mash"; whenever I have asked about the details of their production process in the past, Hofmann or another person from Westland described a sweet-mash system, although that term is very clearly avoided.

Westland filled its first barrel in June 2011, and in 2018 was running near or at maximum capacity given its current equipment. The distillery is producing whiskey seven days a week from its Canadian-made mash house and fermenters and its Vendome-built still. That schedule is enough to produce about 35 casks. To make more, Westland would need to add more fermenters, but future expansions aren't likely to pose much of a problem for the distillery; Westland was acquired by Rémy Cointreau in 2017.

As is common with folks making malt whiskey in the States, some of Westland's production process is inspired by the experiences of the craft brewing industry. It relies on a variety of specialized malts, and more than four-fifths of Westland's grain comes from farms in the distillery's home state. What it cannot find in Washington is sourced out of the UK or from Wisconsin. The yeast used to ferment is a Belgian Saison strain.

Westland is a bit old-fashioned in that it makes still cuts by nose, so those are not precise cuts, but the distillery has established two different entry proofs for its distillate. New make going into new oak is cut to 110 proof, while spirits entered into a used cask are cut to the limit of 125.

Although Westland only makes malt whiskey, it spins many flavors out of that by making multiple distillates from different types of malted barley, aging them in a wide variety of casks. The charred, new white oak 53-gallon barrels come from Independent Stave Company. Westland buys barrels made with staves that have been air-dried for 18 or 24 months; and it employs two separate chars, one with a heavy toast and a light char and one with a light toast and a heavy char.

Past the American Standard Barrels, Westland draws on used wine casks from wineries in Oregon and Washington, as well as importing Sherry casks from Spain. The distillery has several cask exchanges arranged with area brewers, whereby Westland sends them used whiskey casks, the brewers use them to make whiskey beer, and those casks are sent back to Westland to make beer-finished whiskey. Finally, Westland has specially made casks fashioned from their local oak species, *Quercus garryana*.

Westland American Oak Single Malt Whiskey

92 Westland's flagship offering embodies the kinship with American craft brewing that has so infused the modern American malt sector. The whiskey is composed of five different malted barley whiskeys—Washington Select Pale Malt, Munich Malt, Extra Special Malt, Pale Chocolate Malt, and Brown Malt—while a Belgian brewer's yeast adds fruity extras to each type during fermentation. The new make was then entered into both new white oak barrels and used bourbon barrels for at least three years of aging, with these separately aged stocks to be drawn upon for blending later on.

The liquid has a look that sits astride the line between gold and copper. Coating the interior of the glass shows it to be a thin liquid, leaving long legs.

Taking in the nose brings in lightly toasted ice cream cone and berry fruit, the latter either coming from or enhanced by Westland's choice of yeast.

On the palate it is initially quite fruity, a mix of citrus and cherries. This fruity sweetness is later joined by a rising tide of nuts and oak, but this never quite overtakes the fruity character, and ultimately fades away. Lurking in the background throughout that evolution is a note of caramel.

112

The Garryana line is an evolving, limited-edition expression, with each batch drawing on a different selection of malts and barrel stock. The one constant is the use of barrels made from *Quercus garryana*, an oak species particular to the Pacific Northwest. This type of oak is becoming noted for its strongly spicy, not particularly sweet character.

In the 3|1 release, a heavily peated malt whiskey was added to the blend, and the whiskeys were aged in the signature new Garryana barrels, along with a mix of new white oak, used bourbon barrels, former Port casks, and used malt whiskey barrels (recycled within Westland).

Unlike the other Westland whiskeys, this expression is cask strength.

The coloring of an American malt with plenty of used oak in its makeup is pale copper.

Rich, malty honey combines with an earthy puff of smoke and a touch of berry tea to comprise the nose.

On the palate the whiskey has a silken texture. It is honey sweet, spiced with cloves, and seasoned with a touch of earthy, leathery oak. The finish leans on the latter note, turning decisively toward that earthy, leathery, and woody aspect.

MATT HOFMANN

One often finds that people making whiskey outside of Kentucky and Tennessee didn't make their start in life with distilling in mind, and starting or working in a distillery was often a career change. That wasn't the case for Matt Hofmann, who was still at the University of Washington when he became interested in starting a distillery.

Already with an eye to starting a malt whiskey distillery, Hofmann toured the distilleries of Scotland extensively before enrolling in the Institute of Brewing and Distilling for his general certificate in distilling. From there he attended Heriot-Watt University in Edinburgh until 2014, studying brewing and distilling for four years to earn a postgraduate diploma.

All the while, Hofmann was working on Westland Distillery with his cofounder, Emerson Lamb. Although officially founded in 2010, Westland Distillery's first production run was not until June 2011. Indeed, Hofmann was still working on his postgraduate degree when Westland's inaugural release came out in 2013, a 375-milliliter bottling called The Deacon Seat.

Given that Hofmann's technical education was in the UK, it's no surprise that his distillery makes single malt whiskey and draws heavily upon Scottish methods. However, Hofmann did not set out to copy the Scotch industry, but instead to take that knowledge and apply it to the Pacific Northwest. Making the most of the terroir of his Seattle location has been Hofmann's mission at Westland, and that mission is his most consistent challenge. "The whiskey industry isn't set up for a provenance-driven approach," says Hofmann. "Options are limited for not only accessing the raw materials we actually want to use, but finding partners and tradespeople to work with to bring our vision to life."

As a result, Hofmann spends a lot of time away from the distillery, talking to agricultural scientists, malting houses, lumber mills, and basically anyone who will help him develop his vision of Washington State terroir. An example is how he struck upon Garryana oak, a local species Westland is using to make specialized casks. "It was originally our friends in the wine business who turned us on to Garry oak," Hofmann says. "When we were starting nearly a decade ago they had just completed years of experimental trials using this native species of oak." The Garryana didn't work out for the wineries, but Hofmann has put it to good use, and cites it as his most important achievement, representing the cornerstones of his production process (roasted malts, brewer's yeast, and high-quality oak barrels).

Hofmann is uncomfortable with the term master distiller, insisting, "There is no mastering this art." He has also been adamant about refusing to use the terms "craft whiskey" and "craft distillery," which he feels are poor descriptors. "Craft has been co-opted to mean too many different things these days, none of them entirely accurate." And he has a point: they hold a craft license in Washington, but, as he points out, just a few hours north in Vancouver they wouldn't. Nor would Westland be described as a craft distillery in Scotland.

Westland Peated American Single Malt Whiskey

92 After the regional groupings, the two major substyles of Scottish single malts are peated (using barley malted with peat-fueled fires) or Sherried (aged or finished in onetime Sherry casks). That underlines the difference between this and other Westland expressions: a peated malt has been added to the mix. Not just any peated malt, mind you, but using peat harvested in Washington state. Otherwise, the barrel stock used for aging is similar to that of the American Oak: new white oak and used bourbon barrels.

It has a light golden coloring in the glass, and the swish and coat show it to be not especially thin or thick. It streams a handful of long legs, but that is about it.

This is not a big, smoky beast. Instead, the smoke is an accent to the whiskey. The scent carries citrus zest and nuttiness in the main, underscored by a whiff of damp, peaty smoke.

That smoke grows fuller and more like wood smoke once on your palate, but it's still a supporting character to a main body of roasted nuts and sweet, minty herbs. The sweet aspect is what drops out of the picture in the finish, leaving behind smoked nuts.

Westland Sherry Wood American Single Malt Whiskey

92 The new-make spirit is the same as that behind the aforementioned Garryana oak expression; the difference lies in the cask stock chosen for aging. Westland Sherry Wood spends at least three years in a mix of new white oak and former Oloroso and Pedro Ximénez Sherry casks from Tonelería del Sur.

Reflecting the different choice of cask stock, Sherry Wood has a darkened copper look in the glass, and is a thicker, oilier liquid than its oak-aged stablemate. After coating the glass, it takes a noticeable wait for legs and a crown of beads to properly form.

The effects of combining new white oak, Sherry casks, and plenty of dark malts extend beyond the look of the whiskey. The nose smacks of thick maple and oak, malty honey, and cocktail cherry syrup.

On the palate, the profile moves over to oatmeal raisin cookies that lean more sweet than spicy, as if someone snuck some maple syrup into the cookie dough. The finish turns quite tart and woody.

WYOMING

— WYOMING WHISKEY —

Wyoming Whiskey is a small, ambitious distillery in the Equality State. The company was founded in 2009 by the Mead family and David DeFazio, who turned to Steve Nally to help them with the technical side. Thus, Wyoming Whiskey's early work was influenced by Nally's previous work with wheated bourbon at Maker's Mark. However, Nally eventually moved on to other pastures, and to the extent that Wyoming Whiskey still needs advice, it now turns to esteemed industry veteran Nancy Fraley.

WYOMING WHISKEY SMALL BATCH BOURBON WHISKEY

88 This flagship expression is a small-batch bourbon, which was first released in 2012, and received mixed marks in its early years. However, since then the bourbon has been tweaked (batching has risen from 15 barrels to about 40, for example) and gotten a little older. These days it is at least five years old and aged entirely in 53-gallon barrels, but it's still made from a mash of 68% corn, 20% wheat, and 12% malted barley. Its ABV of 44% pays homage to Wyoming's status as the 44th state.

The nose is floral, leaning in the direction of wildflowers and herbs, and letting you know right away that it is a wheated bourbon. The scent also packs a hefty current of caramel.

The liquid has a light character on the tongue, with a flavor that is quite sweet, like a caramel candy topped with a sprinkling of powdered sugar. A note of green, wet wood is present, but not heavy. The flavor is altogether a different creature from the nose, as is the finish, which leaves a warm but quite light afterglow.

88

This is a single-barrel selection of the same stock used to make the small batch, with the pick made by Master Distiller Sam Mead and consultant Nancy Fraley. The stats are identical to the small batch: same mash bill, same age (roughly five years), and same proof.

The nose is orange and vanilla cream filling in the main, with highlights of cocoa also rising.

A sip shows the bourbon to be as soft as one might expect from a solidly wheated bourbon. It's got a richly sweet flavor for the most part, akin to graham crackers with plenty of vanilla drizzle on the top, along with traces of green oak, ginger, and cocoa. The finish lingers, with light currents of more of that ginger spice and a sliver of green oak.

Taken side by side, one can see the clear parallels between the single barrel and the small batch, with the single barrel having a little more character.

100

When Wyoming Whiskey got started, it was largely following a blueprint laid out by Steve Nally, which showed in its initial releases of wheated bourbon. Later on, Sam Mead and David DeFazio began charting their own course, which led the distillery to use rye in their bourbon. Outryder is the first result of that shift, made from whiskeys distilled back in 2011 and released in 2017.

This is a hybrid, a blend of two different types of whiskeys. The first is a bourbon and a lot like the original whiskey used in their small batch and single barrel. The difference is that instead of 20% wheat, it is 20% winter rye. The second is an American whiskey, so named because it has no dominant grain; it's made from a mash bill of 48% rye, 40% corn, and 12% malted barley.

Outryder is also noteworthy because it's a bottled in bond whiskey, part of a crop of bonded craft whiskeys that came out in 2017 and 2018, and that confirmed the rising maturity of the craft whiskey scene.

It's a pale amber whiskey.

Its aroma is that of vanilla bean, maple syrup, and cookie spices.

The flavor runs in waves, starting with allspice, then more maple before turning tropical with some coconut and pineapple. The finish runs long and warm, starting off with a big pinch of orange zest before turning big and spicy, and running spicy down to the end.

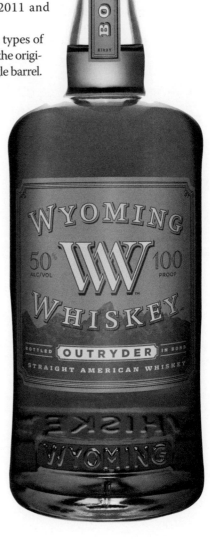

— LOST LANTERN —

Ever since the craft whiskey boom began to take off in the mid-2000s, I had a two-fold vision of the future. The first part is that American whiskey would get back on track to the what-might-have-been if Prohibition had not disrupted the industry. What is often overlooked, however, is that the decades following the repeal of Prohibition in 1933 were little better: those years just happened to coincide with the latter half of the Great Depression, the rationing of World War II, and the broad trend of American industrial consolidation to fewer and smaller producers making national-ized brands.

The forces at work from the 1930s to the 1980s were unfavorable, if not downright hostile, to the reemergence of a sundry class of medium-sized whiskey makers of the style that con-tinued in Scotland. As the craft whis-key movement took off, one could hope for getting back to something like what would have emerged if the American whiskey industry had not suffered Prohibition.

That hope was realized beyond my wildest dreams, with several hundred craft whiskey producers in operation today. That is where Lost Lantern comes into the picture, because once that widespread, coast-to-coast host of whiskey makers was in place, my next vision was the birth of a proper sector of negociants.

One most often encounters this term in relation to the wine trade, but it applies to the whiskey business as well, and the best examples are found in Scotland. They are firms that buy casks of new or partly aged whiskey from distillers, mature it themselves at their own warehouses, and then either bottle it as special single cask editions or blend it into their own products. Oftentimes, they do both. Scotland's advantage for a negociant, such as Douglas Laing or Weymss Malts, is that it has the host of distinctive distillers necessary to make such an enterprise interesting to consumers.

America did not have that host until very recently, and Lost Lantern is the first company to step fully into the negociant role by putting a foot both into in-house blended brands and single cask releases. The company was founded by Nora Ganley-Roper, a former sales manager at New York's Astor Wine & Spirits, and Adam Polo-noski, a one-time writer for Whisky Advocate. The two understood the potential of America's blooming sec-tor of small and midsize distillers per-fectly well, and in 2018 set off on what they called "The Great Whiskey Road Trip" in search of casks to acquire. The results speak for themselves.

105

The term "vatted malt" was invented to further distinguish a Scotch whisky blended from only malt whiskeys from the term "blended whisky," which is a mix of grain and malt whiskeys. Thus, it underlines Lost Lantern's nod toward the Scottish negociants that they chose to make and name their first brand in regular release a vatted malt. This draws on malt whiskeys from six American distillers: Balcones, Copperworks, Santa Fe Spirits, Triple Eight, Westward, and Virginia Distilling.

The coloring was a clear, light amber.

The nose carried Demerara sugar, green applies, and fresh cut, green hay.

The liquid was light, but creamy on the tongue, and tasted of malty honey, caramel, and modest notes of oak and peach. The finish was a subtle one, and fully developed on me only after my shot pour was almost gone, but came out as light touches of oak, dry pepper, and smoke.

Lost Lantern Fall 2021, Single Cask #3: Boulder Spirits Bourbon

138.4 This bottling serves as a prime, recent example of what Lost Lantern does with its single cask business. Boulder Spirits is a Colorado distillery started by Scotsman Alastair Brogan, who brought Scotch-style whiskey making to the Rocky Mountains, complete with a Forsyths copper pot still. That Scottish style is vividly reflected in their bourbon, as it is made with a high malt mash bill: 51% corn, 44% malted barley, and 5% rye. This bottling is a 5-year-old example of that bourbon, matured in a new 53-gallon barrel at mile-high elevation. Keeping in mind that this bourbon is just a hair away from being strong enough to pour straight into your gas tank, my tasting notes reflect a weighty splash of water.

A sniff gave me something like a s'more made with a big, fat caramel candy instead of a marshmallow: toasted graham crackers, oodles of caramel, a little earthy, cocoa edge.

The first sip revealed a whiskey with a decidedly oily texture, which is exactly what I would expect from a very high-malt, pot-distilled, and staggeringly strong bourbon. It has the standard brown sugar and vanilla sweetness and a dollop of fudge, coupled to a bold, but still smooth, current of oak. The finish trails off with mellow spices and wood. For a bourbon that is essentially rocket fuel in a bottle, it's also surprisingly—if not shockingly—smooth.

Angel's share: the name for the portion of whiskey that evaporates as it matures in the barrel.

Barrel: before bottling, whiskey spends time in a barrel, which imparts color and additional flavor; how it's stored, where it's stored, and when it's moved or pulled all help determine the flavor profile of the final product. The most commonly used tree for barrels is white oak (*quercus alba*).

Blended whiskey: an indication that the bottle contains more than one type of whiskey, and may even contain spirits other than whiskey.

Bottled in bond: a straight whiskey that is aged for at least four years and bottled at 100 proof; it must come from a single distilling season, be distilled by one distiller at one distillery, and aged at a federally bonded warehouse.

Bourbon: a whiskey bottled at a minimum of 80 proof, made in the United States, and aged in new charred oak barrels; bourbon must contain at least 51% corn, with the rest made up of rye, wheat, malted barley, and other grains. There is no minimum aging requirement for bourbon, but any bourbon younger than four years must include an age statement on the label; the age statement on any bourbon is determined by the youngest whiskey in the bottle.

Char: before bourbon is put into a barrel to age, the wood must be charred; char levels are determined by the amount of time the wood is allowed to burn: #1 Char—15 seconds of direct flame; #2 Char—30 seconds of direct flame; #3 Char—35 seconds of direct flame; #4 Char (alligator char)—55 seconds of direct flame.

Corn whiskey: A whiskey that is made from at least 80% corn. It can be aged in used or new oak barrels; if it is aged in charred new oak barrels it becomes a bourbon.

Distilling: the process by which a beer or wash is turned into distillate.

Mash bill: the blend of grains used to make the base of the whiskey; many distilleries keep the mash bill a secret, indicating how important the ratio is to the final product.

Rye whiskey: like bourbon, this is a whiskey made in the United States, must be aged in new charred oak, and bottled at a minimum of 80 proof; it contains at least 51% rye grain.

Sour-mash process: incorporating some of the mash from a previous batch of whiskey in the next one. If each batch starts over from scratch, this is known as a sweet-mash process.

Straight whiskey: a whiskey aged a minimum of two years, as mandated by law.

Tennessee Whiskey: made using the same method and ingredients as most bourbons, the factor that distinguishes this spirit is a charcoal "mellowing" known as the Lincoln County Process, where the distillate is passed through a container of heavily charred American maple chips before it is put into new American oak barrels for aging.

ACKNOWLEDGMENTS

When I wrote the first edition of *American Whiskey*, I was simply too overworked to even think of writing acknowledgements. If that sounds lame, it feels lame writing it, but still true. Mercifully, I am now finishing a second edition and have the opportunity to rectify that oversight.

First, I want to acknowledge the longest serving colleagues on my team at The *Whiskey Reviewer*. Although it is true that I do all of the administrative and technical end, and the overwhelming majority of the writing for the website myself, the other writers make a valuable contribution in adding a wider perspective and doing things I cannot. I do not feel like I would have been in a position to be invited to produce *American Whiskey* if it had not been for our team effort during the first several years of the website, leading up to the moment I first put my fingers on the keyboard for this book. That begins with the only other member of the team who was there from day one and is still there today, my brother from another mother and fellow author Kurt Maitland. The other major contributors during that time were Scott Peters, John Rayls, Randall Borkus, Debbie Shocair and Emma Briones. I raise a glass to all of you.

Whether it be writing for a magazine, website, or book, speaking to what distillers are doing across the width and breadth of North America would be impossible without the cooperation of those distillers. All of those folks are passionate and dedicated to their craft and business, which makes it easy to admire what they do. This book is about you, and I couldn't have done it without you in more ways than one. I have been asked by reviews and in person why I didn't cover this distillery or that consultant, and the answer is often "they didn't cooperate with me," which makes me even more grateful for the people that did. The book lists well over 100 of you, so suffice it to say, thanks.

I kicked off my little book tour in February 2020, on the eve of the pandemic lockdown, so that did not go very far. I feel I should call special attention to my hosts at that time and in 2022, as I started doing author's events again. Joe Magliocco, the owner of Michter's, was staggeringly generous in hosting the launch for *American Whiskey* at the Fort Nelson Distillery in Louisville; it was a pleasure to at last meet Alex and Meredith Grelli, the co-founders of Wigle, in Pittsburgh; Mike Vacheresse owns the best whiskey bar in New York and is a great host; and I was thrilled to help fundraise for the Hyde Park Seniors Center in Cincinnati, now called 55North.

For this edition, I must thank Robin Robinson for penning his kind foreword. Not having one was another time-driven oversight of the first edition, now rectified.

And finally, I must thank the folks at Cider Mill Press for asking me to do the two editions of this book. I started working with them in *The New Single Malt* anthology, and it's been a pleasure to continue ever since.

ABOUT THE AUTHOR

Richard Thomas is the owner and managing editor of *The Whiskey Reviewer*, a leading web magazine for whiskey reviews, mixology and trade news, as well as the Whiskey Editor at Large for *Chilled* magazine. Beyond his writing, Thomas's opinions and technical advice on whiskey have appeared in *Style* magazine, and in media outlets such as ABC News and the Discovery Channel. He is also the steward of the Lexington Cocktail Club. When not writing about whiskey, food, and travel, or working on his fiction, you might find him in a boxing gym or hauling a ruck in the forests of Kentucky.

PHOTOGRAPHY CREDITS

Photographs on pages 3, 12, 18, 20, 26, 42-43, 108, 126, 290, 294, 374, 406, 410, 414, 424, 426, 458, 478, 512 are used under official license from Shutterstock.com; images on pages 5-9 and pages 88-89 courtesy of the Library of Congress; photographs on pages 112, 192-193, 216-217, 234, 340-341, 342, 348, 351, 354, 370-371, 373, 390-393, 431-433, 436, 473, 487, 499, and 520-523 courtesy of Richard Thomas; photographs on pages 14-15, 22, 120, 123, 124, 128, 138, 143, 144, 146-147, 150-151, 154, 161-163, 182-183, 204, 252-253, 282, 305, 308-309, 310, 313, 315, and 322-323 courtesy of Cider Mill Press Book Publishers.

All other images courtesy of the respective distilleries.

ABOUT CIDER MILL PRESS BOOK PUBLISHERS

Good ideas ripen with time. From seed to harvest, Cider Mill Press brings fine reading, information, and entertainment together between the covers of its creatively crafted books. Our Cider Mill bears fruit twice a year, publishing a new crop of titles each spring and fall.

"WHERE GOOD BOOKS ARE READY FOR PRESS"

Visit us on the Web at

www.cidermillpress.com

or write to us at

PO Box 454
12 Spring St.
Kennebunkport, Maine 04046

Woodford Reserve Distillery

WOODFORD RESERVE

Woodford Reserve Distillery